MORE PERSONAL JOURNEYS

MORE PERSONAL JOURNEYS

Chaucer-Shakespeare-Augustine-
Newman-Chesterton-Greene

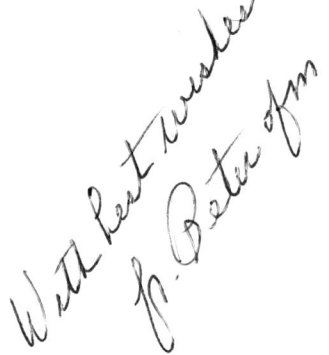

PETER A. FIORE

Copyright © 2005 by Peter A. Fiore.

Library of Congress Number: 2004195697
ISBN :   Hardcover   1-4134-7365-2
                Softcover   1-4134-7364-4

All rights reserved. No part of this book may be reproduced or transmitted in any form or by any means, electronic or mechanical, including photocopying, recording, or by any information storage and retrieval system, without permission in writing from the copyright owner.

This book was printed in the United States of America.

To order additional copies of this book, contact:
Xlibris Corporation
1-888-795-4274
www.Xlibris.com
Orders@Xlibris.com
27133

CONTENTS

Foreword 11

Geoffrey Chaucer 15

William Shakespeare 54

Augustine of Hippo 118

John Henry Newman 155

Gilbert Keith Chesterton 193

Graham Greene 234

Note on Sources 285

Dedication

Siena College is a Catholic liberal arts institution founded by the Franciscan friars in 1937 and is committed to a liberal arts education in the eight hundred year old Franciscan tradition.

This book is dedicated to all the Franciscan friars who over the years devoted their lives to educating young men and women at Siena, to forwarding the tradition of liberal arts, and to perpetuating the Franciscan ideals and values in the world.

Special Acknowledgment

My deepest debt is to Kenneth Kowald, not only for his genuine friendship, his brilliant mind, and his love and support of the arts, all of which have had an enormous impact on my life, but for the generosity with which he read and improved my manuscript. Truly, if this volume is in any way a success, it is due largely to his influence. All limitations in the book, however, are sorely my responsibility.

Foreword

Americans for the Arts, the nation's leading nonprofit organization for the arts in America, lamenting that "there's not enough art in our schools," placed a full page advertisement in the July 29, 2004 New York Times with the bold-faced statement "No Wonder People Say 'Gesundheit' when you say 'Tchaikovsky.'" The article goes on to bemoan the declining standards in schools today and despite the fact that the classical music genius is one of the world's favorite and most famous composers, students still confuse Tchaikovsky with a nasal spasm. Many educators surely smiled at the advertisement, its message all too familiar. The greatest names in music and literature are nearly unknown by our young people, or if known, are confused with politicians, athletes, or whomever. The watering down of our educational standards is showing results. Upon reading the advertisement, I myself was reminded of the little old Iowa lady in Meredith Willson's "The Music Man" who sings and scorns "Shakespeare and all them other highfalutin Greeks."

In the same newspaper on July 11, 2004, Charles McGrath, former editor of The Times Book Review, in an article entitled "What Johnny Won't Read," revealed that the National Endowment for the Arts released what it called a "bleak assessment" of the state of reading in America. According to the endowment's survey, compiled from 2002 Census Bureau data, reading in general has gone down over the last twenty years, and reading of literature in particular. For the first time in our history, less than half the adult population reads fiction, poetry, or plays. And the decline is among 18-to 24-year-olds, the group that twenty years ago was the most likely to pick up a book; now they are the least. None of this is very good news.

Three years ago my book of essays entitled "Personal Journeys: Classic Writers for a New Century." was published. The book was a series of essays on Dante, Donne, Milton, Hopkins, Waugh, and Flannery O'Connor. The reasons for that undertaking were manifold and the same as for this book.

First, I am in love with Chaucer, Shakespeare, Augustine, Newman, Chesterton, and Greene, as well as Dante, Donne, Milton, Hopkins, Waugh, and O'Connor. And I enjoy sharing that love with undergraduates and I particularly relish sharing their responses to the reading experience. Second, it is common knowledge that there has been an unfortunate dumbing down of literature departments in our colleges and universities throughout the country. Political agendas, faculty self interests, and trendy pop art have replaced reading of the great classics as an end in itself, an enrichment of the mind and soul, and as Cardinal Newman reminded us "to foster the culture of the intellect." I would like to think that these books will contribute to the healthy movement afoot in more and more of our colleges: the re-instating of the Great Books and cross-cultural authors in their core curricula. Third, many colleagues in fields other than literature have suggested that I do a book for the general and sometimes uninformed reader on literary figures whose Christian faith was the very impetus for their creative output.

Much has been written about the authors in this book. Chaucer scholarship is doing very well and Shakespeare, as we know, has become an industry. There have been any number of biographies down through the centuries on Augustine, that rogue young man who became one of the Church's greatest saints, and the life and works of Cardinal Newman produce even more scholarship than ever because of his influence on the Second Vatican Council of 1962-1965. Books and articles continue to come out on Chesterton, that most prolific and most often quoted apologist and even if volumes of material on Greene were not coming off the presses, and plenty are, Hollywood itself would and has already immortalized him by using his material for many excellent film productions.

This book however is for the reader who does not want to be overwhelmed by the abundance of material on these writers. It is for the non-specialist reader who desires an introduction and appreciation of the authors without the weight of esoteric research problems and their consequent footnotes. The attempt here is to present a personal and intimate approach to these writers.

There are a number of acknowledgments; my debts are many. I am indebted to William Empson, B.A. Wright, Arthur Brown, Roger Sharrock, Rosalie Colie, Lore Metzger, J. Kirby Neill, professors and colleagues of happy memory. I am indebted to Kevin Mackin, O.F.M., President of Siena College, who appointed me Scholar in Residence at Siena and who facilitated and supported my efforts on this project. The Most Reverend Harry J. Flynn, D.D, Archbishop of St. Paul and Minneapolis and The Rev. Dennis Dease, President of St. Thomas University, provided me with three opportunities to reside at the Bernardi Campus in Rome, the European home of the Catholic Studies Program of St. Thomas University. Sharing my ideas with the students in the program has been invaluable; I hope it was as valuable for them.

I am grateful to the staff of the J. Spencer and Patricia Standish Library at Siena College for all their help, especially Catherine Crohan who is over-accomodating. If in doubt about a source, she will find it. I am thankful to Daniel Nelson, OFM who shared with me his professional expertise in psychology concerning some of the personal problems of the authors. Kenneth Bartmess of Los Angeles, the type of colleague everyone should have, is an ever faithful friend, always ready with support and encouragement. I can always depend upon him for level headed responses to literary queries. I appreciate the support I receive from Rev. Thomas Kelly, Pastor of St. Mary's Parish in Ballston Spa, N.Y. where I engage in weekend pastoral ministry. Edward Le Comte and his late wife Mia have been friends for many years. He continues to share with me his brilliance in literary scholarship, in the matter of this book, Chesterton and Newman. I am so grateful for the friendship and support of Frank and Rose Mary Rossi. Frank was a student of mine and his outstanding success in life and career certainly makes Siena College proud. Patricia Standish did a close reading of the manuscript and saved me from many an error in fact and judgment. She and her husband Spencer have been great supporters of Siena College and of me. I am very grateful.

Geoffrey Chaucer

To this day Londoners love to keep their great literary personalities very much alive, even after seven centuries. One colleague told me that Chaucer studied French at Stratford, East (not Shakespeare's Stratford-on-Avon up north) because his Prioress (Madame Eglantyne) in "The Canterbury Tales" studied her French "After the school of Stratford-atte-Bowe" (that is quite a stretch). And most anyone in the Aldgate East area of London will tell you that the pump (called the Aldgate pump) in front of what is today the Aldgate Underground station is where Chaucer tied his horse when he was in the area. It might well be since the Chaucers were part of that increasingly important middle class that was constantly infiltrating the aristocracy. It is very likely that he owned a horse for transportation.

Geoffrey Chaucer was born about 1342, the exact date is not known, in a London that encompassed an area of about one square mile. His father John was a well-to-do wine merchant and his mother Agnes was the niece of an official at the Mint. They belonged to the parish of St. Martin's-in-the-Vintry. The boy spent a good deal of his childhood in the large middle class wine merchandising area of London, now the London Dock area just east of Tower Bridge. His father's wealth guaranteed him a fine education and the vintry area of London exposed him to many commoners, types who would one day populate his poetry.

When the boy was about six, The Black Death, which had ravaged continental Europe, arrived in England during the summer of 1348, killing a third of the population; it subsided two years later. During this period, John Chaucer took the family to Southampton, not only for safety precautions, but also as part of his profession as a purchaser of wine for the king; by 1350, when Geoffrey was about 10, the Chaucers were back in London living at Thames Street near the river.

Thanks to John Chaucer's employment with King Edward III, Geoffrey was given the position of page in the retinue of the Countess of Ulster, wife of the Duke of Clarence, a younger son of Edward III. Although being a page in such a reputable household meant making beds and running errands, records show that Geoffrey accompanied the countess on visits to Windsor, Oxford, Liverpool, and Yorkshire, which means he was not only making beds. He was receiving a fine education in good manners and courtly decorum.

When he was about 19 he was sent as a squire to fight in one of those many raids into France that were part of the Hundred Years War. He was taken prisoner but soon ransomed by Edward III. Scholars maintain that during this short period, the impressionable 19-year old fell in love with that fascinating cult of courtly love. It was one day to be a major ingredient in his poetry.

The rest of Chaucer's life was spent in close association with the ruling nobility of England, with John of Gaunt who was his most faithful patron and protector; with King Edward III; with Richard II who succeeded to the throne in 1377, and finally with Henry IV, who became king in 1399, the year before Chaucer's death. When he was about 25 years old he was promoted as a courtier.

Chaucer married Philippa de Roet whose father was an official in the household of Edward III's queen. They had a son whom they christened Thomas. By this time Chaucer was about 27 years old and was advancing himself as a courtier. Young Thomas went on to become an eminent man in the next generation, and an Alice Chaucer, quite possibly Chaucer's granddaughter, was sufficiently important to marry successively the Earl of Salisbury and the Duke of Norfolk, the premier duke of England. The Chaucer family was certainly in the forefront of bridging the gap between commoner and aristocracy. The times were changing.

When John of Gaunt's first wife died, Chaucer wrote one of his most beautiful early poems in her honor, "The Book of the Duchess." He went on to do a verse translation of the French classic, "Le Roman de la Rose." This was followed by another early classic work, "The Legend of Good Women." He did a prose translation of the sixth century Roman writer Boethius' "De Consolatione Philosophiae," one of the most valued books of the whole Middle Ages and one that influenced immeasurably the poet's life and works. He did his own version of the tragic love story "Troilus and Criseide." These were followed by "The Parliament of Fowls" and "The House of Fame."

The rest of his career was such that one wonders how he ever had time to write, poetry, that is. He was sent on military and diplomatic missions to France, Spain, and Flanders. He joined a trade and diplomatic mission to Genoa with a side trip to Florence where he began his love affair with Dante's "La Divina Commedia." He got to know the writings of Petrarch and Boccaccio as well, authors whose works were a great influence on his creative output. He was appointed the Controller of the Customs and Subsidies on wool for the port of London, the wool trade being England's largest trade. He became Justice of the Peace and Member of Parliament for the county of Kent. (Records show that he gave up his lease on the Aldgate house in order to move to Kent.) Throughout his life he received grants and annuities; often he requested money and more money. This may explain his late work "The Complaint of Chaucer to his Purse," addressed to Henry IV. The requests were often granted and finally Henry awarded him a sizable annuity which made him a wealthy man in his last days.

In the final months of his life, he rented a house in the garden of Westminster Abbey, a stone's throw from Westminster Hall, the ancient seat of English government. He died on October 25, 1400. That Chaucer was buried in Westminster Abbey was due primarily to the fact that his last residence was on the abbey grounds. So important was he deemed as a poet that the space around the tomb was later dubbed the Poet's Corner, and luminaries of English letters have been laid to rest around him down through the centuries.

Chaucer's outlook on life was basically a Christian one. He believed in the Creed and the Sacraments, and was influenced by the rich intellectual and spiritual traditions of Christianity. This was a Christianity where the Catholic Church was omnipresent. The ordinary citizen, spoon-fed with the Sacraments, was comfortably cared for from birth to death. It was a Christianity devoid of the Puritanism, Victorianism, and Jansenism of the later centuries, that is, a Christianity that was not always on the defensive.

He held Catholic Church dogmas, believed in the Incarnation and Redemption, knew the New Testament and the teachings and parables of Christ, and had a medieval grasp of what one had to do to go to heaven. Yet being a man of the court, an intellectual, and an artist, he was not constrained blindly to these teachings. He was never a part of that large uneducated citizenry that was so constrained.

This was a time when educated people learned to write poetry and several of his friends wrote verse; none, however, reached his stature. Music was a part of education and the cultured world; music accompanied Mass, meals, and entertainments. Society was surrounded by ornate tapestries, beautifully illustrated books, and brightly colored statues in the churches. Courtiers and clergy alike wore scarlet and ermine. No wonder the Parson in "The Canterbury Tales" attacked this extravagance. The Court Chaucer trafficked in was an exciting center of affairs and ideas, of affluence and comfort.

We can deduce from his works that he had a basic intellectual background in philosophy, having translated Boethius' "Consolation of Philosophy," science, rhetoric, and literature. Dante is evident everywhere, so too Boccaccio. He was not a university man and we are not certain of where he took his early education, although it is thought that he had some early schooling at St. Paul's Almonry.

He knew Latin and French. As a matter of fact most of the upper class of England still spoke French in their daily lives. They were still Normans some three centuries after the Norman Conquest of 1066, and their French kept them separated from the lower-class Saxons. Though Chaucer was not of the upper class, it was with them that he was associated from his early life.

So many of the literary works that the Englishman read were translated from the author's language into Latin. It was a curious phenomenon then that Chaucer wrote in English, the first English author and thereby the Father of English Poetry. Dante began his "Commedia" in Latin but when he discovered that he was not proficient enough in Latin to describe the horrors of Hell he reverted to Italian. And the trend picked up across the channel. Things were changing and English was coming into its own. Two great masterpieces were written in the late fourteenth century, "Sir Gawain and the Green Knight," by an unknown author, and "Piers Plowman" by William Langland. And then came "The Canterbury Tales."

It is safe to say that the Europe of Chaucer's England was a community with an international language, an international church, and a concept of a united Christendom. But a new era was coming in with the vernacular as a literary language, also the emergence of modern ideas, such as nationalism, Protestantism, and secularism. Chaucer lived in this transition period and it gave him the advantage of presenting, artistically speaking, the balance of the two worlds.

Chaucer's orthodoxy is plain enough. He makes no secret of his belief in the necessity of confession to a priest, of his reverence for saints and sacraments, his acceptance of pilgrimages, all practices condemned by the Wyclifites, who were so intent on attacking authority and reforming the Church that their founder John Wyclif ultimately denied the doctrine of Transubstantiation which led to his condemnation in 1380. Ruth Margaret Ames says "Everything we know about Chaucer, the body of his work, the records of his life, his self-image, contribute to a picture of a man who held orthodox views without worrying about conformity, who practiced intellectual freedom, who was zealous for truth and charity, and who had great breadth of humor and humanity." His was an inclusive Christianity.

Chaucer's lesser works have a value and charm all of their own. I hesitate to call them minor works because they are crafted in near perfect fashion, revealing the poet as a master of the literary genres prevalent at the time; also they are precursor to his classic, "The Canterbury Tales."

"The Book of the Duchess" is a dream-poem in 1,334 lines lamenting the death of Blanche of Lancaster, first wife of John of Gaunt. The love-lorn poet falls asleep reading the story of Ceix and Alcyone and follows a hunting party. He meets a knight in black who laments the loss of his lady. The knight tells of her virtue and beauty and of their courtship, and in answer to the dreamer's question declares her dead. The hunting party reappears and a bell strikes twelve, awakening the poet who finds his book still in his hand. It is an accomplished and charming work founded on the French tradition of the dream as a vehicle for love poetry.

"Roman de la Rose," written by Guillaume de Lorris and Jean de Meun and translated by Chaucer in verse, is an allegorical presentation of courtly love. In the first part, the allegorical figures mostly embody various aspects of the lady whom the love-narrator meets in his endeavor to reach the rose which symbolizes the lady's love. In the second part, love is shown in a wider context of scholarship, philosophy, and morals. The poem, in its allegorical dream form and in its presentation of both the courtly and the philosophical discussions of love, was an immense literary influence all through the later Middle Ages throughout Europe.

"Consolation of Philosophy," a work by the sixth century Roman Boethius, written when the author was in prison awaiting his execution, was probably one of the most valued books of the whole Middle Ages. The author laments his fate but asserts that Philosophy reminds him of the caprices of fortune, and of the vanity of those things, riches, honors, power, which the world esteems good. The only real good is God. Philosophy answers the question of the true nature of Providence, and the reconciliation of free will with the foreknowledge possessed by God. Chaucer's own philosophical attitude, that of living fully in the world while remaining spiritually away from it, is very much in the spirit of Boethius.

"Troilus and Criseide" can hardly be considered one of Chaucer's lesser works since it is his longest complete poem, some 8,239 lines, and one of great beauty. Chaucer takes his story from Boccaccio's "Il Filostrato" and uses it as a vehicle for some of his philosophical attitudes that he shares with Boethius. The story of the love of Troilus and Criseide and its betrayal, against the setting of the siege of Troy by the Greeks, is conventional. But Chaucer introduces an adjuration to young lovers to withdraw from worldly vanity and to place their trust, not in the unstable fortune of young love, courtly love in particular, but in God.

"The Legend of Good Women" is an unfinished poem by Chaucer which begins with a rebuke of the sleeping narrator by the god of love because of the disparaging things he has written about women (a commonplace convention). Chaucer vows to make amends by composing this work in praise of women celebrated for their fidelity in love. The women are Cleopatra, Thisbe, Dido, Hypsipyle and Medea, Lucrece, Ariadne, Philomena, Phyllis and Hypermnestia.

"The Parliament of Fowls" is a dream poem centering on a conference of birds to choose their mates on St. Valentine's Day. The poet falls into a sleep in which he expresses the Boethian lament that he has not what he wants, and has what he does not want (this usually refers to unrequited love in medieval writing). He then has a vision of a garden in which the goddess of Nature presides over the choosing of mates. The argument centers on the opposition between courtly love and pragmatic love. The debate is unresolved, and the birds agree to assemble again a year later to decide. The poem is a brilliant example of the bestiary genre which lends itself so well to irony and satire (the word 'parliament" in the title has any number of undertones); the bestiary was used to great advantage in the twentieth century by George Orwell in his novel "The Animal Farm."

Chaucer's most celebrated work, "The Canterbury Tales," was probably designed about 1387 and extended to 17,000 lines in prose and verse, although most of it is rhyming couplets. The General Prologue describes "Some nine and twenty in a company / Of sundry folk" at the Tabard Inn in Southwark (in fact they add up to 31). They are pilgrims on their way to the shrine of the famous English saint, Thomas a Becket, the Archbishop of Canterbury who was murdered in his cathedral in 1170.

Detailed pen-pictures are given of 21 of the pilgrims, vividly described and corresponding to traditional lists of the orders of society, clerical and lay. There is every possibility that Chaucer saw these departures since at the time of composition he was living in Greenwich and could see the road taken for the journey. The distance from London to Canterbury is about ninety minutes by rail, but the tradition of a walking tour of the pilgrims' journey by Chaucer lovers and university students continues to this day.

Medieval people were notorious story tellers, so the host of the Tabard Inn, Harry Bailey, a natural leader with fine organizational skills, proposes that the pilgrims should shorten the road by telling four stories each, two on the way to Canterbury and two on the way back. He will accompany them and a free supper paid by the others will be awarded to the teller of the best story on their return. The work is incomplete; only twenty-three pilgrims tell stories, and there are only twenty-four stories told altogether (Chaucer tells two). In the scheme the stories are linked by narrative exchanges between the pilgrims and by prologues and epilogues to the tales.

Chaucer uses an imaginative frame-story format to present the twenty-four tales. The stories cover a wide range of subjects, most often reflecting the personality and the class in society of the teller. It is interesting to note that the frame story format was not particularly new and had been a favorite of writers for centuries and for sometime before Chaucer.

"The Arabian Nights," more properly called "The Thousand and One Nights," was a group of loosely told tales passed down by word of mouth in many lands throughout the East. They took the form of a collection in Cairo sometime in the fifteenth century. Boccaccio's "Decameron" (1353), a far more cohesive collection of stories, had for its occasion a plague in Florence whereby wealthy persons, twelve nobles to be exact, flee the city and in so doing tell stories to pass the time. The tales, all one hundred of them, are completed; the plague ends in Florence, and the nobles return to the city. It is probably the strongest influence on Chaucer. What makes Chaucer's work more memorable, however, is the diversity of characters. Far from being nobles, Chaucer's tale-tellers run the spectrum of the middle class.

The twentieth century saw John Steinbeck's "Wayward Bus" (1947) where a group of people stranded on a bus begin to reveal their inner selves, their conflicts, heartaches. Katherine Anne Porter's "Ship of Fools" (1945), a favorite novel of the last century, has a shipload of passengers on a voyage just before World War II revealing their life situations. In each case, the pilgrimage, the plague, the bus, the ship, provide the setting that will become a microcosm of the world, each little world a reflection of the outer and larger world.

Concerning "The Canterbury Tales," Chaucer himself is included as a principal character on the pilgrimage, a departure from the frame-story device. A mild-mannered, retiring person, he tells two tales. Whereby, the Haberdasher, the Carpenter, the Weaver, the Dyer, and the Tapestry Maker, usually considered as one by critics, who are all members of a guild, each wealthy and smart enough to be an alderman, are assigned no tales by the author.

The Knight is a courtly medieval fighting man who has served king and religion all over the known world. Modest in dress and speech, though the highest in rank of the pilgrims to Canterbury, he rides with only his son and a yeoman in attendance. Quite obviously, the narrator admires the Knight very much. He is the first one to be portrayed and he is the first to tell a tale. More so he embodies all the noble characteristics of the ideal military gentleman, "chivalry, truth, honour, generousness and courtesy . . . a true, a perfect gentle-knight." He could be a medieval version of Castiglione's "Il Cortegio," the ideal gentleman.

His is a tale of courtly love in which Theseus, duke of Athens, imprisons Arcite and Palamon, two knights from

Thebes (another ancient city in Greece). From their prison, the knights see and fall in love with Theseus' sister-in-law Emelye. Through the intervention of a friend, Arcite is freed, but he is banished from Athens. He returns in disguise and becomes a page in Emelye's chamber. Palamon escapes from prison, and the two meet and fight over Emelye. Theseus apprehends them and arranges a tournament between the two knights and their allies, with Emelye as the prize. Arcite wins, but he is accidentally thrown from his horse and dies. Palamon then marries Emelye.

As tedious as this four-part story may be for the modern reader, it is one that Chaucer's reader would find very enjoyable. It is fitting that the knight would choose a story filled with knights, love, honor, chivalry, and adventure. Also the many elements of Chance (Fortune or Destiny) in the story are what the reader would expect because these were so much a part of the literary decorum of the day. Yet the most important contribution to Chaucerian literature that the story makes is the element of Courtly Love. This was a code of chivalrous love originating in the twelfth century in the lyrics of the troubadours of northern Italy and Provence, probably deriving from Ovid and popular Oriental ideas. A lover, smitten from afar by a beautiful married woman of equal or higher status, must long agonize and weep in sleepless silence, then reveal his love, then prove it in mighty exploits, adhering to pledges of secrecy and faithfulness until death. Then, finally he achieves consummation. The cult of the Virgin Mary and Neo-Platonism contributed the heightening of the ideal over the sensual. In a sense, the Knight's tale is probably the most representative of the literary taste of the times.

The Squire, the Knight's son, is a young man of 20 who has fought in several battles. Like his father, he exudes knightly courtesy, but he also enjoys a good time. He is a strong, curly-haired young man, a bit foppish with his clothes embroidered with dainty flowers; he fights in the hope of winning the favor of his "lady." His talents are those of the courtly lover, "He loved so hotly that till dawn grew pale / He slept as little as a nightingale," singing, playing the flute, drawing, writing, and riding. He is dutiful to his father and even "carved to serve his father at table."

He tells a story of adventure and enchantment in a distant land. The story he leaves unfinished tells of four gifts sent to Canace, daughter of King Cambuscan. Each of the gifts has magical powers: a ring that enables the bearer to talk to birds, a brass horse that will take its rider anywhere, a mirror that shows the truth and the future, and a sword that can slay any beast. The ring enables Canace to learn the story of a lovelorn female hawk, deserted by her mate. She related the story of how a handsome young, male hawk wooed her and won her in marriage. When he tired of her he took up with a beautiful kite. So remorseful was the female hawk that she left her homeland and wandered aimlessly about the earth. Canace took her to the palace and restored the hawk back to health. The Squire intends to tell of the other three gifts but suddenly the Franklin breaks in and insists on telling his story. Scholars have puzzled over the reasons why Chaucer never finished this story. The story aptly fits the character of the Squire but, unfortunately, is less than half told.

The Yeoman, the Knight's attendant, is a forester "whose face was brown. / He knew the whole of woodcraft up and down." He takes excellent care of his gear. He wears green from head to toe and he carries an enormous bow and beautifully feathered arrows, as well as a sword and a small shield. And "a medal of St. Christopher he wore / Of shining silver on his breast." Chaucer assigns no story to him.

The Prioress, who goes by the name Madame Eglantyne, travels with another nun and three priests as her attendants to the shrine of St. Thomas. A woman of conscience and sympathy, she wears a curious brooch upon which appears the ambiguous statement, in Latin, "Amor vincit omnia." Although she is not part of the royal court, she does her best to imitate its manners, "straining / To counterfeit a courtly kind of grace." She takes great care to eat her food daintily, to reach for food on the table delicately, and to wipe her lips clean of grease before drinking from her cup. "No morsel from her lips did she let fall." She speaks French, but with a provincial English accent. She is compassionate towards animals, weeping when she sees a mouse caught in a trap, and feeding her dogs roasted meat and milk. The narrator says that her features are pretty, "Her way of smiling very simple and coy," and even her enormous forehead had a certain charm.

Her story is that of a little schoolboy murdered for his religion by Jews. In a Christian town in Asia, there was a quarter of the town where Jews lived, kept there by the lord of the town for usurious purposes. Nearby there is a Christian school where the children were free to come and go. One of the children had not learned to read as yet, but did learn, however, to sing the Latin hymn 'O Alma Redemptoris' which he heard the older students sing. Not only did he memorize it but learned its meaning, that it was a song in praise of the Virgin Mary. Every day he would sing the song loudly and devoutly as he walked through the ghetto. The serpent Satan whispered to the Jews that this was an affront to the Jews and an insult to their Jewish Holy Laws. A murderer was hired and one day he grasped the child, slit his throat, and threw the body into a cesspool. The child's mother was beside herself with the child's disappearance but by the direction of Jesus, she discovered the pit where the child was cast. As she approached the place the child's voice broke out in song, the 'O Alma Redemptoris'; the Christian townspeople gathered around in astonishment. The Provost had the Jews rounded up and eventually executed. The child was taken to a neighboring abbey, still singing the 'O Alma,' until the Virgin Mary appeared at his burial and laid a grain upon his tongue. Then the singing stopped. Later a tomb of marble was erected as a memorial to the young martyr.

Certainly the story is in keeping with the nun's character and position. She is a nun whose order relies heavily on the patronage of the Blessed Mother. Yet Chaucer's description of her is so vivid and so detailed many readers have come to see many contradictions in her. One could say that she, and some of the other clergy on the journey, tells us much as to why there was need for a reformation. Her broach can be interpreted in many contradictory ways. The "Amor vincit omnia," we can hope, refers to God. That she travels with three priests (not one, it only takes one to celebrate Mass) tells us that she is a woman of extravagence. That she puts on airs at the dinner table, "she could carry a morsel up and keep / the smallest drop from falling on her breast" seems to go beyond good dinner manners into affectation. Her French from Stratford-atte-Bowe, as noble as it is to have a second language, is still watered-down (and learned in the East End of London, no less!). Her concern for her dogs, and even a mouse, propels us to wonder what is her concern for suffering mankind, the poor and the hungry outside her convent. Since she has the title of Madam we can presume that she was a major administrator of her religious community, consequently the privilege to join a pilgrimage to Canterbury. She seems to be out of place in the group, not because she is a nun but because of her airs that do not reflect the humility that her vocation calls for. I am not saying that she has to have the earthiness of the Wife of Bath, but she is expected to have the humility and the poverty that are part of her calling. Chaucer is saying much in this creation and the narrator's remark "She certainly was very entertaining" smacks of a certain irony. The tale she tells represents Medieval England's hatred for the Jews. There is nothing new about the tale, as a matter of fact there were hundreds of them floating around and so many of them were passed along as true. Some critics see the bland story, which has no specific source, as a comment on her uncritical nature and a reflection of her lack of creative imagination.

The Second Nun, who accompanies the Prioress, tells a Christian legend of the martyrdom of St. Cecilia, a story typical of medieval hagiography. Cecilia, a noble young woman of Rome, on her wedding night convinces her new husband to go to the Appian Way and there be converted to Christianity by Pope Urban. Urban is amazed to see the power that Cecilia had that she could convince a young man to be converted. Valerian, elated by his own conversion, prays to an angel that his brother, Tiburce, also be baptized. Tiburce objects but through the instruction of Cecilia becomes converted. Later an official named Almachius discovers the Christians, has them arrested, and orders them to sacrifice to pagan gods. They refuse and all three are sentenced to death. Cecilia, after insulting the pagan gods and inferring that Almachias is vain and ignorant, is placed in boiling water by executioners; but this fails. They then try three times to cut off her head but do not completely succeed. She lives for three more days, converting many people to Christianity, and then finally dies.

It is fitting that the nun would tell this tale since in her convent, much of their time is spent in discussing the lives of the saints. More interesting is the fact that Chaucer knew so much about this saint and was able to recount it in such detail, especially since little is known about the historical Cecilia. But the story was generally a familiar one to the people and despite its improbabilities and over the top use of the supernatural, it satisfied the peoples' need for legends of noble ideals and martyrs dying for the faith.

The Nun's Priest, whose name is John, is not described in the prologue but the tale that he tells, a beast epic, is clever, didactic, and often hilarious. We see that he is a very witty man. The tale is one of the masterpieces of "The Canterbury Tales."

The tale begins by telling of a poor, elderly widow who lives a simple life in a cottage with her two daughters. Her few possessions include three sows, three cows, a sheep, and some chickens. One chicken, her rooster, is named Chanticleer (which in French means 'sings clearly'). True to his name, Chanticleer's clear clucking sound makes him the master of all roosters. He crows the hour more accurately than any church clock. His crest is redder than fine coral, his beak is black as jet, his nails whiter than lilies, and his feathers shine like burnished gold. Understandably, such an attractive cock would be the Don Juan of the barnyard. Chanticleer has many hen-wives, but he loved most truly a hen named Pertelote. She is as lovely as Chanticleer is magnificent.

As Chanticleer, Pertelote, and all of Chanticleer's adjunct hen-wives are roosting one night, Chanticleer has a terrible nightmare about an orange houndlike beast who threatens to kill him while he is in the yard. Fearless Pertelote berates him for letting a dream get the better of him. She believes the dream to be the result of some physical malady, and she promises him that she will find some purgative herbs. She urges him once more not to dread something as fleeting and illusory as a dream. In order to convince her that his dream was important, he tells the stories of men who dreamed of murder and then discovered it. His point in telling these stories is to prove to Pertelote that "Mordre will out"—murder will reveal itself—even and especially in dreams. Chanticleer cites textual examples of famous dream interpretations to further support his thesis that dreams are prophetic. He then praises Pertelote's beauty and grace, and the aroused hero and heroine make love in barnyard fashion, copulating with her 20 times before "it was pryme" (6:00 am, the hour of Prime).

One day in May, Chanticleer has just declared his perfect

happiness when a wave of sadness passes over him. That very night, a hungry fox stalks Chanticleer and his wives, watching their every move. The next day, Chanticleer notices the fox while watching a butterfly, and the fox confronts him with duplicitous courtesy, telling the rooster not to be afraid. Chanticleer relishes the fox's flattery of his singing. He beats his wings with pride, stands on his toes, stretches his neck, closes his eyes, and crows loudly. The fox reaches out and grabs Chanticleer by the throat, and then slinks away with him back toward the woods. No one is around to witness what has happened. Once Pertelote finds out what has happened, she burns her feathers with grief, and a great wail arises from the henhouse.

The widow and her daughters hear the screeching and spy the fox running away with the rooster. The dogs follow, and pretty soon the whole barnyard joins in the bedlam. Chanticleer very cleverly suggests that the fox turn and boast to his pursuers. The fox opens his mouth to do so, and Chanticleer flies out of the fox's mouth and into a high tree. The fox tries to flatter the bird into coming down, but Chanticleer has learned his lesson. He tells the fox that flattery will work for him no more. The moral of the story, concludes the Nun's Priest, is never to trust a flatterer. Do not let flattery ravish reason (Chanticleer); do not open your mouth when it should be closed (Fox); do not close your eyes when you should be vigilant (Chanticleer); do not allow yourself to be fooled twice (Chanticleer).

The tale is a classic example of the Bestiary (or Beast Epic), probably an elaboration of Aesop's fables which date back to the sixth century B.C. and similar folklore in which talking animals satirize human foibles and institutions, particularly church and court. (Paulus Diaconus, an Italian monk respected by Charlemagne, is said to have written the first beast epic, but the form flourished in northern France, western Germany, and Flanders in the twelfth and thirteenth centuries.) Reynard the fox, Isegrym the wolf,

Chanticleer the cock, Tybert the cat, Bruin the bear, and Courtoys the hound are prominent characters in the bestiary tradition.

Of course, the 1945 George Orwell novel "Animal Farm" is a classic example of the beast fable for the modern reader. It is a satire on Revolutionary and post-Revolutionary Russia, and, by extension, on all revolutions. The animals of Mr. Jones' farm revolt against their human masters and drive them out, the pigs becoming the leaders. Eventually the pigs dominated by Napoleon, their chief, become corrupted by power and a new tyranny replaces the old. The ultimate slogan runs "All animals are equal, but some animals are more equal than others." Napoleon, ruthless and cynical, represents Stalin, and Snowball, the idealist whom he drives out, Trotsky. Boxer, the noble carthorse, stands for the strength, simplicity, and good nature of the common man.

The satirical affect of the beast fable rests on dramatic irony, a discrepancy between the speaker and what is being said, a clash between appearance and reality. "The Nun's Priest Tale" reads like a simple fable about animals that concludes with a moral lesson. But it is more than that. Chanticleer's learned allusions to the 'Dream of Scipio', Daniel and Joseph's interpretations of dreams, and Andromache's dream, as well as his quote of the Latin phrase "In principio, mulier est hominis confusio" is a wonderful send-up of medieval scholarship and, as well, the court intellectuals and their pretentiousness which Chaucer saw first-hand. And to allude to the traitors Judas and Ganelon and then expound on the theology of divine foreknowledge is parody at its richest.

The rooster's plumage is described as shining like burnished gold, certainly a parody of the Homeric hero and his shield. Milton uses the same epic device three centuries later in describing Satan's shield in "Paradise Lost," but certainly not as parody. As a matter of fact, the tale uses any number of epic devices (apostrophes, invocations, epic hero) to enhance the stature of the story. And the reader roars at all this fuss over the doings in a chicken coop. Also the tale is an ironic retelling of the fable of the fox and the rooster in the guise of a courtly romance. It is hilariously done, since into the struttings of a rooster's life, Chaucer transposes scenes of a hero's dreaming of death and courting his lady love, in a manner that imitates the overblown, descriptive style of courtly romances. Chanticleer's beating his wings, standing on his toes, stretching his neck, closing his eyes, and crowing loudly as the fox flatters him is right out of the tradition of the prima donna taking her curtains. (Opera did not get started until a much later date, but the court singers certainly anticipated the opera diva.) And the hilarious chaos in the barnyard that results from the rooster's abduction can easily be seen as a precursor of the Marx Brothers statesroom antic or to the bedlam they caused during the opera house's "Il Trovatore." The tale is an example of Chaucer at his greatest. (The host's attraction to the priest's muscles, large neck, and big chest has some sexual implications: his observation that if the priest were not in holy orders, he would be as sexually potent as Chanticleer supports this.)

The Monk, who prefers to be out of his cloister, is a fat hedonist whose favorite food is "a fat swan best, and roasted whole." It is quite possible that his administrative position in the monastery was one that required him to have contact with the business or commercial world in order to take care of the needs of the cloister. And the things of the world have overtaken him. He is no lover of books and learning which is strange for a monk of the Middle Ages when a monk's primary vocation was to pray, reflect, study, and excel in learning. Chaucer is almost cynical in describing him as "one of the finest sort / Who rode the country." He prefers to hunt and eat. He owns horses that are richly dressed and he loves his dogs, "Greyhounds he had, as swift as birds." He himself is richly dressed "With fine grey fur, the finest in the land." He is bald and quite upbeat in personality. The tale he tells is in direct contrast to his personality. The tale reads like a catalog of tragic figures of the past.

He defines tragedy as being the story of a man fallen from high degree and then offers many examples, including anecdotes of Lucifer, Adam, Samson, Hercules, Balthasar, Nebuchadnezzar, Zenobia, King Peter of Spain, King Peter of Cyprus, Bernarbo of Lombardy, Holofernes, Antiochus, Ugolino of Pisa (one of Dante's most vivid accounts in the Inferno), Alexander, Julius Caesar, and Croesus. One is grateful that he is interrupted by the knight, which makes his tale unfinished, since the account of the tragic figures is bleak, boring, and repetitious. It's a difficult read. And how does the monk know so much about so many historical figures and yet be an unlearned monk?

The Friar, who is named Hubert, is a merry man who "knew the taverns well in every town / And every innkeeper and barmaid too / Better than lepers." Since he is an exempt religious he holds authority directly from the Pope and has the privilege of hearing confessions, a privilege given only to mendicant orders of the time. He abuses the privilege by dispensing penances in proportion to the pay-off from the penitent. "Sweetly he heard his penitents at shrift / With pleasant absolution, for a gift." He is a complete contradiction of his Franciscan calling and sees himself as well above "dealing with a scum / Of wretched lepers." He has the reputation of being the best beggar in the friary and he gets his alms from taverns and inns. It is significant that Chaucer mentions lepers twice in his portrayal of the friar. The very first of the three great moments in St. Francis' journey to God was when he, a wealthy young man with an aversion to lepers, dismounted his horse upon seeing a leper on the road, leaned over, gave him some money, and kissed him. (The other two moments were his receiving the message of his ministry from God while praying before the Cross in the Damiano chapel and his receiving the stigma, the five wounds of Christ on his body during his last days.) In kissing the leper Francis learned that Christ's message is that we are to love all people, regardless of whatever makes them different.

The Friar's story tells of a summoner (a diocesan priest) who is engaged by his bishop to spy on parishioners, record their immoral deeds, and then by entrapment, extort large sums from them to get their names off the record. The summoner one day meets a yeoman who turns out to be the devil himself. They enter into a pact and by a number of twists of fate the summoner finally loses his soul and is dragged into hell by the devil. The story arouses the discomfiture of the Summoner in the group of pilgrims and acquaints the reader of the conflict that existed in Chaucer's time between diocesan priests of the national church and the exempt priests of the mendicant orders. And it is ironic that an extortionist priest tells a story about a priest given to entrapment. And when the narrator concludes that there were none so good as Hubert in his profession, we see Chaucer at his most ironic.

The Merchant is a tight-lipped man of business who is a member of the rich and powerful rising middle class. He rides "high on his horse," wears a forking beard, "a Flemish beaver hat," and daintily buckled boots. He is smooth and knows a good bargain. He looks and talks so impressively and transacts his business with such flair that "none knew he was in debt." He tells a story of the evils of marriage between old men and young women.

His tale tells of January, an old husband, and May, his young wife, and problems with obedient fidelity involved in this relationship. January ignores the good advice of Justinus in favor of the time-serving opinion of Placebo and marries May. When he goes blind she makes love to her suitor in a pear tree. Pluto mischievously restores January's sight, but Proserpine inspires May to explain that the restoration of his sight was brought about by their activities in the pear tree and that this has been their purpose.

The Clerk of Oxford is a serious young scholar who loves philosophy and prefers books to worldly pleasures. He was probably working for a Masters degree, aspiring for some ecclesiastical position. He has a gaunt, hollow look, and his horse, like himself, "was thinner than a rake" and his clothes were threadbare since he preferred buying books rather than food and clothes. Whatever money he had for his education and buying books, he received from friends and "prayed for them most earnestly, returning / Thanks to them thus for paying for his learning." He did not talk much but when he did it was with poise and moral virtue. Chaucer's treatment of the Clerk is filled with love.

His tale is an answer to the Wife of Bath's idea that in marriage the woman ought to have dominion. The Clerk's tale is of an infinitely patient wife named Griselda, who endures all manner of ill-treatment from her husband, the Marquis Walter. When the Marquis married Griselda, he decided to put her to gruelling tests of her fidelity, which included his request that she abandon their daughter, later that she abandon their son, still later that she return home to her father so that he could take a second wife. In all of this Griselda perseveres and finally, the Marquis, guilt-ridden, confesses to her what he has done, takes her back, returns the children to her, and pronounces to the world that Griselda is the perfect, steadfast wife, a model for all wives.

The Man of Law, a busy man who "was less busy than he seemed to be," makes a great show of his learning, and can cite "every judgement, case and crime / Ever recorded since King William's time." He has a brilliant memory and can cite every word and comma of every judgment, a feat that earned him high distinction in the profession and enormous fees for his work. One has the impression that he can work his way around the law for himself and for his clients without ever violating the letter of the law.

His tale tells of a Muslin sultan of Syria who converts his whole sultanate and himself to Christianity so that he can win the hand of Custance, daughter of the emperor of Rome. The sultan's mother, who remains faithful to the Muslim faith, stages a banquet at which she has her son and all the Christians massacred. Custance who survives is set adrift in a rudderless ship and after several years of floating is rescued in Northumberland by a constable and his wife, Hermengyld. Custance converts them to Christianity. One night at the instigation of Satan, a young knight murders Hermengyld and places the bloody knife near the sleeping Custance. The constable returns home with Alla, the king of Northumberland, and after Alla hears the whole story about Custance, takes pity on her and probes deeply into the murder. The knight while accusing Custance of the murder is struck down and his eyes burst out of his face which convinces Alla that he is the murderer. He is executed and Alla, converted to Christianity, marries Custance. Alla's mother, the evil Donegild, through manipulation and interception of letters, has Custance exiled while Alla is away. When Alla returns he learns what his mother has done and kills her. After many mishaps at sea, including an attempted rape, Custance is reunited with Alla in Rome and they return to England. After Alla's death she returns to Rome to live out her life. In some way this complicated and detailed story reflects the lawyer's exceptional memory and his fanatic commitment to detail, as convoluted as the story may be.

The Franklin is a rich landlord who loves to eat. "His bread, his ale were finest of the time / And no one had a better stock of wine." He was "Epicurus' very son." In his time he had been sheriff of his county, "a model among landed gentry." His story is an old Breton lay, a tale of chivalry and the supernatural. He apologizes for the story and its telling, saying he is an uneducated man. His tale, a folk ballad of ancient Brittany, tells of Dorigen who awaits the return of her husband, Arveragus, who has gone to England to win honor in feats of arms. She worries that the ship bringing her husband home will wreck itself on the coastal rocks, and she promises Aurelius, a young man who falls in love with her, that she will give her body to him if he clears the rocks from the coast. Aurelius hires a student who is learned in magic to create the illusion that the rocks have disappeared. Arveragus returns home and tells his wife that she must keep her promise to Aurelius. Aurelius is so impressed by Arveragus' honorable intention he generously absolves her of the promise, and the magician, in turn generously absolves Aurelius of the money he owes. Chaucer then poses the question: "Woman the most noble?"

The Haberdasher, the Carpenter, the Weaver, the Dyer, and the Tapestry Maker are Guildsmen who are listed together and appear as a unit. English guilds were a combination of labor unions and social fraternities, craftsmen of similar occupations joined together to increase their bargaining power, and live communally. All five Guildsmen are clad in the livery of their brotherhood. "They were so trim and fresh their gear would pass / For new." Their wives enjoyed their wealth, flaunting it by going to church and by being called 'Madam' and having their "mantle carried, like a queen." Chaucer assigns no tales to them.

The Cook, named Roger, was hired by the Guildsmen to serve them during their journey. As chef, he knew all the proper spices, he knew all "London ale by flavour," he could roast, broil, and fry, and "Make good thick soup and bake a tasty pie." He is a rollicking individual who loves the bawdy tales of the Miller and the Reeve. He insists on telling his own bawdy tale but Chaucer leaves it unfinished.

The Cook tells of an apprentice cook working in London named Perkin Reveler who was full of love as he was full of sin. At every wedding he would dance and sing rather than attend the shop. And when he was not dancing or singing, he was gambling. His master finally decided that one rotten apple could spoil the whole barrel. Thus, the master dismissed Perkin. The young man, obeying another proverb, "birds of a feather flock together," joined another young man of the same habits as his and who was married to a prostitute. The tales breaks off after fifty-eight lines.

The Shipman is the captain of the Maudelayne of Dartmouth. He is a good skipper and a smuggler, huge in appearance and uncouth in manner. "The nicer rules of conscience he ignored." He knew all the ports from the Mediterranean to the Baltic. He could read the stars and knew how to handle himself in a fight. But he did not ride a horse well and he looked like a fish out of water on his horse. Like others of the company, he tells a fabliau, a bawdy tale. He relates the misadventures of a merchant of St. Denis, in Belgium, who is cheated of his wife's favors and his money by a sly monk named John, who tricks the wife into having sex with him by borrowing money from the merchant, then giving it to the wife so she can repay her own debt to her husband, in exchange for sexual favors. When the monk sees the merchant next, he tells him that he returned the merchant's money to his wife. The wife realizes that she has been duped, but she boldly tells her husband to forgive her debt and that she will repay it in bed.

The Doctor of Physic, a great talker, is a materialistic man greatly interested in money; he "had a special love of gold." He knows all the great medical authorities but "did not read the Bible very much." He knows his astrology and something of nature and could tell what humour was responsible for a sickness. Everyone thought he was in league with the druggist. He made a lot of money during the plague but he is tight with it.

The Physician's tale tells of the judge Appius who lusts

after Virginia, the beautiful daughter of Virginius. Appius persuades a churl named Claudius to declare her his slave, stolen from him by Virginius. Appius declares that Virginius must hand over his daughter to Claudius. Virginius tells his daughter that she must die rather than suffer dishonor, and she virtuously consents to her father's cutting her head off. Appius sentences Virginius to death, but the Roman people, aware of Appius' evil, throw him into prison where he commits suicide.

The Wife of Bath, the most colorful character of all the pilgrims, is a clothmaker. "She'd had five husbands, all at the church door, / Apart from other company in youth." Her name is Alice and she is gap-toothed and deaf in one ear. Apparently wealthy from her marriages, she has traveled a great deal, including three trips to Jerusalem. She is well-versed in marriage and love-making. "and knew the remedies for love's mischances / An art in which she knew the oldest dances." Her theory is that the woman must dominate in marriage, and to make her point tells a tale of an ugly lady who, when her husband is obedient, becomes fair.

If Chaucer had created no other character for his pilgrimage and only the Wife of Bath he still would have gone down in the history of English literature for this brilliant characterization. The Wife of Bath has become many things for many people: readers, scholars, critics, love her or hate her; all admit she is an extraordinary creation. For our times she has become the first person to liberate herself from the strictures of an institutional church, the first feminist, the first shrew anticipating Shakespeare's Katarina letting Petruchio think that he has tamed her.

The Wife of Bath begins her prologue by announcing that she has always followed the rule of experience rather than that of authority. And since she has had five husbands at the church door, she has had a great amount of experience. She sees nothing wrong with having five husbands, and cannot understand Jesus' rebuke to the woman at the well who also had five husbands. She prefers the biblical injunction to "increase and multiply." She reminds the pilgrims of several biblical incidents: Solomon and his many wives, the command that husband must leave his family and join with his wife, and St. Paul's warning that it is better to marry than to burn. Having shown herself to have a knowledge of the bible, she asks where it is that virginity is commanded. It is, she admits, advised for those who want to live the perfect life, but she admits that she is not perfect. Moreover, she asks, what is the purpose of the sex organs? They were made for both functional purposes and for pleasure. And like many cold and coy women, she was always willing to have sex whenever her husband wanted to. The Pardoner interrupts and says that he was thinking of getting married, but having heard the Wife of Bath, he is glad that he is single. She responds that she could tell more, and the Pardoner encourages her to do so.

The Wife then relates stories concerning her five husbands. She recalled that three of them were very old and good and rich. And she will now reveal how she was able to control each one. Her techniques were very simple. She accused her husbands (the first three) of being at fault. She scolded them when they accused her of being extravagant with clothes and jewelry when her only purpose was to please her husband. She railed at one husband when he refused to disclose the worth of his land and the value of his coffers. She derided the husband who considered her as property. She denounced men who refused her the liberty of visiting her friends, for women, like men, like liberty. She decried the husband who suspected her chastity was in danger every time she smiled at another gentleman to whom she wished only to be courteous. She denounced the husband who hired spies to determine if she was unfaithful, and indeed, hired her own witnesses to testify to her faithfulness to her marriage bed.

Each time she gained complete mastery over one of her husbands, he would then die. But her fourth husband was different. He kept a mistress and this bothered her, because the Wife was still in the prime of life and full of passion. Thus, while not being actually unfaithful to her fourth husband, she made him think so. Thus "in his own grease I made him fry." But now he is dead, and when she was burying him, she could hardly keep her eyes off a young clerk named Jankyn whom she had already admired. Thus, at the month's end, she married for the fifth time even though she was twice the clerk's age. And this time she married for love and not riches. But as soon as the honeymoon was over, she was disturbed to find that the clerk spent all of his time reading books, especially books which disparaged women. In fact, he collected all the books he could which told unfavorable stories about women and he spent all his time reading from these collections.

One night he began to read aloud from his collection. He began with the story of Eve and read about all the unfaithful women, murderesses, prostitutes, etc. which he could find. The Wife of Bath could not stand this any more, so she grabbed the book and hit Jankyn so hard that he fell over backwards into the fire. He jumped up and hit her with his fist. She fell to the floor and pretended to be dead. When he kneeled over her, she hit him once more and pretended to die. He was so upset that he promised her anything if she would live. And this is how she gained "sovereignty" over her fifth husband. And from that day on, she was a true and faithful wife to him.

The Wife of Bath's tale, while carrying out her theme of female dominance is somewhat flat after such a colorful prologue, for it tells of a young knight of King Arthur's court who rapes a maiden. To atone for his crime, Arthur's queen sends him on a quest to discover what women want most. An ugly old woman promises the knight that she will tell him the secret if he promises to do whatever she wants for saving his life. He agrees, and she tells him woman want control of their husbands and their own lives. They go together to Arthur's queen, and the old woman's answer turns out to be correct. The old woman then tells the knight that he must marry her. When the knight confesses later that that he is repulsed by her appearance, she gives him a choice: she can either be ugly and faithful, or beautiful and unfaithful. The knight tells her to make the choice herself. With that she rewards him for giving her control of the marriage by rendering herself both beautiful and faithful.

The Parson, a "holy-minded man of good renown," seemingly the only devout churchman in the company, lives in poverty and is rich in holy thoughts and deeds. The pastor of a large town, he preaches the Gospel and makes sure to practice what he preaches. He is everything that the Monk, the Friar, and the Pardoner are not. He visits the sick, does not criticize other priests, gives to the poor, and tends his sheep (parishioners) with love. Chaucer loves his parson and has the narrator exclaim, "I think there never was a better priest." Refusing to tell an idle tale to his fellow pilgrims, he tells what he terms a merry tale about the Seven Deadly Sins.

The Parson's Tale, probably Chaucer's dullest piece in the whole work, is really a sermon on the Seven Deadly Sins. He begins by reminding the pilgrims that everyone wants to be saved and this can come only by Penitence, and the resolve to sin no more. The root of Penitence is contrition; the branches and the leaves are confession; the fruit is satisfaction; the seed is grace; and the heat in that seed is love of God. He then goes on to discuss the seven deadly sins, first Pride which takes upon itself the form of arrogance, boasting, hypocrisy, and joy of having done someone harm. The remedy for Pride is humility. He then discusses Envy, Anger, Sloth, Avarice, Gluttony, and Lechery. It is fitting that he should preach this sermon. He is a holy man whom Chaucer loves and he feels the evil of the times require good preaching. Although it is a tiresome sermon, it appears near the end of the storytelling to give the whole experience a high moral tone.

The Plowman is the Parson's brother and is equally holy. A member of the peasant class, he pays his tithes to the Church and leads a good life. Like his brother "he would help the poor / For love of Christ and never take a penny." Chaucer assigns him no tale.

The Miller is stout and brawny, "a chap of sixteen stone," with a wart on his nose. He has a big mouth, both figuratively and literally. He threatens the Host's notion of propriety when he drunkenly insists on telling the second tale, after the Knight's tale. The Miller seems to enjoy overturning all conventions: he ruins the Host's careful planned storytelling order; he rips doors off hinges; and he tells a tale that is somewhat blasphemous, ridiculing religious clerks, scholarly clerks, carpenters, and women. "A wrangler and buffoon, he had a store / Of tavern stories, filthy in the main."

The Miller's tale is as earthy as the knight's is elevated. Nicholas, an Oxford student boarding with a carpenter named John, lusts for Alison, the latter's young wife. He convinces his landlord that a great flood is imminent but assures him that they can escape if John will make three tubs, one for each of them, and hang them from the eaves of the house in readiness. When John falls asleep in his tub, Nicholas and Alison climb down from theirs and make love in John's bed. Toward morning another admirer, Absalom, a dandified parish clerk, comes to the bedroom window and begs a kiss. Alison gleefully presents her posterior over the windowsill. When Absalom discovers which end of Alison he has kissed, he vows revenge. Returning from a blacksmith's forge with a hot coulter, he asks for another kiss. This time Nicholas decides to repeat the ruse by exposing his posterior; at the precise moment of the kiss he expels gas thunderously. Absalom applies the smoking implement, the stricken Nicholas shouts "Water!" and John awakens. When he cuts lose his tub and crashes to the ground, the confusion brings out the neighbors in the gathering dawn, who laugh at the disorder, especially John's "madness."

The Reeve, a slender, choleric man named Oswald, was the manager of a large estate. He was a skinny man with a bad temper. His close cut beard and short haircut accentuated his thinness and long legs. He was an able, efficient, and shrewd man who had reaped riches from his master. He was flawless in keeping his masters accounts, "No one ever caught him in arrears." The serfs, herdsmen, and workers fear him dreadfully because of his unrelenting perseverance. Having been a carpenter, he is incensed by the Miller's tale.

The Reeve tells the story of two students, John and Alayn, who go to the mill to watch the miller grind their corn, so that he won't have a chance to steal any. But the miller unties their horse, and while they chase it, he steals some of the flower he has just ground for them. By the time the students catch the horse, it is dark, so they spend the night in the miller's house. That night Alayn seduces the miller's daughter, and John seduces his wife. When the miller wakes up and finds out what has happened, he tries to beat the students. His wife, thinking that her husband is actually one of the students, hits the miller over the head with a staff. The students take back their stolen goods and leave.

The Manciple was a steward for a law school who took care of the needs of lawyers living in the dormitory. He was an uneducated man who was shrewd enough to steal a great deal from the learned lawyers, thirty of them, who hired him to look after their establishments. The narrator says that it is a marvel of God's grace that "an illiterate fellow can outpace / The wisdom of a heap of learned men."

The Manciple, after criticizing the Cook for his drunkeness and for his inability to tell a tale, tells a fable of the tell-tale crow, probably not that unfamiliar to the pilgrims. Phebus has a crow which is white and can speak. It reveals to Phebus the infidelity of his wife and Phebus kills her in a rage. Then in remorse, he plucks out the crow's white feathers, deprives it of speech, and curses it with blackness, which is why crows are now black. The manciple ends the tale by admonishing people to restrain their tongues.

The Summoner, a man employed to summon sinners for a trial before a church court, has a fire red complexion, pimples and boils, a scaly infection around the eye, a moth-eaten beard, and has leprosy. Children were terrified of him. To make matters worse, he loved to eat garlic, onions, leeks, and drink strong wine. He could quote a few lines of Latin to impress people. Forgiving the sinner was ordinary for him. "Why, he'd allow—just for a quart of wine—/ Any good lad to keep a concubine." He was well-acquainted with ladies of questionable reputation; "he was as hot and lecherous as a sparrow." Angered by the Friar's tale about a summoner, he tells a tale about a friar who becomes the subject of coarse humor.

The Summoner tells his listeners that there is no difference between friars and fiends. Once when an angel took a friar down to hell to show him the torments there, the friar asked why there were not friars in hell. The angel then pulled up Satan's tail and twenty thousand friars came out of his rectum. In the Summoners's Tale, a friar begs for money from a dying man named Thomas and his wife, who have recently lost their child. The friar shamelessly exploits the couple's misfortune to extract money from them; so, Thomas tells the friar that he is sitting on something that he will bequeath to the friars. The friar reaches for his bequest, and as he does Thomas breaks wind. The friar is then instructed to devise an ingenious stratagem to divide it with perfect justice among the friars.

The Pardoner, a church official who had authority from Rome to sell pardons and indulgences to sinners, has just returned from Rome with a bag filled with fake pardons, "Brimful of pardons come from Rome, all hot," which he planned to sell at a great profit to himself. He claims, for example, that he has the veil of the Virgin Mary. He has long, yellow, greasy hair and is beardless and furthermore would never have a beard. Chaucer implies that he is sexually ambivalent. He knew how to sing and preach so as to frighten everybody into buying his pardons at a great price.

The Pardoner's Tale tells of three rioters who set out to find Death who has killed their companion. A mysterious old man tells them they will find him under a particular tree, but when they get there they find instead eight bushels of gold, which they plot to sneak into town after dark. The youngest goes into town to fetch food and drink, but brings back poison, hoping to have the gold all to himself. His companions kill him to enrich their own shares, then drink the poison and die under the tree. The tale, one of Chaucer's greatest, is a classic example of dramatic irony.

The Canon is a traveler who joins the pilgrims briefly on the road to Canterbury but leaves when it is hinted that he is a cheating alchemist. His Yeoman however remains with the pilgrim company to tell an anecdote about an alchemist. The Canon Yeoman's Tale begins with the yeoman bragging about his and his master's skill at alchemy. He speaks of the alchemist's arcane practice and its futility. The tale proper tells of how an alchemical canon (who is not his master, he protests) tricks a priest out of forty pounds by pretending to teach him the art of making precious metals. It is no more than an anecdote but it is fitting since the dishonesty of alchemists' practice was much discussed and condemned in the fourteen century, every bit as much as the corrupt practice of selling indulgences.

Finally, the author, who has put himself into his poem as a quiet, unassuming person, tries, at the instigation of the host, to recite the "Rime of Sir Thopas," a dreary parody of bad poetry which the host interrupts as too dull. He begins again, at the instigation of the host, to tell a second story, the Tale of Melibee.

Melibee's house is raided by his foes, who beat his wife Prudence, and severely wound his daughter Sophie, in her feet, hands, ears, nose, and mouth. Prudence advises him not to rashly pursue vengeance on his enemies, and he follows her advice, putting his foes' punishment in her hands. Prudence forgives them for the outrages done to her, in the model of Christian forbearance and forgiveness.

Chaucer, the first great poet of English literature, left behind him a work of perennial attraction and enjoyment. Not only was "The Canterbury Tales" popular from the time of its composition, it has been read ever since, edited, reprinted endlessly, taught in schools, adapted in part for the stage, and used for political parody. It is obvious why Chaucer's work has held the interest of readers for six centuries. He was quite simply a brilliant writer; he had an amazing gift for adapting styles to fit a character or occasion; he was an astute observer of the human comedy, recording flawlessly the most intimate and minute details of a character.

The collection of pilgrims making their way to the shrine is a fair cross section of people from various walks of life and professions. Chaucer draws them with detailed individual characteristics yet with universal qualities which allow them to come alive in any generation. Unlike Dante and Boccaccio, he does not use one consistent style for all the tales. On the contrary, he has taken great care to match the stories to their tellers, the styles to their speakers. The knight talks like a knight, the nun talks like a nun, the miller talks like a miller. It was the prevailing medieval view that coarseness should be described coarsely, regardless of shocking readers and ladies. So it was natural for "The Miller's Tale" be recited in front of the Prioress and her entourage. Part of being faithful to the truth is part of

Chaucer's defense that in the use of rough language the word is cousin to the deed.

Indeed "The Miller's Tale" is a crude tale told in a very crude style. Chaucer as a Christian may strongly argue that sexual immorality in the tale is a serious criticism of life. But Chaucer is not telling the tale, the Miller is, and the Miller certainly suggests that sexual immorality of the tale's sort is perfectly all right, as a matter of fact, great fun. Chaucer in creating the character reveals himself a multi-talented, multi-faceted artist, fine-tuning the techniques of tone, point of view, and narrative voice to create a desired experience for his reader.

We see this again in his introduction of the character of Chaucer as one of the pilgrims. We are told he is a quiet, unassuming, wimp of a person which Chaucer certainly was not. In his "Tale of St. Thopas" he burlesques a certain kind of bad verse (and himself) to perfection. It is such bad doggerel verse that the Host has to cover his ears. Everyone knows that Chaucer was a perfectionist in his verse and certainly did not write that way. But what Chaucer has done is create a character named Chaucer with a specific personality and an atrocious style of writing. And such a creation brings home again not only what a sophisticated stylist the poet actually was but more so what a great sense of humor he had. Chaucer knew how to laugh at himself.

The subtlety of Chaucer's art has been an object lesson for writers for centuries. By implication, by suggestion, and by innuendo, he says more by saying less. No one, for example, can ever forget the brief portrait in the Prologue of the Wife of Bath, a florid woman, gaudy and bold in appearance. She is a lower-middle-class weaver from near Bath and has had five husbands. Chaucer slyly adds, "not to speak of other company in her youth." The innuendo stated almost as if it is an aside is subtle and important. Yet the story she tells is an Arthurian romance, stressing the virtues of courtesy and gentilesse. It is obviously a wish-fulfillment tale in which the ugly old woman wins sovereignty over her unwilling youthful husband and then turns young and beautiful. Careful study of this tale with the Wife's Prologue portrait, her conversation with other pilgrims, and her lusty confessional prologue reveals an antithetical side of this apparently crude and vulgar woman. She is more complex than one at first realizes, and Chaucer conveys this psychological dimension of her personality subtly without ever stating the fact.

Another pilgrim who fascinates readers is the Pardoner, a thorough charlatan, admittedly evil, who brags of his scandalous treatment of those he should serve. It is again important that Chaucer never says the Pardoner is a rogue; as with all the characters, he is allowed to reveal his character through quarrels with other pilgrims or by the type of story he tells. Furthermore, Chaucer never says he is homosexual but by inference suggests that he is sexually ambivalent.

The purposeful ambiguity in the portrait of the Nun, who concentrates on genteel social concerns—feeding delicate morsels to her pet dogs and watching her table manners—instead of showing more Christian traits, the concerns of social justice and the rights of depressed individuals, makes a comment, though again indirect. And Chaucer never explicitly states that she is extravagant but implies that she is by telling us that she travels with three priests, as attendants to boot. The fact that the tale she tells, a typical miracle story she might have learned by rote, expresses so little sympathy and compassion makes a strong statement about her character.

And so throughout "The Canterbury Tales," Chaucer, who places himself along with the other pilgrims as a naïve, unobservant traveling companion, uses this persona to effect satire and irony in the portraits. Chaucer does not condemn clerics, trades people or any other group. Instead he allows them to reveal their own faults and makes clever asides to the reader to suggest a viewpoint. We see the pilgrims as they are with all their virtues and vices, and we can readily identify with their humanness.

The question of anti-clericalism in Chaucer still perplexes readers even though reputable critics have noted that the freedom with which everybody criticized the clergy and argued theology, much to the surprise of today's reader, was an old medieval custom. Anti-clericalism has always been more predominant in cultures where there was no pluralism and where a religious denomination was identified with the whole people, e.g., Italy, Spain, France, and now Ireland.

In Chaucer's England, everyone wanted reform in the Church, everyone condemned selling of pardons, everyone condemned the worldliness of the clergy, bishops, priests, professors, clerks, knights, merchants, and poets. And it is against this background that the clerics are portrayed in "The Canterbury Tales." Ten of the twenty-nine Canterbury pilgrims are either members of the clergy or minor functionaries of the Church. Only four of these, the Parson, the Clerk, the Nun's Priest, and the Second Nun, pass without criticism, the last two not being described at all in the General Prologue. Further, the monks, priests, friars, and clerks who figure in the tales told by the pilgrims are a pretty notorious group of rogues. Indeed there are more good pagans in the stories than there are good clerics. However to conclude that Chaucer is either atheist or heretic because of these creations is to miss the point. These are all his creations and Chaucer the man, the artist, desired the reform of the Church in an orthodox way, as did most of the country, and he described what he saw, and what he saw was often downright funny. Maybe clergy, professors, writers, and merchants should follow Chaucer's example and learn to laugh at themselves.

Another reason for this great work's popularity lies in the variety of the tales. The stories range from bawdy burlesques to tales of chivalry, from local folk legends to sermons. Chaucer handles with equal facility different genres and stylistic devices of medieval literature, from the courtly romance told by the Knight down to the bawdy tales of the Miller and the Reeve. He uses the dream sequence as a vehicle for love poetry in the "The Book of the Duchess"; allegory in the "Romance of the Rose" and "The Merchant's Tale"; worldly vanity in "Troilus and Criseide,"; the bestiary in "The Parliament of Fowls" and "The Nun's Priest Tale"; the morality play concept in "The Second Nun's Tale"; the fabliau in "The Shipman's Tale"; the Breton lay in "The Franklin's Tale"; dramatic irony in "The Pardoner's Tale"; chance, fortune and destiny in "The Knight's Tale"; satire and dramatic irony in the creation of Chanticleer, just to name a few. And of course he uses the ever-popular frame story device which had great appeal to the reader, as it does today. Even Chaucer himself said of the variety in his work that if a reader is not satisfied with one thing, "turn over the leaf and choose another tale." If you don't like lechery, then go to a saint's legend.

Chaucer's handling with dexterity the different levels of language—that is, courtly speech, bawdy expression, elegant prayers, language of the church, street, or tavern—is second only to his genius for vivid and precise description of his pilgrims. Readers of the Tales will never forget the Pardoner's greasy blond hair, the Nun's huge forehead, the Miller's nose wart, the Wife of Bath's gap-tooth, the Summoner's garlic breath, and Chanticleer's head high, neck stretched, eyes shut tight, cackling with all his might.

One other reason for the lasting quality of this first great work of English literature is that, like Shakespeare's dramas, it opens innumerable possibilities to the reader. It poses questions about human motivation and aspirations. It probes into established attitudes, questions existing institutions. That is why it is futile for critics to find an encompassing theme in the work. Like Dante's

"Commedia" and Shakespeare's plays, the work is too big, too vast, as vast as humanity itself. The Canterbury collection represents a panorama of representative humanity, a comedie humaine, not only of the fourteenth century but of all ages. "The Canterbury Tales" reveals the tensions of Chaucer's time, the alternatives for man in a changing world, where many long-cherished customs and opinions were disintegrating. But these tensions, these alternatives, these changes are not peculiar just to Chaucer and his times; they are endemic to all men of all times and of all places

Chaucer's pilgrims with their tales reveal the hopes and uncertainties of life, the heights to which a person can climb as well as the depths to which people can descend. All these qualities make this great unfinished work the masterpiece we all acknowledge.

Major Works

The Book of the Duchess (about 1369)
Le Roman de la Rose (translation, during the 1360s)
The Legend of Good Women (between 1372 and 1386)
De Consolatione Philosophiae
(translation, probably during the 1370s)
Troilus and Criseide (about 1385)
The Parliament of Fowls (between 1375 and 1385)
The House of Fame (in the 1370s)
The Canterbury Tales (designed about 1387)

WILLIAM SHAKESPEARE

Certainly any literary masterpiece has a right to be read and enjoyed on its own terms, devoid of all kinds of props to assist in discerning its 'meaning.' Great works of art are monuments that are lastingly independent of their particular era; indeed the test of a work's greatness is that it transcends its time and speaks to any number of societies, cultures, and religious and philosophical traditions.

But to think that a work, or for that matter, an artist, is totally independent of the historical, social, cultural, and religious background is simply unrealistic. One can read James Joyce's "Portrait of An Artist as a Young Man" without an awareness of the Dublin Catholicism which prompts the protagonist to cry out "I will not serve." But the richness of the Joyce readers' experience is certainly diminished without some awareness of that background. Shakespeare's "Measure for Measure" does not need a full awareness of Matthew's chapter 7, verses 1-5 where the play got its title. But the whole context of the gospel incident, that of Christ's Sermon on the Mount, is relevant to the themes of the play and gives added meaning and depth to the reading experience.

This essay attempts to present a broad overview of Shakespeare's life as laid against his sixteenth century backgound, a brief survey of the major plays, and then an investigation of various scenes and passages from the plays that reflect doctrinal tenets of traditional Christian theology which give richness to the moments, scenes, or plays as a whole. The intention here is not to categorize the poet's personal faith in any way, either as early Renaissance Anglican, or as Roman Catholic, although we know from documentary evidence that he and his children lived and died Church of England. But how deep his Church of England faith was will always be conjecture. There must have been some church attendance; failure in this obligation could be dangerous and expensive. Many a heretic went to church under Elizabeth simply for the reason of personal safety.

But Shakespeare did live in an age where the broad spectrum of theology was Augustinian, that the churchmen and upcoming Puritan preachers proclaimed the word from an Augustinian point of view, and that Christian and Augustinian spirit penetrated the religious air the people breathed. Also as a youth he must have heard older people, like his own parents, recall with nostalgia the Latin Mass, the Divine Office chanted in monasteries, 'Bare ruin'd choirs, where late the sweet birds sang,' the authority of the Pope holding the whole thing together, unlike the chaos unleashed by Henry's assertion to be 'supreme head' of the Church of England. The currents and cross-currents of the times had to have some influence on the dramatist, even though the plays are persistently secular, temporal, and non-theological.

The Early Years

William Shakespeare, actor, playwright, poet, theater administrator, and landowner was baptized in Holy Trinity Church, Stratford-upon—Avon, on Wednesday, 26 April 1564, the third child and the first son of John Shakespeare and his wife Mary Arden. His actual date of birth, traditionally celebrated on April 23, St. George's Day, is not known. At the time because of plague, very few days ever elapsed between birth and baptism; so, April 23 or 24 is accurate enough. He probably grew up in the Henley Street house known as the Birthplace with his younger sisters Anne and Joan, and his younger brothers Gilbert, Richard, and the late-born Edmund, who like him eventually became an actor. Two sisters, Joan and Margaret, had died in infancy, and William himself was very fortunate to have escaped the plague. Just a few months after he was born, toward the end of 1564, at least 237 burials are recorded, something like one-eighth of Stratford's population.

Stratford had lovely homes, a fine grammar school, and a beautiful church. For the most part, the townsmen were educated and wealthy. Contact with London was surprisingly good because of carriers. Visiting companies of actors frequently came to Stratford during Shakespeare's boyhood and youth. His father was a bailiff (mayor), an officer who carried out commands and moderately enforced the law, even with the power to make arrests. The position afforded him privileges for his family.

William more than likely went to petty school, a preschool where the children got the rudiments of grammar and arithmetic from clergymen or itinerant teachers. He and his brothers would get here reading, writing, and how to pronounce English properly. At the age of six or seven, they would proceed to the King's New School, an established grammar school with well-qualified teachers and only a five minute walk from the Shakespeare home. There are no lists of the school's pupils, but his father's position would qualify him to attend. Emphasis was placed on grammar, logic, and rhetoric. His education would have been furthered by the compulsory attendance at Church of the families. Here he would learn the Bible, the Book of Common Prayer, and the Homilies. The hours were long and arduous, and the school was cold, but there was time for sports and recreation in the surrounding countryside.

The curriculum offered at the King's New School was such that it provided the student with a solid classical education. William would have been grounded in Latin and be given a background in Greek that would have developed in him a facility for languages such as French and Italian. He would have become familiar with such authors as Aesop, Caesar, Cicero, Sallust, Livy, Virgil, Horace, Ovid, and Seneca. He would have studied logic and rhetoric as well, and also the principles of composition and oratory. Memorizing classical texts was a must in this classical education. It is interesting to note that many of the references in the plays about education, schooling, and schoolmasters imply that the whole experience of formal education was an extremely arduous one. If he is speaking from his personal experience then we can presume that Shakespeare's formal education was a strict and rigid discipline. It served his artistic sensibility well.

He is likely to have left school when he was about 15 years old. What he did then has been the subject of much speculation for centuries. About three years later in late 1582 he married Anne Hathaway; a daughter, Susanna, was baptized on May 26 of the following year, and twins Hamnet and Judith were baptized on February 2, 1585. Anne was eight years his senior and there is evidence that she was pregnant when the marriage license was issued by the Bishop of Worcester on November 27, 1582; Susanna was baptized in Holy Trinity Church six months later on May 26, 1583. The fact that there was only one reading of the banns (the customary announcement in church preceding a wedding that allowed time for any legal impediments to be brought forward was read three times) implies there was haste.

Some have conjectured that William became a schoolmaster for awhile to earn a living, others have claimed that he began to write, (maybe so, but not seriously enough to make a living), and still others feel he worked for his father in the family business as a glover, which seems quite likely. He was very young and it is quite possible that the family extended itself in every way to these two young people who found themselves in the state of marriage. Maybe it was at this time that he joined the Queen's Men when they visited Stratford, but we will never know.

We do know that in 1592, ten years after his marriage to Anne, he was well known on the theatrical scene. He had probably already written his earlier comedies and history plays. "Venus and Adonis" and "The Rape of Lucrece," Ovidian narrative poems, were published successively in 1593 and 1594. Both works were dedicated to the young Henry Wriothsley, 3rd Earl of Southampton, who probably had become Will's patron. Dedications at the time were ordinarily to patrons, and it has been suggested that he was the "Fair Youth" of Shakespeare's Sonnet.

No one disputes the fact that William and Anne were not inseparable lovers. After the christening of Hamnet and Judith, they lived more than one hundred miles apart for the greater part of twenty years during which Shakespeare was employed in the London theater. If there were frequent visits to Stratford we will never know. If we are to read the sonnets as somewhat autobiographical, a "Dark Lady," to whom William's lustful desires provokes in him a certain disgust, can suggest an affair. Also the fair "Young Man" of many of the poems is the recipient of many of his deepest and most tender feelings. If there is reason to speculate that William was not faithful to Anne as a lover, there is reason to suggest that he was a good provider as a husband. In 1597 he purchased a beautiful house in Stratford—New Place where he settled his wife and children and where he retired as a country gentleman, at the end of his theatrical career.

But there are so many unaccounted for years, called the "dark years," from the time of the christening of the twins in 1585 and the positive evidence of Will's affiliation with a particular theater company in London in 1595. The company was the Lord Chamberlain's Men with whom he remained for the rest of his working life. He may have studied law, as some have suggested, as many young men did in London at the time without seriously intending to practice it as a profession. See John Donne and his colleagues at the Inns. A very likely suggestion by biographers was that he taught school for awhile. He certainly had a first class classical education to qualify him. And then there is the possibility of traveling to the Continent. I find this very plausible because of the Italian element in the plays. His knowledge of Italy, the cities where he places the action of plays (Verona, Venice, Sicily, Rome, Messina), the names he uses for his characters (Lucentio, Romeo, Mercutio, Claudio, Emilia—even in "Measure for Measure" which takes place in Vienna, the principal characters all have Italian names); all suggest a first hand knowledge of the country. Of course there were travel books around where he could have learned much about the country, but too often intimate details occur that would not be found in travel books. He probably did not have the money to finance a trip, but at the same time, many young men in London at the time did not either, but they managed a trip to the Continent. What was to stop a smart, enterprising, creative young man like Shakespeare from doing the same?

We are not certain about the terms of the agreement with the Lord Chamberlain's Men, but it seems that he was to produce two plays a year for them. He had already written the Senecan tragedy "Titus Andronicus" and the Plautine comedy "Comedy of Errors," as well as "Henry VI." It is quite obvious that as early as 1590, Will Shakespeare was a name around London to be reckoned with. Robert Greene, the once-prominent poet and playwright, and one of the "University Wits" who dominated the London theater scene in the late 1580s, in a written testament warned his colleagues about an "upstart crow" who was not content to be just an actor but was aspiring (threatening is more like it) to be a professional playwright. Greene was anxious over the fact that in the next twenty years the dominant force in the London theater scene was going to be not Kyd, not Greene, not Marlowe, not even Ben Jonson, but Will Shakespeare.

In Shakespeare's day, London was a vibrant center of bustling activity with a population of some 175,000 people. It was not all the majesty of the court. It was a place of everyday affairs. Its market-places were filled with assorted goods of every variety. The streets were crowded with country people in their peculiar styles and wealthy citizens in their elegant and decorative apparel. The taverns were the gathering places, like the pubs of today, with an array of diverse types and personalities. Urban lowlife rubbed elbows with gentry, pickpockets drank, ate, conversed with the best of them, who would find themselves missing their purse when they went home that night. London was an immensely stimulating social and cultural environment. As with Chaucer, who absorbed from London his Wife of Bath, Miller, Parson, Clerk, and Knight, Will Shakespeare had plenty to draw from for his Mistress Quickly, Hotspur, Mistress Overdone, Pistol, and Bassanio.

Shakespeare's reputation as a dramatist in the 1590s is witnessed by documentary evidence. In 1598 his name appeared for the first time on the title pages of his plays "Richard II" and "Richard III," the second quartos, and "Love's Labour's Lost" the first quarto. Also he is listed as one of the principal tragedians in Ben Jonson's "Sejanus" and one of the principal comedians in Jonson's "Every Man in his Humour." It is presumed that he gave up acting after these two performances, maybe in 1603, in order to give himself fully to writing.

All was not 'merrie Englande' all the time. The encroaching Puritans were on the loose, condemning cosmetics worn by women, especially make-up in the theater. Every chance they had to close down a theater, they did. They cursed the use of pieces of jewelry and other ornaments on clothing worn by the theatergoer. The city fathers had to contend with gambling, drunkenness, prostitution and other 'liberties' that took place in the Bankside district south of the Thames and in Shoreditch, where James Burbage had erected the first permanent commercial playhouse called the Theater. It was in this area of pickpockets and vagabonds that Will Shakespeare wrote and helped perform the greatest theatrical works the world has ever experienced. The Bankside and Shoreditch districts blossomed into being the finest theatrical centers of the age and the 'villainous' element stayed right there with them. It was because of this that acting and theater were considered such shady forms of entertainment.

The Theater

The Theater was largely devoid of scenery. The playwright and the actors made efficient use of language, the resources of rhetoric and symbolism, and gestures to establish time, locale, situation, and atmosphere. The actors, the dramatis personae, imitated humanity in such a way as to create what the author and his company intended for a scene, an act, or a full dramatic sequence. By today's standards this would seem too primitive: no spots, very little furnishings, a minimum of setting, no curtain to signal beginning and end of acts, and only the crudest of sound effects. The results were brilliant because the focus was on the text, the words, the sparkling poetry of the playwright. After four centuries we have returned to what is important in theater, the words and the action.

About three thousand spectators could be crammed into the ninety-nine-foot-wide structure of the Theater. It opened in 1576 and was dismantled in 1598 because the owner of the land would not negotiate on a lease acceptable to Shakespeare's acting company. They moved across the Thames and constructed a more handsome playhouse called the Globe. More than half the audience stood in the yard (groundlings who paid a penny and risked getting soaked in the event of rain, which, in London, was often), about fifty-five feet in diameter, and the remainder sat in three galleries that encircled the yard and were covered by a thatched roof.

The stage was about forty-three feet wide and it was thrust some twenty-seven feet into the yard from the 'tiring house' at the rear of the building. It was covered by a superstructure, the heavens, that protected the actors and their costumes from the elements. In the floor of the stage platform was a trapdoor that could be opened for ascending and descending, depending on the context. It could be used for a pit, a grave, even for hell. At the back of the stage in the tiring house, the actors did their costume changes and waited for their cues. At the back of the stage, in front of the tiring house, were three doors, two being used for right and left entrances and exits, and the larger one center could be used for scenes or tableaux. At the sides of the stage there were elevated balconies that contained bays for the higher paying theater goer, but these balconies also could be used as part of the show as an upper stage.

Since the main playing area was so close to the spectators, the playwright and the players could confide with the audience through asides, even soliloquies, and establish a close relationship with the audience. This may seem a bit artificial to a modern audience but, on the contrary, the device shows just how intimate the dramatist and his work was with the audience. And it attests to the sophistication of the Elizabethan audience which expected such intimate communication with the dramatist and his players.

The audience was a wide assortment of people. Afternoon performances drew a wealthier class since they had the leisure time; they paid slightly more than a penny. Dramatists have always complained about the quality of the audiences and the Elizabethan writer was no different. The outdoor theater such as the Theater and the Globe drew a more common crowd. Those standing in the yard could be rowdy and the pickpockets and prostitutes found this area more productive. As the indoor theaters became more popular, like the Blackfriars where the price was six pence, the profession gained respectability. Women who attended the Globe were usually considered suspect, but with the indoor theaters their attendance became more acceptable.

One of the most powerful of court officials was the Lord Chamberlain who was responsible for assigning lodgings in the palace, for the court's travel arrangements, for reception of overseas dignitaries, and for the court's entertainments, including plays. The Revels Office, and its Master, were a part of the Lord Chamberlain's vast responsibility. Henry Carey, Lord Hundston, was appointed Lord Chamberlain on the 4th of July, 1585 and he formed a playing company, the Chamberlain's Men, which included Shakespeare. Will's position with the Lord Chamberlain's Men was a source of professional stability and had a great deal to do with his maturation and success. He bought stock in the company and this freed him from the frustrations of other writers who free-lanced selling their material, consequently losing any real say about their plays and their productions. Of course, being so tied up with the Court restricted somewhat his hand to freely write about deficiencies of the monarch but this did not seem to be much of a problem with Shakespeare. He was a prudent man with no particular ax to grind and his focus was on creating good plays. Being a stockholder of the particular theatrical organizatioin for which he wrote, he shared in all the profits that the company took in at the gate, and he was a participant in many of the major decisions being made concerning the company's welfare. Being an artist, his major benefit, aside from finances, was his freedom to write, change, and supervise his productions. He could write for certain personages in mind for particular roles: for example, Richard Burbage in "Othello" and "King Lear." And he prospered financially from this arrangement. Like his father, he invested wisely in real estate and purchased property in both Stratford and London. Quite obviously he was not a flaky man about town, but a serious writer with Court connections. Working so closely to Court supervision had far more advantages than disadvantages. And being an actor, he probably loved the prestige.

The Apprentice Years and Sonnets

In 1593 Shakespeare came out with his "Venus and Adonis," a long mythological poem based on Ovid's "Metamorphoses," employing the ababcc metrical form of Spenser. Despite its ornamental style and lack of metrical virtuosity it was an immediate success. Within a year's time he produced his second poem, "The Rape of Lucrece," again drawing on Ovid and again dedicating the work to "the Right Honorable Henry Wriothesley, Earl of Southampton." The poem was an immediate success and despite its correctness and its adherence to a traditional form, the poem, like "Venus and Adonis" brings home that Shakespeare's talent is definitely for theater. The poems were written during his 'apprenticeship' period, that is, before his membership with the Lord Chamberlain's Men. Yet his early plays, the three parts of Henry VI, Titus Andronicus, The Two Gentlemen of Verona, The Comedy of Errors, and The Taming of the Shrew came out during this 'apprenticeship' period and despite their immaturity they tower over the two Ovid adaptations.

Shakespeare's attempts at the poems tell us much about his talent. The "Venus" and the "Lucrece," along with "A Lover's Complaint," a narrative poem written in rhyme royal attributed to him, and "The Phoenix and Turtle," a curious poem written in the John Donne 'metaphysical' tradition, in no way come up to the plays in stature. It would seem that Shakespeare was far more comfortable in writing in a genre that was directed to the play-going public rather than to a noble patron and a cultivated public to whom the narratives were directed. Of course this does not apply to the sonnets, all 154 of them, that are equal in stature to the plays and at times surpass them in value. He was able to compress great depth of thought and feeling in the tightness of the fourteen liner as he did in the plays, but in the long narrative form he simply did not succeed.

The sonnets, which were published in an unauthorized edition in 1609, probably reveal to us more about the personality of Shakespeare than any other source simply because the genre is so personal. Shakespeare's sonnets are in the tradition of Petrarch's in Italy in the fifteenth century, and such late sixteenth-century English sequences as those of Philip Sidney and Edmund Spenser. They are conventional in some respects but in others they are not. In the 4-4-4-2 sequence (abab cdcd efef gg), a variation of the 8-6 of the Italian (abbacddc efgefg), Shakespeare will introduce an unexpected twist in the final couplet that will turn the tradition upside down. Furthermore the sonnets, like the plays, portray humanity so credibly that the reader is almost forced to read them autobiographically. It is always risky to read autobiographical aspects into the sonnets because the bottom line is that they are fictions. Like the plays and narrative poems, they tell a story, but unlike the plays and poems, they are so intimately confessional and they convey so poignantly a deeply felt personal situation.

If we read the sonnets as evidence of the inner man, then we see beneath the controlled exterior a turbulent inner life ("Desiring this man's art, and that man's scope"); passions not easily mastered ("The expense of spirit in a waste of shame / Is lust in action"); self-knowledge wrested with difficulty ("Sin of self-love possesseth all mine eye"); a desire to idealize and immortalize the beloved through verse

("So long as men can breathe, or eye can see, / So long lives this, and this gives life to thee."); the realization that true love never dies ("Let me not to the marriage of true minds / Admit impediments"); a demanding need for love that can embrace male or female ("Two loves I have of comfort and despair, / Which like two spirits do suggest me still: / The better angel is a man right fair, / The worser spirit a woman colour'd ill."); the experience of male love relationships ("To me, fair friend, you never can be old, / For as you were when first your eye I ey'd, / Such seems your beauty still."); a belief in the power of the imagination ("Not marble, nor the gilded monuments / Of princes, shall outlive this powerful rime."); the transience of youth and beauty ("When forty winters shall beseige thy brow, / And dig deep trenches in thy beauty's field."); an inner conflict of the spirit ("Poor soul, the centre of my sinful earth, / [Fool'd by] these rebel powers that thee array"); and the reality of death ("So shalt thou feed on Death, that feeds on men, / And Death once dead, there's no more dying then"). We see a genius who has suffered the extremities of passion summoning up the self-control, the discipline to shape and contain it within the demanding verse structures of the sonnet form.

The Early Plays

Concerning the plays, the four known as Shakespeare's 'first tetralogy' are the three parts of "Henry VI" and "Richard III," all written by 1592. The plays in the 'second tetralogy' are "Richard II," "Henry IV," parts 1 and 2, and "Henry V," written between 1595 and 1597. Despite the fact that "Richard III" is part of the 'first tetralogy', and quite a masterpiece, the earlier plays seem less artistic than the later ones. In any case, the plays most read and performed from the early period, the 'apprenticeship' period, and, for the most part, those written before

Shakespeare became associated with the Lord Chamberlain's Men, are "Richard III," "The Comedy of Errors," "The Taming of the Shrew," "The Two Gentlemen of Verona," and "Titus Andronicus." "Richard II," "Henry IV, Part 1" and "Henry V," also frequently read and performed, really come from a later period.

"Richard III" (1591) centers on the character of Richard of Gloucester, afterwards King Richard III, ambitious and bloody, bold and subtle, treacherous, yet brave in battle, a murderer, and usurper of the crown. The play begins with the deformed Richard's announcement: "Now is the winter of our discontent / Made glorious summer by this son of York." That is the King Edward IV, his brother, who is dying. Richard is determined that he shall succeed to the crown and sets out to eliminate any opposition to this and to secure his position. He has his brother the duke of Clarence, who has been imprisoned in the Tower, murdered. As she accompanies the corpse of her dead father-in-law, Henry VI, Anne, the widow of Edward, Prince of Wales, is wooed by Richard, and they are later married.

When the king dies Richard begins his attack on Queen Elizabeth's family and supporters with the help of the duke of Buckingham. Hastings, Rivers, and Grey are all executed, and Buckingham persuades the citizens of London to proclaim Richard king. After his coronation he murders his nephews, the princes in the Tower, and following the death of his wife Anne, which he encourages, tries to marry his niece, Elizabeth of York. However, Buckingham rebels and goes to join Henry Tudor, earl of Richmond, who has landed in Wales at Milford Haven to claim the crown. Buckingham is captured and Richard has him executed, but he now has to face Richmond's army at Bosworth. On the night before the battle the ghosts of those whom Richard has killed appear to him and foretell his defeat. In the battle the next day he loses his horse and is killed by Richmond, who is then proclaimed Henry VII, the first of the Tudor monarchs.

The role of Richard from its beginning has been a 'must' for great actors in the British theater. Richard Burbage owned it in Shakespeare's own theater, David Garrick in the eighteenth century, Edmund Kean in the nineteenth, and Laurence Olivier in the twentieth. The complexity of the character presents a tremendous challenge for the player. He is physically ugly, a "poisonous hunch-backed toad," yet admirable in his eloquence and resourcefulness. He is Machiavellian in his politics, foxlike in his cunning. He is the totalitarian dictator who tramples on any social or religious institution to achieve his psychopathic ends. He is the consummate alienated rebel who challenges any form of discipline or order.

Of course, the role lends itself to over the top scenery chewing; some costuming had the hunch-back Richard looking three times the size of Rigoletto. But the importance of Richard and his climb to power, which the more learned Elizabethan audience would have recognized and which is a moral lesson for today, is in prophetic Queen Margaret's (widow of Henry VI) reminder over and over again that had there not been such back-stabbing corruption in the kingdom prior to the advent of Richard, there would have been no ripe occasion for the "dreadful minister of hell" to ascend the throne in the first place.

There have been some six film adaptations of the play in the twentieth century. Laurence Olivier's characterization overshadows most of them. Ian McKellen's version created quite a stir, heavy in irony, filled with contemporary allusions and modern settings, and scenes in derelict hotels and seedy pub toilets.

"King John" (sometime in the 1590s), the play, with some departures from historical accuracy, deals with various events in King John's reign, and principally with the tragedy of young Arthur. It ends with the death of John at Swinstead abbey. The tragic quality of the play, the poignant grief of Constance, Arthur's mother, and the political complications depicted, are relieved by the wit, humor, and gallantry of the Bastard, supposed son of Faulconbridge, actually the son of Richard Coeur de Lion.

"The Comedy of Errors" (probably as early as 1590) is the story of numerous misunderstandings and mistaken identities. Syracuse and Ephesus being at enmity, any Syracusan found in Ephesus is put to death unless he can pay a ransom of one thousand marks. Egeon, an old Syracusan merchant, has been arrested in Ephesus and on the duke's order explains how he came there.

He and his wife Emilia had twin sons exactly alike and each named Antipholus; the parents had purchased twin slaves, also exactly alike, each named Dromio, who attended on their sons. Having in a shipwreck been separated, with the younger son and one Dromio, from his wife, Egeon had never seen them since. The younger son (Antipholus of Syracuse) on reaching manhood had gone (with his Dromio) in search of his brother and mother and had no more been heard of, though Egeon had now sought for five years over the world, coming at last to Ephesus.

The duke, moved by this tale, gives Egeon until evening to find the ransom. Now, the elder Antipholus (Antipholus of Ephesus), with one of the Dromios, has been living in Ephesus since his rescue from shipwreck and is married. Antipholus of Syracuse and the other Dromio have arrived there that very morning. Each twin retains the same confusing resemblance to his brother as in childhood. From this the comedy of errors results. Antipholus is summoned home to dinner by Dromio of Ephesus; he is claimed as husband by the wife of Antipholus of Ephesus, the latter being refused admittance to his own house, because he is supposed to be already within; and Antipholus of Syracuse falls in love with Luciana, his brother's wife's sister. Finally Antipholus of Ephesus is confined as a lunatic, and Antipholus of Syracuse takes refuge from his brother's jealous wife in a convent.

Meanwhile evening has come and Egeon is led to execution. As the duke proceeds to the place of execution, Antipholus of Ephesus appeals to him for redress. Then the abbess of the convent presents Antipholus of Syracuse as claiming redress. The simultaneous presence of the two brothers explains the numerous misunderstandings. Egeon recovers his two sons and his liberty, and the abbess turns out to be Emilia.

The play is early Shakespeare and has elements, such as confusion of identities, the friendship theme, and miraculous reunions in the end, that the poet will use right to the end of his career. Despite the farcical elements of a plot where a husband and wife are lost by shipwreck, each with a son and his slave, with an additional plot of dinner confusion including one wife and her sister, the stupid business of naming twins the very same name and finding slave twins with the same name and the ridiculous mother turning out to be the abbess completing the hilarity, most critics are now agreed that it is a play of some sophistication and insight. It became the basis for the long-running (1938) Broadway hit by Richard Rodgers and Lorenz Hart, "The Boys from Syracuse"

"The Taming of the Shrew" (probably 1592) begins with an induction in which Christopher Sly, a drunken Warwickshire tinker, picked up by a lord and his huntsman on a heath, is brought to the castle, sumptuously treated, and in spite of his protestations is assured that he is a lord who has been out of his mind. He is set down to watch the play that follows, performed solely for his benefit by strolling players.

Baptista Minola of Padua has two daughters, Katherina the Shrew, who is the elder of the two and Bianca who has many suitors, but who may not marry until a husband has been found for Katherina. Petruchio, a gentleman from Verona, undertakes to woo the shrew to gain her dowry and to help his friend Hortensio win Bianca. To tame her he pretends to find her rude behavior courteous and gentle and humiliates her by being late for their wedding and appearing badly dressed. He takes her to his country house and, under the pretext that nothing there is good enough for her, prevents her from eating or sleeping. By the time they return to Baptista's house, Katherina has been successfully tamed, and Lucentio, a Pisan, has won Bianca by disguising himself as her schoolmaster, while the disappointed Hortensio has to console himself with marriage to a rich widow. At the feast which follows the three bridegrooms wager on whose wife is the most docile and submissive. Katherina argues that "Thy husband is thy lord, thy life, thy keeper / Thy head, thy sovereign" and Petruchio wins the bet.

The play with all its slapstick and vulgar physicality has a good deal of subtle psychology about it. The so-called happy ending of Kate's sudden submission to her "loving lord" is pretty unbelievable given what we see and know of her throughout the play. Her final wink to the audience (not in the text but often used in modern day productions) calls into question her being tamed and his winning the bet. The play became the source for the very successful 1948 Cole Porter musical "Kiss Me Kate," the title coming from Petruchio's three time request "kiss me, Kate" and the not very successful Zeffirelli film with Elizabeth Taylor and Richard Burton. Certainly the best twentieth century adaptation of the play is the beautiful American opera, Vittorio Giannini's "The Taming of the Shrew" (1953).

"The Two Gentlemen of Verona" (probably 1592-3) are the two friends, Valentine and Proteus. Proteus is in love with Julia, who returns his affection. Valentine leaves Verona for Milan "to see the wonders of the world abroad," and there falls in love with Silvia, the daughter of the duke of Milan. Presently Proteus is sent also on his travels, and exchanges vows of constancy with Julia before starting. But arriving at Milan, Proteus is at once captivated by Silvia, and, betraying his friend and his former love, reveals to the duke the intention of Valentine to carry off Silvia. Valentine is banished and becomes a captain of outlaws and Proteus continues his courting of Silvia.

Meanwhile Julia, pining for Proteus, comes to Milan dressed as a boy and takes service as Proteus' page, unrecgonized by him. Silvia, to escape marriage with Thurio, her father's choice, leaves Milan to rejoin Valentine, is captured by outlaws and rescued from them by Proteus. Proteus is violently pressing his suit on Silvia when Valentine comes on the scene. Proteus is struck with remorse, and his contrition is such that Valentine is impelled to surrender Silvia to him, to the dismay of Proteus' page, the disguised Julia. She swoons, and is then recognized by Proteus, and the discovery of her constancy wins back his love. The duke and Thurio arrive. Thurio shows cowardice in face of Valentine's determined attitude, and the duke, approving Valentine's spirit, accords him Silvia and pardons the outlaws. Launce, the clownish servant of Proteus, and his dog Crab, 'the sourest-natured dog that lives,' provide much humor.

The play has never been popular in the theater. Because of its many flaws scholars have conjectured that it was probably Shakespeare's very first work. It does have two strong women, two very engaging clowns, and a dog (Crab) who invariably steals the show. Because of its weakness directors have taken many liberties with it in order to engage the audience. Musical adaptations of it have been successful, notably Joseph Papp's 1971 revival in New York and David Thacker's 1994 RSC production at the Swan which used songs from Cole Porter.

"Titus Andronicus" (probably as early as 1590) deals with the return of Titus Andronicus to Rome after his sixth victory over the Goths. He brings with him their queen Tamora and her three sons, the eldest of whom Alarbus, is sacrificed to avenge his own sons' deaths. Titus is offered the imperial mantle, but gives it instead to the late emperor's son Saturninus, to whose marriage with his daughter, Lavinia, Titus consents. Saturninus' brother claims Lavinia as his own and, while taking her off, Titus kills his son Mutius, who had tried to block his way. Saturninus now changes his mind, renounces Lavinia, and marries Tamora who engineers a false reconciliation between the emperor and Titus, whom she plans to destroy. She does this with the help of her lover Aaron, the Moor, who gets Tamora's sons Chiron and Demetrius to murder Bassianus, whose body is thrown into a pit, rape Lavinia, and cut off her tongue and hands. Titus' sons Quintus and Martius are then lured by Aaron to fall into the pit, where they are found and accused of Bassianus' murder. Aaron tells Titus that his sons will not be executed if he sacrifices his hand and sends it to the emperor. Titus does this, but gets it back again with the heads of his two sons.

In the second half of the play Titus discovers who raped and mutilated his daughter, and with his brother Marcus, and last remaining son Lucius, vows revenge. Lucius leaves Rome, but returns with an army of Goths, which captures Aaron and his child by Tamora. Tamora and her sons Demetrius and Chiron visit Titus disguised as Revenge, Rapine, and Murder and ask him to have Lucius banquet at his house, where the emperor and the empress and her sons will be brought. Titus recognizes his enemies and with the help of Lavinia slits the throats of Chiron and Demetrius and uses their flesh in a pie, some of which Tamora eats at the banquet before Titus kills her. He also stabs Lavinia, but is killed by Saturninus, who is in turn killed by Lucius. He is elected emperor and sends Aaron to be buried breast deep in the ground and starved to death.

Despite the fact that the revenge motif appears in many Shakespeare plays, this early play is not a history play but a revenge tragedy almost outdoing Thomas Kyd's "Spanish Tragedy." It is a blood bath. Julie Taymor's stylized 2000 Hollywood film "Titus" with Anthony Hopkins is impressive.

The Middle Years

"Romeo and Juliet" (probably 1595) tells the story of the Capulets and Montagues, the two chief families of Verona, who are bitter enemies. Escalus, the prince, threatens anyone who disturbs the peace with death. Romeo, son of old Lord Montague, is in love with Lord Capulet's niece Rosaline. But at a feast given by Capulet, which Romeo attends, disguised by a mask, he sees and falls in love with Juliet, Capulet's daughter, and she with him. After the feast, he overhears, under her window, Juliet's confession of her love for him, and wins her consent to a secret marriage. With the help of Friar Laurence, they are wedded the next day. Mercutio, a friend of Romeo, meets Tybalt of the Capulet family, who is infuriated by the discovery of Romeo's presence at the feast, and they quarrel. Romeo comes on the scene and attempts to reason with Tybalt, but Tybalt and Mercutio fight and Mercutio falls. Then Romeo draws and Tybalt is killed. The prince, Montague, and Capulet come up, and Romeo is sentenced to banishment.

Early next day, after spending the night with Juliet, he leaves Verona for Mantua, counselled by the friar, who intends to reveal Romeo's marriage at an opportune moment. Capulet proposes to marry Juliet to Count Paris, and when she seeks excuses to avoid this, peremptorily insists. Juliet consults the friar, who bids her consent to the match, but on the night before the wedding drink a potion which will render her apparently lifeless for forty-two hours. He will warn Romeo who will rescue her from the vault on her awakening and carry her to Mantua. The friar's message to Romeo miscarries and Romeo hears that Juliet is dead. Buying poison he comes to the vault to have a last sight of Juliet. He chances upon Count Paris outside the vault; they fight and Paris is killed. Then Romeo, after a last kiss on Juliet's lips, drinks the poison and dies. Juliet awakes and finds Romeo dead by her side, and the cup still in his hand. Realizing what has happened, she stabs herself and dies. The story is unfolded by the friar and Count Paris's page, and Montague and Capulet, faced by the tragic results of their enmity, are reconciled. The play begins with a sonnet spoken by the chorus and in its poetry, language and plot reflects the sonnet craze of the 1590s, from which period Shakespeare's own sequence dates.

Often referred to as the greatest love story ever told, "Romeo and Juliet" has been filmed more often than any other play of Shakespeare's, save "Hamlet." And in at least seven languages. There are a series of silent films, one from Italy which for the first time used the original settings. George Cukor's 1936 sound version had Norma Shearer (Juliet), Leslie Howard (Romeo), Basil Rathbone (Tybalt), and John Barrymore (Mercutio), everyone pretty over-aged for their parts. Shearer actually looked matronly and Howard went on to play Ashley Wilkes in "Gone With the Wind," embalmed looking for the part, just a few years later. It was lavishly done and in black and white. Renato Castellani's colorful version in 1954 with Laurence Harvey came out when Italy was going through its neo-realism period in film making. Franco Zeffirelli's 1968 film appealed greatly to the 60s generation with its emphasis on sincere innocence in conflict with indomitable parental attitudes. The Italian settings are gorgeous and Zeffirelli's choice of two unknown actors in the lead roles gave the story the youthful freshness that the play requires. It is a masterful production. Baz Luhrmann's 1996 version is in blazing color, clever, filled with energy, erratic, with music often drowning out the lines, and set in Florida. But contemporary culture forced on Shakespeare's world often feels strained. The exciting Bernstein-Sondheim-Robbins "West Side Story" was very successful on Broadway and has become a staple in some European opera houses and performed even more often than the more familiar Gounod operatic version.

"Romeo and Juliet", in one form or another, will continue to hold its position as one of the great classic love stories of the dramatic repertory.

"Love's Labour's Lost" (1595) tells the story of the king of Navarre and three of his lords who have sworn for three years to keep from the sight of women and to live studying and fasting. The arrival of the princess of France on an embassy with her attendant ladies, obliges them "of mere necessity" to disregard their vows. The king is soon in love with the princess, his lords with her ladies, and the courting proceeds amidst disguises and merriment, not too unlike Mozart's "Cosi fan tutte." The other characters contribute to the fun: Don Adriano de Armado, the Spaniard, a master of extravagant language, Holofernes the schoolmaster, Dull the constable, Costard the clown, and Sir Nathaniel the poor curate in the hilarious Pageant of the Nine Worthies. News of the death of the princess' father interrupts the wooing, and the ladies impose a year's ordeal on their lovers. The play ends with the beautiful owl and cuckoo song, "When icicles hang by the wall."

Kenneth Branagh's film version of the play in 2000 with some dancing to the music of Cole Porter, the Gershwins, and Jerome Kern is pretty much of an embarrassment, given that Branagh has been quite successful in bringing Shakespeare to the screen. This is best forgotten.

"A Midsummer Night's Dream." (1595 or 1596) Hermia, ordered by her father Egeus to marry Demetrius, refuses, because she loves Lysander, while Demetrius has formerly professed love for her friend Helena, and Helena loves Demetrius. Under the law of Athens, Theseus, the duke, gives Hermia four days, in which to obey her father, else she must suffer death or enter a nunnery. Hermia and Lysander agree to leave Athens secretly in order to be married where the Athenian law cannot pursue them, and to meet in a wood a few miles from the city. Hermia tells Helena of the project, and the latter tells Demetrius.

Demetrius pursues Helena to the wood, as Helena pursues Demetrius, so that all four at that night are in the wood. This wood is the favorite haunt of the fairies.

Oberon and Titania, king and queen of the fairies, have quarreled, because Titania refuses to give up to him a little changeling boy for a page. Oberon tells Puck, a mischievous sprite, to fetch him a certain magic flower of which he will press the juice on the eyes of Titania while she sleeps, so that she may fall in love with what she first sees when she wakes. Overhearing Demetrius in the wood reproaching Helena for following him, and desirous to reconcile them, Oberon orders Puck to put some of the love-juice on Demetrius' eyes, but so that Helena will be near him when he does it. Puck, mistaking Lysander for Demetrius, applies the charm to him, and as Helena is the first person Lysander sees he at once woos her, enraging her because she thinks she is being made a jest of. Oberon, discovering Puck's mistake, now places some of the juice on Demetrius' eyes; he on waking first sees Helena, so that both Lysander and Demetrius are now wooing her. The ladies begin to abuse one another and the men go off to fight for Helena.

Meanwhile Oberon has placed the love-juice on Titania's eyelids, who wakes to find Bottom the weaver near her, wearing an ass's head (Bottom and a company of Athenian tradesmen are in the wood to rehearse a play for the duke's wedding, and Puck has put an ass's head on Bottom); Titania at once becomes enamored of him, and toys with his "amiable cheeks" and "fair large ears." Oberon, finding them together, reproaches Titania for bestowing her love on an ass, and again demands the changeling boy, whom in her confusion she surrenders; whereupon Oberon releases her from the charm. Puck at Oberon's orders throws a thick fog about the human lovers, and brings them all together, unknown to one another, and they fall asleep. He applies a remedy to their eyes, so that when they awake they return to their former loves. Theseus and Egeus appear on the scene, the runaways are forgiven, and the couples married. The play ends with the 'play' of "Pyramus and Thisbe," comically acted by Bottom and his fellow tradesmen, to grace these nuptials and those of Theseus and Hippolyta.

Considered by many scholars as Shakespeare's most charming comedy, the play is certainly different from anything thus far. In many ways it is the most original work in the entire Shakespeare canon and has given inspiration to such artists as the composer Felix Mendelsson, the painter William Blake, the director Peter Brook, and the filmmakers Max Reinhardt and Woody Allen. The play clearly offers attractive possibilities for visual realization and the film and TV industries have certainly exploited those possibilities, none however so brilliantly as Max Reinhardt in his 1936 film featuring Olivia de Haviland as Hermia, Mickey Rooney as Puck, and James Cagney as Bottom. It is a remarkable display of festive comedy, evoking the folk rituals associated with May Day and Midsummer Eve; its final mood is one of romantic fulfillment. The casting was a stroke of genius and Mickey Rooney's impish Puck has gone down in the annals of great screen performances.

"The Merchant of Venice" (between 1596 and 1598) begins with Bassanio, a noble but poor Venetian, asking his friend Antonio, a rich merchant, for three thousand ducats to enable him to prosecute fittingly his suit of the rich heiress Portia at Belmont. Antonio, whose money is all employed in foreign ventures, undertakes to borrow the sum from Shylock, a Jewish usurer, whom he has been wont to upbraid for his extortions. Shylock consents to lend the money against a bond by which, if the sum is not repaid at the appointed day, Antonio shall forfeit a pound of flesh.

By her father's will Portia is to marry that suitor who selects of three caskets (one gold, one silver, one lead) the one which contains her portrait. Bassanio makes the right choice—the leaden casket—and is wedded to Portia, and

his friend Graziano to her maid Nerissa. News com
Antonio's ships have been wrecked, that the debt h
been repaid when due, and that Shylock claims his pound
of flesh. The matter is brought before the duke. Portia
disguises herself as an advocate, Balthazar, and Nerissa as
her clerk, and they come to the court to defend Antonio,
unknown to their husbands.

Failing in her appeal to Shylock for mercy, Portia admits the validity of his claim, but warns him that his life is forfeit if he spills one drop of blood, since his bond gives him right to nothing beyond the flesh. Pursuing her advantage, she argues that Shylock's life is forfeit for having conspired against the life of a Venetian citizen. The duke grants Shylock his life, but gives half his wealth to Antonio, half to the State. Antonio surrenders his claim if Shylock will turn Christian and make over his property on his death to his daughter Jessica, who has run away and married a Christian and been disinherited, to which Shylock agrees. Portia and Nerisa ask as rewards from Bassanio and Graziano the rings that their wives have given them, which they have promised never to part with. Reluctantly they give them up, and are taken to task accordingly on their return home. The play ends with the news of the safe arrival of Antonio's ships.

"The Merchant of Venice" has been labeled by many scholars as a 'problem comedy' and then by others as a 'romance.' Whatever the label, the play gives the reader a great deal to think about, not the least being its anti-semitism. But it is a popular play, loved by many viewers, a wonderful challenge for actors, and a real delight for teachers. It is a mystery that such an enjoyable work can have so many ugly elements about it. The three couples end happily in the tradition of the romance but at some price, and Jessica, Shylock's daughter, can be viewed as despicable. The "sweet harmony" that the lovers have at the end is achieved by bringing Shylock to justice, which would have been enough, but compelling him to convert to Christianity, as an act of mercy, is reprehensible, and here Portia too is despicable. Audiences will always feel a twinge of guilt as they watch the three couples contemplate the serenity of the spheres in the mythical and symbolic Belmont while knowing what has happened in far-off Venice to bring it about. Shylock's grim exit casts a pall over the festivities of the final act in Belmont. (I saw the Jonathan Miller National Theater production [1970] with Laurence Olivier as an Edwardian Shylock whose off-stage wailing after his final exit, which gave his agony an indelible poignancy, paralyzed the audience. It was the day that Queen Elizabeth announced that he had been elevated to Lord Olivier.)

"Richard II" (probably 1595) begins with the quarrel between Henry Bolingbroke, son of John of Gaunt, and Thomas Mowbray, duke of Norfolk, which King Richard resolves arbitrarily by exiling Mowbray for life and Bolingbroke for ten years. When 'time honoured' John of Gaunt dies Richard confiscates his property to pay for his Irish wars, for which he leaves the country. Bolingbroke returns to claim his inheritance and takes Berkeley Castle, which the duke of York has as regent to yield him. The king returns to Wales, hears that his Welsh supporters have deserted him and that Bolingbroke has executed the king's favorites Bushy and Green. Accompanied by York's son Aumerle, he withdraws to Flint Castle, where Bolingbroke accepts his surrender. The first half of the play ends with a discussion between a gardener and Richard's Queen Isabel about the government of the garden-state and the possibility of the king's deposition.

In London Richard relinquishes his crown to Bolingbroke, who sends him to the Tower. The earl of Carlisle's and Aumerle's plot to kill Bolingbroke who has now proclaimed himself Henry IV, is foiled by York. Richard is transferred to Pomfret Castle, where he hears of Henry's coronation and is murdered by Sir Pierce of Exton.

The play is written entirely in verse and it contains some of Shakespeare's most famous speeches, classics in their own right and much anthologized, including John of Gaunt's evocation of England as "this royal throne of kings, this sceptred isle, this earth of majesty . . . . this other Eden, demiparadise . . . this happy breed of men, this little world . . . this blessed plot, this earth, this realm, this England." Richard's plea "Let's talk of graves, of worms, and epitaphs . . . For God's sake let us sit upon the ground / And tell sad stories of the death of kings!" contributed to its potent appeal. But the basic statement of the play is so important and applicable to all eras where people of power are involved. At the beginning of the play Richard's security in his presumption that he is God's deputy and thus above the law leads him to disregard those principles which are the basis of his own position as king and head of state. His disregard for all administrative protocal sets in motion the rebellion that brings about his downfall. And his murder by Henry IV's henchmen becomes a blood bath. His musings in the Tower and his meditations on "the death of kings," some of Shakespeare's greatest lines up to this point in his career, make him something of a martyr.

"Henry IV" (about 1597) part 1 tells of the rebellion of the Percys, assisted by Douglas and in concert with Mortimer and Glendower and its defeat by the king and Prince Hal, the prince of Wales, at Shrewsbury (1403). Falstaff first appears in this play. The prince of Wales associates with him and his boon companions, Poins, Bardolph, and Peto, in their riotous life. Poins and the prince contrive that the others shall set on some travelers at Gadshill and rob them, and be robbed in their turn by themselves. The plot succeeds, and leads to Falstaff's well-known fabrication to explain the loss of the booty, and his exposure. At the battle of Shrewsbury, Prince Hal kills Hotspur in a heroic single combat, and then discovers Falstaff feigning death, whom he mourns with the words "I could have better spar'd a better man." After Hal's exit Falstaff resourcefully claims credit for having slain Hotspur.

Part 2 deals with the rebellion of Archbishop Scroop, Mowbray, and Hastings, while in the comic under-plot the story of Falstaff's doings is continued, with those of the prince, Pistol, Poins, Mistress Quickly, and Doll Tearsheet. Falstaff, summoned to the army for the repression of the rebellion, falls in with Justices Shallow and Silence in the course of his recruiting, makes a butt of them, and extracts one thousand pounds from the former. Henry IV dies, reconciled to his son, and Falstaff hastens from Gloucestershire to London to greet the newly crowned king, who rejects him in the speech beginning "I know thee not, old man. Fall to thy prayers,' banishing him from his presence but allowing him "competence of life."

"Henry V" (1599) opens with the newly ascended Henry astonishing clergy and courtiers by his piety and statecraft. The archbishop of Canterbury demonstrates, in the long 'Salic Law' speech, Henry's claim to the throne of France, and the Dauphin's jesting gift of tennis balls gives him an immediate pretext for invasion. Henry unmasks the three traitors, Scrope, Grey, and Cambridge, and sets out for France. He besieges and captures Harfleur, and achieves a resounding victory at Agincourt (1415), a battle for which he prepares his soldiers in the 'Crispin Crispian' speech. Comic relief is provided by the old tavern companions of Falstaff, who have fallen on hard times, and by some of Henry's soldiers, especially the pedantic but courageous Welsh captain Fluellen. The new, patriotic, comic characters symbolically defeat the old when Fluellen compels the braggart Pistol to eat a leek. The last act is given to Henry's wooing Katherine of France.

The two outstanding "Henry V" films were made by Laurence Olivier (1944) and Kenneth Branagh (1989) who, like Olivier before, was director and played the title role. Olivier's film, which is heavy with wartime patriotism, remains a classic and his delivery of the 'Crispin Crispian' speech is one of the great moments in film history. William Walton's sparkling orchestral score rousingly punctuates the films many dramatic moments. Branagh's film, on the other hand, in no way glamorizes war and makes Henry a much less aristocratic military leader. The scene when he finds the slain body of the Boy from Agincourt and carries it, grieving, across the battlefield is heartbreaking.

"The Merry Wives of Windsor." (possibly 1597) Falstaff, who is "out of heels", determines to make love to the wives of Ford and Page, two gentlemen dwelling at Windsor, because they have the rule of their husband's purses. Nym and Pistol, the discarded followers of Falstaff, warn the husbands. Falstaff sends identical love letters to Mrs. Ford and Mrs. Page who contrive the discomfiture of the knight. At a first assignation at Ford's house, on the arrival of the husband, they hide Falstaff in a basket, cover him with foul linen, and have him tipped into a muddy ditch. At a second assignation, they disguise him as the "fat woman of Brainford," in which character he is soundly beaten by Ford. The jealous husband having been twice fooled, the plot is now revealed to him, and a final assignation is given to Falstaff in Windsor Forest at Herne's oak, where he is beset and pinched by mock fairies and finally seized and exposed by Ford and Page.

The sub-plot is concerned with the wooing of Anne, the daughter of Page, by three suitors: Dr. Caius, a French physician, Slender, the foolish cousin of Justice Swallow, and Fenton, a wild young gentleman whom Anne loves. Mistress Quickly, servant to Dr. Caius, acts as go-between for all three suitors, and encourages them all impartially. Sir Hugh Evans, a Welsh parson, interferes on behalf of Slender and receives a challenge from the irascible Dr. Caius, but hostilities are confined to hacking of the English tongue. At the final assignation with Falstaff in the forest, Page, who favors Slender, arranges that the latter shall carry off his daughter, who is to be dressed in white; while Mrs. Page, who favors Dr. Caius, arranges that he shall carry her off dressed in green. In the event both of these find themselves fobbed off with a boy in disguise, while Fenton has run away with and married the true Anne.

These four plays—"Henry IV," 1 and 2, "Henry V," and "The Merry Wives of Windsor"—introduce us to some of the most fascinating characters in all of the Shakespeare canon: the youthful Prince Hal, the fiery Hotspur, the immortal Falstaff, the very clever women, Mistress Ford and Mistress Page, the witty Mistress Quickly, and so many other well-drawn characters. Falstaff however is the most memorable of them all.

Falstaff according to Samuel Johnson is a 'compound of sense and vice.' He is fat, witty, a lover of sack and of jests, and skilful at turning jokes on him to his own advantage, "I am not only witty in myself, but the cause that wit is in other men." He is a drinking companion of Prince Hal, and anticipates great advancement when Hal becomes king. Hal humors him and allows him to give his own version the Gadshill encounter with the men 'in buckram,' to mimic his father, Henry IV, and even take credit for the death of Hotspur at the battle of Shrewsbury. In 2 Henry IV, he is seen little with Hal, and is portrayed as old, ill, unscrupulous in his financial dealings with Mistress Quickly. On succeeding the throne Hal/Henry V rejects him in the speech "I know thee not, old man. Fall to thy prayers," which Falstaff throws off by assuring his friends that he will be sent for privately. But he pleads to the King, "we have heard the chimes of midnight," a far cry from his lecture on honor that Prince Hal allows him to deliver in the tavern. In "Henry V" however, Mistress Quickly tells us that "the king has kill'd his heart'" and goes on to describe his death in a tavern. The Falstaff of the "The Merry Wive of Windsor" is a buffo figure, whose attempts to mend his fortunes by wooing two citizens' wives simultaneously end in his discomfiture in Windsor Forest. It is this Falstaff, subject of some nine operas, which Verdi chose for what is probably the greatest operatic masterpiece to be composed in the late nineteenth century. It is Verdi's greatest work, pure genius from beginning to end.

"Much Ado About Nothing" (probably 1598-9) tells the story of the prince of Aragon, with Claudio and Benedick in his suite, who visits Leonato, duke of Messina, father of Hero and uncle of Beatrice. The sprightly Beatrice has a teasing relationship with the sworn bachelor Benedick. Beatrice and Benedick are both tricked into believing the other is in love, and this brings about a genuine sympathy between them. Meanwhile Don John, the malcontented brother of the prince, thwarts Claudio's marriage by arranging for him to see Hero apparently wooed by his friend Borachio on her balcony—it is really her maidservant Margaret in disguise. Hero is publicly denounced by Claudio on her wedding day, falls into a swoon, and apparently dies. Benedick proves his love for Beatrice by challenging Claudio to a duel. The plot by Don John and Borachio is unmasked by the "shallow fools" Dogberry and Verges, the local constables. Claudio promises to make Leonato amends for his daughter's death, and is asked to marry a cousin of Hero's; the veiled lady turns out to be Hero herself. Benedick asks to be married at the same time; Beatrice, "upon great persuasion; and partly to save your life, for I was told you were in a consumption," agrees and the play ends with a dance.

Critics have been quick to observe that the word 'nothing' was ambiguous in Shakespeare and that in this work it is a play on the word 'note' or 'noting.' Much of the play's action takes place by someone noting what someone else is doing or saying. "Notings" have been made by friends of Beatrice and Benedict and much ado has been made of Beatrice and Benedict's "notings" of others. Kenneth Branagh filmed the play on a grand scale in a lavish Italian setting in 1993 with himself and his then wife Emma Thompson in the leads. Nothing was spared in terms of gorgeous color, glorious music, beautiful Hollywood faces, and emphatic repartee. You have never seen or heard so much laughing, laughing, laughing. It is a gem.

"As You Like It" (probably earlier than 1599). Frederick has usurped the dominions of the duke his brother, who is living with his faithful followers in the forest of Arden. Celia, Frederick's daughter, and Rosalind, the duke's daughter, living at Frederick's court, witness a wrestling match in which Orlando, son of Sir Rowland de Boys, defeats a powerful adversary, and Rosalind falls in love with Orlando and he with her. Orlando, who at his father's death has been left in the charge of his elder brother Oliver, has been driven from home by Oliver's cruelty. Frederick, learning that Orlando is the son of Sir Rowland, who was a friend of the exiled duke, has his anger against the latter revived, and banishes Rosalind from his court, and Celia accompanies her. Rosalind assumes a countryman's dress and takes the name Ganymede; Celia passes as Aliena his sister. They live in the forest of Arden, and fall in with Orlando, who has joined the banished duke. Ganymede encourages Orlando to pay suit to her as though she were his Rosalind. Oliver comes to the forest to kill Orlando, but is saved by him from a lioness, and is filled with remorse for his cruelty. He falls in love with Aliena, and their weding is arranged for the next day. Ganyhmede undertakes to Orlando that she will by magic produce Rosalind at the same time to be married to him. When all are assembled in the presence of the banished duke to celebrate the double nuptials, Celia and Rosalind put off their disguise and appear in their own characters. News is brought that Frederick the usurper, setting out to seize and destroy his brother and his followers, has been converted from his intention "by an old religious man" and has made restitution of the dukedom.

Entertainment rather than plot dominates this play; much of it is provided by reflections of Jaques and Touchstone, and by the large number of songs, more than in any other Shakespeare's plays, including such lyrics as 'Under the greenwood tree' and 'Blow, blow, thou winter wind.'

The Plays: The Final Years

"Julius Caesar" (probably 1599) begins with the events of the year 44 B.C., after Caesar, already endowed with the dictatorship, had returned to Rome from a successful campaign in Spain, and when there are fears that he will allow himself to be crowned king. Distrust of Caesar's ambition gives rise to a conspiracy against him among Roman lovers of freedom, notably Cassius and Casca; they win over to their cause Brutus, who reluctantly joins them from a sense of duty to the republic. Caesar is slain by the conspirators in the Senate house. Antony, Caesar's friend, stirs the people to fury against the conspirators by a skillful speech at Caesar's funeral. Octavius, nephew of Julius Caesar, Antony, and Lapidus, united as triumvirs, oppose the forces raised by Brutus and Cassius. The quarrel and reconciliation of Brutus and Cassius, with the news of the death of Portia, wife of Brutus, provide one of the finest scenes in the play. Brutus and Cassius are defeated in the battle of Philippi (42 B.C.) and kill themselves.

One is amazed at the beauty and brilliance of this play. Since for many years it was required reading for students on a secondary level in schools, many mistakenly thought it was less profound than the other plays. On the contrary, Shakespeare's grasp of Roman life, politics, and rhetorical style, as well as his knowledge of the philosophy, specifically Roman Stoicism, of 44 B.C., have formed our impressions of how the ancient Romans thought and talked and conducted their civic affairs. There were nine silent film versions of this play but it was the 1953 Joseph L. Mankiewicz production with Louis Calhern (Caesar), James Mason (Brutus), John Gielgud (Cassius), and Marlon Brando (Mark Antony) that surprised the viewing public. Made on a shoe-string budget the film turned out to be a classic. Marlon Brando is amazing.

"Twelfth Night" (1601) tells the story of Sebastian and Viola, twin brother and sister and closely resembling one another, who are separated in a shipwreck off the coast of Illyria. Viola, brought to shore in a boat, disguises herself as a youth, Cesario, and takes service as page with Duke Orsino, who is in love with the lady Olivia. She rejects the duke's suit and will not meet him. Orsino makes a confidante of Cesario and sends her to press his suit on Olivia, much to the distress of Cesario, who has fallen in love with Orsino. Olivia in turn falls in love with Cesario. Sebastian and Antonio, captain of the ship that had rescued Sebastian, now arrive in Illyria. Cesario, challenged to a duel by Sir Andrew Aguecheek, a rejected suitor of Olivia, is rescued from her predicament by Antonio, who takes her for Sebastian. Antonio, being arrested at that moment for an old offence, claims from Cesario a purse that he had entrusted to Sebastian, is denied it, and hauled off to prison. Olivia, coming upon the true Sebastian, takes him for Cesario, invites him to her house, and marries him out of hand. Orsino comes to visit Olivia. Antonio, brought before him, claims Cesario as the youth he has rescued from the sea, while Olivia claims Cesario as her husband. The duke, deeply wounded, is bidding farewell to Olivia and the "dissembling cub" Cesario, when the arrival of the true Sebastian clears up the confusion. The duke, having lost Olivia, and becoming conscious of the love that Viola has betrayed, turns his affection to her, and they are married.

Much of the play's comedy comes from the sub-plot dealing with the members of Olivia's household: Sir Toby

Belch, her uncle; Sir Andrew Aguecheek, his friend; Malvolio, her pompous steward; Maria, her waiting gentlewoman, and her clown Feste. Exasperated by Malvolio's officiousness, the other members of the household make him believe that Olivia is in love with him and that he must return her affection. In courting her he behaves so outrageously that he is imprisoned as a madman. Olivia has him released and the joke against him is explained, but he is not amused by it, threatening, "I'll be reveng'd on the whole pack of you." The play's gentle melancholy and lyrical atmosphere is captured in Feste's two beautiful songs "Come away, come away, death" and "When that I was and a little tiny boy, / With hey, ho, the wind and the rain."

The title of the play comes from the name traditionally associated with the Feast of the Epiphany (January 6, the twelfth day of Christmas), a time when Folly was allowed to reign supreme under the guise of a Feast of Fools presided over by a Lord of Misrule. So this sets the tone of fun. Misrule is represented by Sir Toby Belch and his friends, Sir Andrew, Feste, and the gentlewoman Maria, who make life miserable for Olivia's stuffy steward Malvolio, whose name means 'bad will.' He is to be banished so that 'good will' can reign supreme. The gulling scene is Shakespeare comedy at its best. Malvolio is tricked into thinking that his Lady is in love with him. In an effort to allure her he wears cross-gartered yellow stockings in her presence; it has the opposite affect since she concludes that he is deranged. Laughingly they all poke fun and torment him until he exits vowing revenge "on the whole pack" of them. There have been many TV productions of the play; Alec McCowen and Alec Guinness played Malvolio in two of them. Trevor Nunn's film in 1996 done in Cornwall, stressing the sea imagery, is the best fun, with Nigel Hawthorne as Malvolio.

"Troilus and Cressida" (1602) Shakespeare's treatment of the love of Troilus and Cressida and its betrayal, against the setting of the siege of Troy by the Greeks, is conventional.

As well as Homer's and Chaucer's handling of the material, Shakespeare knew Ovid's "Metamorphoses," books XI and XII. The play contains much formal debate and takes the story up to the death of Hector at the hands of Achilles: Troilus fails to kill his rival Diomedes, and the cynically railing Thersites escapes death. Modern criticism has tended to agree with Coleridge's view that 'there is none of Shakespeare's plays harder to characterize."

"All's Well that Ends Well" (1603-4) tells the story of Bertram, the young count of Rousillon, who, on the death of his father, is summoned to the court of the king of France, leaving his mother and with her Helena, daughter of the famous physician Gerard de Narbon. The king is sick of a disease said to be incurable. Helena, who loves Bertram, goes to Paris and effects his cure by means of a prescription left by her father. As a reward she is allowed to choose her husband and names Bertram, who unwillingly obeys the king's order to wed her. But under the influence of the worthless braggart Parolles, he at once takes service with the duke of Florence, writing to Helena that until she can get the ring from his finger "which never shall come off," and is with child by him, she may not call him husband. Helena, passing through Florence on a pilgrimage, finds Bertram courting Diana, the daughter of her hostess there. Disclosing herself as his wife to them, she obtains permission to replace Diana at a midnight assignation with Bertram, having caused that day him to be informed that Helena is dead. Thereby she obtains from Bertram his ring, and gives him one that the king had given her. Bertram returns to his mother's house, where the king is on a visit. The latter sees on Bertram's finger the ring that he had given Helena, suspects Bertram of having destroyed her, and demands an explanation on pain of death. Helena herself now appears, explains what has passed, and claims that the conditions named in Bertram's letter have been fulfilled. Bertram, filled with remorse, accepts her as his wife. The sub-plot concerning the braggart Parolles, has been felt by some readers to dominate the play, and in performance it has often done so.

"Hamlet" (1599, completed 1601). Old Hamlet, king of Denmark, is recently dead, and his brother Claudius has assumed the throne and married his widow Gertrude. Young Hamlet, returning from university in Wittenberg, learns from the ghost of his father that Claudius murdered him by pouring poison into his ear, and is commanded to avenge the murder without injuring Gertrude. Hamlet warns his friend Horatio and the guards Bernardo and Marcellus (who have also seen the apparition) that he intends to feign madness, and swears them to secrecy. Immediately after his famous speech of deliberation beginning "To be, or not to be' he repudiates Ophelia whom he has loved, while spied on by Claudius and by Ophelia's father Polonius.

He welcomes a troupe of visiting players, and arranges a performance of a play ('the Mouse-trap') about fratricide, which Claudius breaks off, in apparently guilty and fearful fury, when the player Lucianus appears to murder his uncle by pouring poison into his ear. Hamlet refrains from killing Claudius while he is at prayer, but stabs through the arras in his mother's bedroom, killing the old counsellor Polonius, before reprimanding his mother for her affection for Claudius.

Claudius sends Hamlet to England with sealed orders that he should be killed on arrival. Hamlet outwits him, however, returning to Denmark, having arranged the deaths of his old friends Rosencrantz and Guildenstern, who were his uncle's agents. During Hamlet's absence Ophelia has gone mad with grief from Hamlet's rejection of her and her father's death, and is found drowned. Her brother Laertes, having returned from France, determines to avenge his sister's death. Hamlet and Laertes meet in the graveyard where Ophelia is to be buried, and fight in her grave. Claudius arranges a fencing match between

Hamlet and Laertes, giving the latter a poisoned foil; an exchange of weapons results in the deaths of both combatants, not before Gertrude has drunk a poisoned cup intended for her son, and the dying Hamlet has succeeded in killing Claudius. Fortinbras, prince of Norway, whose resolute military heroism has been alluded to throughout the play, appears fresh from wars with Poland and gives Hamlet a military funeral.

There has never been a shortage of Hamlets, even amongst women, with Sarah Bernhardt as the most notorious. Laurence Olivier's 1948 film version with the forty year old Olivier playing the role and directing is an elegiac journey into loneliness and nostalgia very much reflecting the mood of post-war Europe. The black and white photography is perfect. Tony Richardson's 1969 adaptation makes Nicol Williamson much more the student. Zeffirelli's 1990 version boasts such wonderful people as Glenn Close, Ian Holm, Paul Scofield, Alan Bates and all filmed on location, but it is hardly a faithful adaptation; he uses little more than 30% of the full text. Mel Gibson as Hamlet is a bit precious, facial tics and all. Kenneth Branagh's Hamlet is the full four hour text lavishly done with an array of famous actors even in the smallest roles. Kevin Kline and Ralph Fiennes have done it for stage and TV in modern dress.

"Measure for Measure" (summer of 1604) a tragicomedy often categorized as a 'problem play' because of the unpleasantness of its subject—matter, tells of the duke of Vienna, who, on the pretext of a journey to Poland, hands over the government to his virtuous-seeming deputy Angelo, who enforces strict laws against sexual license which for the past fourteen years had been neglected. Angelo at once sentences to death Claudio, a young gentleman who has got his betrothed Julietta with child. Claudio's sister Isabella, who is a novice in a sisterhood of nuns, pleads with Angelo for her brother's life, urged on by Claudio's friend Lucio.

In response to her repeated pleas Angelo offers to spare Claudio's life if she will consent to be his mistress. Isabella refuses, and will not be persuaded even by the desperate entreaties of Claudio in prison.

The duke, disguised as a friar, has made a visit of spiritual comfort to Claudio, and now devises a way of saving his life. Isabella is to agree to a midnight assignation with Angelo, but her place is to be taken by Mariana, who was betrothed to Angelo and still loves him. Mariana is first seen listening to the song 'Take, O, take those lips away.' The scheme is successful, but Angelo still proceeds with the order for Claudio's execution, though unknown to Isabella Claudio is saved by the substitution of the head of Ragozine, a pirate, who has died that night in the same prison. The duke lays by his disguise, simulates a return to Vienna, and pretends to disbelieve the complaints of Isabella and suit of Mariana, in favor of Angelo's hypocritical denial. When Angelo is forced to confess, both Mariana and Isabella plead for his life; Mariana is married to Angelo, Lucio to a whore, and at the end of the baffling final scene the duke appears to propose marriage to the novice Isabella.

This bare outline in no way conveys the richness of the play, especially the accompanying roles played by the bawds and all the dramatic irony. It may not be the best of Shakespeare's plays, but it is, as far as I am concerned, the most fun to teach. And students love it. Since it is a tragicomedy it offers the student so much to argue about, so many serious issues to be resolved. Should Isabella give in to Angelo's proposition to save her brother's life, a challenge Puccini's Tosca will someday have to resolve? And isn't the rigid Isabella a bit too strong-willed for a postulant who is anticipating a vow of obedience? And doesn't Angelo have a problem with the abuse of power, certainly an issue which concerns undergraduates today? And that wonderful ending where Isabella is offered the marital state and what will she do; many a director and actress has had to grapple with that one. Can the 'bed trick' be considered ethical? After all this is a play whose title is from the Sermon on the Mount. Yet, the 'bed trick,' as seen also in "All's Well that Ends Well" comes from Genesis, 35 and that it was associated in the Old Testament with providential intervention. And in this play we have the wonderful example of Shakespeare's low-life bawds having more insight and perception than the people of court, a great Shakespeare device. Research may come and go but Roy Battenhouse's essay on this play quite some years ago is still the definitive study of the play. ('Measure for Measure and Christian Doctrine of the Atonement', PMLA, 61, 1946).

"Measure for Measure" qualifies as a tragicomedy; but for the intervention of some characters and situations it could have ended up being a revenge tragedy. Certainly Angelo would have been executed if there had not been an intervention. It is quite possible that Shakespeare turned himself entirely to tragedy in his next three plays, tragedies that have plenty of revenge and are probably the greatest tragedies in classical literature: "Othello," "King Lear," and "Macbeth." Three plays in three years, 1604, 1605, 1606.

"Othello" (between 1602 and 1604). The play's first act is set in Venice. Desdemona, the daughter of Brabantio, a Venetian senator, has secretly married Othello, a Moor in the service of the state. Accused before the senators and the duke of having stolen Brabantio's daughter, Othello explains and justifies his conduct, and is asked by the Senate to lead the Venetian forces against the Turks who are about to attack Cyprus.

In the middle of a storm that disperses the Turkish fleet, Othello lands on Cyprus with Desdemona. Cassio, a young Florentine, who helped him court his wife and whom he has now promoted to be his lieutenant, and Iago, an older soldier, bitterly resentful of being passed over for promotion, who now plans his revenge, meet them. Iago uses Roderigo, 'a gull'd Gentleman' in love with Desdemona, to fight with

Cassio after he has got him drunk, so that Othello deprives him of his new rank. Iago then persuades Cassio to ask Desdemona to plead in his favor with Otello, which she warmly does. At the same time Iago suggests to Othello that Cassio is, and has been, Desdemona's lover, finally arranging through his wife Emilia, who is Desdemona's waiting-woman, that Othello should see Cassio in possession of a handkerchief which he had given to his bride. Othello is taken in by Iago's promptings and in frenzied jealousy smothers Desdemona in her bed. Iago sets Roderigo to murder Cassio, but when Roderigo fails to do this Iago kills him and Emilia as well, after she has proved Desdemona's innocence to Othello. Emilia's evidence and letters found on Roderigo prove Iago's guilt; he is arrested, and Othello, having tried to stab him, kills himself.

The play's strength is in its starkness; no sub-plots, little spectacle, quick movement. So much happens in the time span of two or three days. Such swiftness makes credible Othello's quick downfall. He has so little time to evaluate Iago's true motives, and to reflect on his blind jealousy. Orson Welles' film "Othello" is brilliant with its Moroccan locations and black and white imagery. John Dexter's film of the National Theater production captures Laurence Olivier's towering performance, almost too overpowering. Oliver Parker's "Othello" features the Hollywood actor Laurence Fishburne. Critics were quick to observe that his performance capitalized on the media dramatization of the O. J. Simpson trial. Verdi's opera "Otello" is one of the great operas in the Italian tradition. The role of Otello is written for a dramatic tenor and has the glorious lyricism of the Moor's Shakespearean poetic utterances. The role of Iago is written for a baritone, capturing all the darkness of Iago's revenge poetry. It is amazing how faithful Verdi is to Shakespeare's text and spirit, using, of course, Arrigo Boito's Italian libretto. An interesting class project is to have students listen to a recording of the Shakespeare play and then a recording of the Verdi opera for comparison; invariably the students prefer the Verdi.

"King Lear" (1604-5). Lear, king of Britain, a petulant and unwise old man, has three daughters: Goneril, wife of the duke of Albany, Regan, wife of the duke of Cornwall, and Cordelia, for whom the king of France and the duke of Burgandy are suitors. Intending to divide his kingdom among his daughters according to their affection for him, he bids them say which loves him most. Goneral and Regan make profession of extreme affection, and each receives one-third of the kingdom. Cordelia, self-willed, and disgusted by their shallow flattery, says she loves him according to her duty, not more nor less. Infuriated with this reply, Lear divides her portion between his older daughters, with the condition that he and one hundred knights shall be maintained by each daughter in turn. Burgundy withdraws his suit for Cordelia and the king of France accepts her without dowry. The earl of Kent, taking her part, is banished. Goneril and Regan reveal their heartless character by grudging their father the maintenance that he has stipulated, and finally turning him out of doors in a great storm. The earl of Gloucester shows pity for the old king, and is suspected of complicity with the French, who have landed in England. His eyes are put out by Cornwall, who receives a death wound in the affray. Gloucester's son Edgar, who has been traduced to his father by his bastard brother Edmund, takes the disguise of a lunatic beggar, and tends his father until the latter's death. Lear, whom rage and ill-treatment, have deprived of his wits, is conveyed to Dover by the faithful Kent in disguise, where Cordelia receives him. Meanwhile Goneril and Regan have both turned their affections to Edmund. Embittered by this rivalry, Goneril poisons Regan and takes her own life. The English forces under Albany defeat the French, and Lear and Cordelia are imprisoned; by Edmund's order, Cordelia is hanged, and Lear dies from grief. The treachery of Edmund is proved by his brother Edgar. Gloucester's heart has "Twixt two extremes of passion, joy and grief, / Burst smilingly". Albany, who has not abetted Goneril in her cruel treatment of Lear, takes over the kingdom.

For many this is Shakespeare's most profoundly and philosophically intense drama. And what makes the play such a masterpiece is that against such dense and profound happenings, Lear's reunion and reconciliation with his dead Cordelia just before he dies is done so simply, touchingly, and with such heart-breaking sensitivity. The mistakes of a father, the betrayal of two children, and the death of a loyal daughter, certainly the height of domestic tragedy, is all performed on a near empty stage except for an upper level for Lear to cry out his storm soliloquy. It may well be the height of English literature in any form.

"Macbeth" (about 1606). Macbeth and Banquo, generals of Duncan, king of Scotland, returning from a victorious campaign against rebels, encounter three weird sisters, or witches, upon a heath, who prophesy that Macbeth shall be thane of Cawdor, and king hereafter and that Banquo shall beget kings though he be none. Immediately afterwards comes the news that the king has created Macbeth thane of Cawdor. Stimulated by the prophecy, and spurred on by Lady Macbeth, Macbeth murders Duncan, who is on a visit to his castle. Duncan's sons, Malcolm and Donalbain escape, and Macbeth assumes the crown. To defeat the prophecy of the witches concerning Banquo, he orders the murder of Banquo and his son Fleance, but the latter escapes. Haunted by the ghost of Banquo, Macbeth consults the three weird sisters and is told to beware of Macduff, the thane of Fife; that none born of woman has power to harm Macbeth; and that he never will be vanquished till Birnam Wood shall come to Dunsinane. Learning that Macduff has joined Malcolm, who is gathering an army in England, he surprises the castle of Macduff and causes Lady Macduff and her children to be slaughtered.

Lady Macbeth goes mad and dies. The army of Malcolm and Macduff attacks Macbeth; passing through Birnam Wood every man cuts a bough and under these 'leavy screens' marches to Dunsinane. Macduff, who was "from his mother's womb / Untimely ripp'd" kills Macbeth. Malcolm is hailed king of Scotland.

Where Othello's tragedy comes from his blinding jealousy and the savage plottings of an evil Iago, and Lear's comes from a miscalculation born of a certain arrogance, pride, and self-consumption, Macbeth's comes from premeditated murder in the service of uncontrollable ambition. The fanatic desire for power has taught Macbeth that life is "but a walking shadow," "a tale / Told by an idiot, full of sound and fury, / Signifying nothing." Again when students are given the opportunity to experience and compare Verdi's operatic version of "Macbeth" and Shakespeare's play, they invariably prefer the Verdi. They are in good company. Verdi himself loved his "Macbeth" more than any of his other creations.

"Antony and Cleopatra" (1606-7). The play presents Marc Antony, the great soldier and noble prince, of Alexandria, enthralled by the beauty of the Egyptian queen Cleopatra. Recalled by the death of his wife Fulvia and political developments, he tears himself from Cleopatra and returns to Rome, where the estrangement between him and Octavius Caesar is terminated by his marriage to Octavia, an event which provokes the intense jealousy of Cleopatra. But the reconciliation is short-lived, and Antony leaves Octavia and returns to Egypt. At the battle of Actium, the flight of the Egyptian squadron is followed by the retreat of Antony, pursued to Alexandria by Caesar. There after a momentary success, Anthony is finally defeated. On the false report of Cleopatra's death, he falls upon his sword. He is borne to the monument where Cleopatra has taken refuge and dies in her arms. Cleopatra, fallen into Caesar's power but determined not to grace his triumph, takes her own life by the bite of an asp.

Because of the vividness of its central figures and the exoticism and luxuriousness of its language and structure, Antony and Cleopatra has long been one of the bard's most popular plays. Audiences have been willing to forget the problems of the play, such as its failure to be true to the Roman and Egyptian way of doing things, its too British treatment of what is essentially a Roman play. One does not learn much of Roman philosophy here but there is plenty about gorgeous writing in the lush poetry of the two lovers. There is a British film with Robert Speaight as Antony (Eliot's choice for his first Beckett in "Murder in the Cathedral") and several TV productions by Trevor Nunn and Jonathan Miller, all emphasizing lavishness of production.

"Coriolanus" (about 1608). Caius Marcius, a proud Roman general, performs wonders of valor in a war against the Volscians and captures the town Corioli, receiving in consequence the surname of Coriolanus. On his return it is proposed to make him consul, but his arrogant and outspoken contempt of the Roman rabble makes him unpopular with the fickle crowd, and the tribunes of the people have no difficulty in securing his banishment. He goes to the Volscian general, Aufidius, his enemy of long standing, is received with delight, and leads the Volscians against Rome to effect his revenge. He reaches the walls of the city, and the Romans, to save it from destruction, send emissaries, old friends of Coriolanus, to propose terms, but in vain. Finally his mother Volumnia, his meek wife Virginia, and his son come to beseech him to spare the city and he yields to the eloquence of his mother, suspecting that by doing so he has signed his own death warrant, makes a treaty favorable to the Volscians, and returns with them to Antium, a Volscian town. Here Aufidius turns against him, accusing him of betraying the Volscian interests, and with the assistance of conspirators of his faction, publicly kills Coriolanus.

"Coriolanus" is one of Shakespeare's least popular plays. It is the third and last of the "Roman plays" and it is stark and barren in its language and spectacle. It seems the play's unpopularity is due to what is in a sense its strength. Coriolanus dominates the action; he is almost super-human in leadership and battle. He has only contempt for those whom he dislikes, he is unbearable while participating in civil affairs, and he is completely undiplomatic in his relationship with the public. When he brings down upon himself the wrath of the Volscians he is actually bringing down upon himself his own destruction. He is the least attractive of Shakespeare's heroes and that may be the reason the play is seldom performed. Yet, the character has such stature and the role is so challenging one would think it would be as desired a challenge for actors as is Hamlet. One of the great successes in the career of Laurence Olivier was his Coriolanus, a performance filled with energy and bravado. Others who have assumed the role are Richard Burton, Alan Howard, Ian McKellen, and Kenneth Branagh.

"Timon of Athens" (about 1607). Timon, a rich and noble Athenian of good and gracious nature, having ruined himself by his prodigal liberality to friends, flatterers, and parasites, turns to the richest of his friends for assistance in his difficulties, and is denied it and deserted by all who have previously frequented him. He surprises these by inviting them once more to a banquet; but when the covers are removed from the dishes, as Timon cries "Uncover, dogs, and lap", they are found to contain warm water, which with imprecations he throws in his guests' faces. Cursing the city, he betakes himself to a cave, where he lives solitary and misanthropical. While digging for roots he finds a hoard of gold, which has now no value for him. His embittered spirit is manifested in his talk with the exiled Alcibiades, the churlish philosopher Apemantus, the thieves and flatterers attracted by the gold, and his faithful steward Flavius. When the senators of Athens, hard pressed by the attack of Alcibiades, come to entreat him to return to the city and help them, he offers them a fig-tree, on which to hang themselves as a refuge from affliction. Soon his tomb is found by the seashore, with an epitaph expressing his hatred of mankind.

"Timon of Athens" is the last of Shakespeare's tragedies and significantly so. Probably the playwright himself realized his progressive weakness in creating tragic heroes (Timon has a lot of Coriolanus in him) and that the public was not interested in misanthropical losers. Ralph Richardson, Paul Scofield, and Jonathan Pryce attempted the role in England, each bringing a very personal understanding of Timon' s plight.

"Pericles, Prince of Tyre" (between 1606 and 1608). The play is presented by John Gower, author of "Confessio Amantis", who acts as Chorus throughout, and tells how having solved the riddle of King Antiochus and discovered his incestuous relationship with his daughter, Pericles, prince of Tyre, finds his life in danger. He leaves his government in the hands of his honest minister, Helicanus, and sails from Tyre to Tarsus where he relieves a famine. Off the coast of Pentapolis, Pericles alone survives a wreck of his ship, and in a tournament defeats the suitors for the hand of Thaisa, daughter of King Simonides, whom he marries.

Hearing that Antiochus has died, Pericles sets sail for Tyre, and during a storm on the voyage Thaisa gives birth to a daughter, Marina, and faints. Apparently dead, Thaisa is buried at sea in a chest, which is cast ashore at Ephesus, where Cerimon, a physician, opens it and restores Thaisa to life. She, thinking her husband drowned, becomes a priestess in the temple of Diana. Pericles takes Marina to Tarsus, where he leaves her with its Governor Cleon and his wife Dionyza.

When the child grows up Dionyza, jealous of her being more favored than her own daughter, seeks to kill her; but Marina is carried off by pirates and sold in Mytilene to a brothel, where her purity and piety win the admiration of Lysimachus, the governor of the city, and the respect of the brothel-keeper's servant, Boult, and secure her release. In a vision Pericles is shown Marina's tomb, deceivingly erected by Cleon and Dionyza. He puts to sea again and lands at Mytilene, where through Lysimachus and to his intense joy Pericles discovers his daughter. In a second vision, Diana directs him to go to her temple at Ephesus and there recount the story of his life. In doing this, the priestess Thaisa, his lost wife, recognizes him, and is reunited with her husband and daughter. At the end of the play the Chorus tells how Cleon and Dionyza are burnt by the citizens of Tarsus as a penalty for their wickedness.

Most scholars are agreed now that "Pericles" was not written by Shakespeare alone. The play is not very often performed, although Marina is one of the bard's most beautifully crafted characters. Audiences are moved by a beloved child's power to regenerate her father and renew his faith in life. She has been compared to Cordelia in "King Lear" and she is the source for T. S. Eliot's lovely lyric "Marina." The play is immediately recognizable as something very different for Shakespeare and is probably a precursor of what is to come in the final three works, "Cymbeline," "The Winter's Tale," and "The Tempest."

"Henry VIII" also known as "All is True" was co-authored with Fletcher; its performance of June 1613 resulted in the burning down of the Globe Theater as a result of a cannon shot during a performance. It deals with the fall and execution of the duke of Buckingham; the question of the royal divorce; the pride and fall of Cardinal Wolsey and his death; the advancement and coronation of Anne Boleyn; the triumph of Cranmer over his enemies; and the christening of the Princess Elizabeth.

The play is probably the least performed of all Shakespeare's works.

"Cymbeline" (1609-10). Imogen, daughter of Cymbeline, King of Britain, has secretly married Leonatus Posthumus, a poor but worthy gentleman. The queen, Imogen's stepmother, determined that her clownish son Cloton shall marry Imogen reveals the secret marriage to the king, who banishes Posthumus. In Rome Posthumus boasts of Imogen's virtue and makes a wager with Iachimo that if he can seduce Imogen he shall have a diamond ring that Imogen had given him. Iachimo is repulsed by Imogen, but by hiding in her bedchamber he observes details of Imogen's room and her body which persuade Posthumus of her infidelity, and he receives the ring.

Posthumus writes to his servant Pisanio directing him to kill Imogen; but Pisanio instead provides her with male disguise, sending a bloody cloth to Posthumus to deceive him that the deed is done. Under the name Fidele Imogen becomes a page to Bellarius and the two lost sons of Cymbeline, Guiderius and Arviragus, living in a cave in Wales. Fidele sickens and is found as dead by the brothers. Left alone, she revives, only to discover at her side the headless corpse of Cloten, which she believes, because of his borrowed garments, to be that of her husband Posthumus.

A Roman army invades Britain; Imogen falls into the hands of the general Lucius and becomes his page. The Britons defeat the Romans, thanks to the superhuman valor in a narrow lane of Bellarius and his two sons aided by the disguised Posthumus. However, Posthumus, pretending to be a Roman, is subsequently taken prisoner and has a vision in gaol of his family and Jupiter, who leaves a prophetic document with him. Lucius pleads with Cymbeline for the life of Fidele/Imogen: moved by something familiar in her appearance, he spares her life and grants her a favor. She asks that Iachimo be forced to tell how he came by the ring he wears. Posthumus, learning from this confession that his wife is innocent but believing her dead, is in despair until Imogen reveals herself. The king's joy at recovering his daughter is intensified when Bellarius restores to him his two lost sons, and the scene ends in a general reconciliation. Posthumus's words to Imgen on being reconciled with her, "Hang there like fruit, my soul, / Till the tree die!" were described by Tennyson as the tenderest lines in Shakespeare.

This strange and complicated play, coming toward the end of Shakespeare's literary career, is especially noteworthy because it has a woman at the heart of the action. Imogen, a woman of exemplary chastity and loyalty, is in the tradition of Griselda in Chaucer's "The Clerk's Tale." Episodic in structure the play attempts to synthesize British and Roman qualities which sixteenth century Renaissance theater-goers believed to be the very essence of each nation's greatness. But the complexity of events and the pace at which the various plot strands are unraveled at the end make Verdi's "Il Trovatore" seem like simple narration.

"The Winter's Tale" (1610 or 1611). Leontes, king of Sicily, and Hermione, his virtuous wife, are visited by Leontes' childhood friend Polixenes, king of Bohemia. Leontes presently convinces himself that Hermione and Polixenes are lovers, attempts to procure the death of the latter by poison, and on his escape imprisons Hermione, who in prison gives birth to a daughter. Paulina, wife of Antigonus, a Sicilian lord tries to move the king's compassion by bringing the baby to him, but in vain. He orders Antigonus to leave the child on a desert shore to perish. He disregards a Delphian oracle declaring that Hermione is innocent. He soon learns that his son Mamillius has died of sorrow for Hermione's treatment, and shortly after that Hermione herself is dead. Leontes is filled with remorse.

Meanwhile Antigonus leaves the baby girl, Perdita, on the shore of Bohemia (sic), and is himself killed by a bear.

Perdita is found and brought up by a shepherd. Sixteen years pass. When she grows up, Florizel, Perdita, son of Polixenes, and the old shepherd flee from Bohemia to the court of Leontes, where the identity of Perdita is discovered, to Leontes' great joy, and the revival of his grief for the loss of Hermione. Paulina offers to show him a statue that perfectly resembles Hermione, and when the king's grief is intensified by the sight of this, the statue comes to life and reveals itself as the living Hermione, whose death Paulinus had falsely reported in order to save her life. Polixenes is reconciled to the marriage of his son with Perdita, on finding that the shepherd girl is really the daughter of his former friend Leontes. The rogueries of Autolycus, the pedlar and the 'snapper-up of unconsidered trifles', add amusement to the later scenes of the play; and his songs "When daffodils begin to peer" and "Jog on, jog on, the footpath way" are famous.

Again we have in this play the husband consumed with jealousy, like Othello, but coming to enlightenment and contrition to give the play a happy ending, like "Cymbeline." This device of all the pieces falling into place at the end, all's well that ends well, which is seen in so many of the plays, especially in "Measure for Measure", which has contrition and redemption so integral to the action, is prominent here and in "The Tempest."

"The Tempest" (1611). Prospero, duke of Milan, ousted from his throne by his brother Antonio, and turned adrift on the sea with his child Miranda, has been cast upon a lonely island. This had been the place of banishment of the witch Sycorax. Prospero, by his knowledge of magic, has released various spirits (including Ariel) formerly imprisoned by the witch, and these now obey his orders. He also keeps in service the witch's son Caliban, a misshapen monster, the sole inhabitant of the island. Prospero and Miranda have lived thus for twelve years.

When the play begins a ship carrying the usurper, his confederate Alonso, king of Naples, his brother Sebastian and son Ferdinand, is by the art of Prospero wrecked on the island. The passengers are saved, but Ferdinand is thought by the rest to be drowned, and he thinks this is their fate. According to Prospero's plan Ferdinand and Miranda are thrown together, fall in love, and plight their troths. Prospero appears to distrust Ferdinand and sets him to carrying logs. On another part of the island Sebastian and Antonio plot to kill Alonso and Gonzalo, 'an honest old Councellor' who had helped Prospero in his bnishment. Caliban offers his service to Stephano, a drunken butler, and Trinculo, a jester, and persuades Sebastian and Antonio to try to murder Prospero. As their conspiracy nears him, Prospero breaks off the masque of Iris, Juno, and Ceres, which Ariel has presented to Ferdinand and Miranda. Caliban, Stephano, and Trinculo are driven off and Ariel brings the king and his courtiers to Prospero's cell. There he greets "My true preserver" Gonzalo, forgives his brother Antonio, on the condition that he restores his dukedom to him, and re-unites Alonso with his son Ferdinand who is discovered playing chess with Miranda. When Alonso repents for what he has done, Antonio and Sebastian do not speak directly to Prospero, but exchange ironical and cynical comments with each other. The boatswain and master of the ship appear to say that it has been magically repaired and that the crew is safe. Before all embark for Italy Prospero frees Ariel from his service, renounces his magic, and leaves Caliban once more on the island.

This is reputed to be Shakespeare's last play before his retirement to Stratford and critics have conjectured that Prospero's renouncing magic was Shakespeare's farewell to the magic of theater. This has long been a favorite of readers and audiences and what a grand finale it is. It has young love, magic, the effervescent Ariel, the human brute Caliban, the problem of transcendent power and its political and religious implications, the exploration of poetic and dramatic art, and the issue of Prospero's (Shakespeare's) achievement of wisdom in the culmination of his career. The end of the masque very significantly relates to Shakespeare's 'farewell' to the stage.

"Our revels now are ended. These our actors, / As I foretold you, were all spirits and / Are melted into air, into thin air: / And, like the baseless fabric of this vision, / the cloud-capp'd towers, the gorgeous palaces, / the solemn temples, the great globe itself, / Yea, all which it inherit, shall dissolve / And, like this insubstantial pageant faded, / Leave not a rack behind. We are such stuff / As dreams are made on, and our little life / Is rounded with a sleep."

What happened in England between the time of Shakespeare's "Richard III" in 1591 and his "The Tempest" in 1611, a mere twenty years, can only be described as amazing. The greatest works in the history of theater and dramatic literature were written by William Shakespeare. Some thirty-three plays came out of London, a superhuman and miraculous feat of genius.

Christian Influences

Readers have always been fascinated with Shakespeare's background, particularly those aspects of the Christian tradition that had so much to do with shaping and influencing his creative output. Certainly there are many non-Christian influences here and a number of the plays are in a non-Christian setting. But the fascination seems to be more for Christian influences, particularly the realm of theology.

There is a fairly wide range of theological subjects and materials in Shakespeare's plays which attest to the playwright's theological sophistication. They are virtues and theological commonplaces which are found in the Sacred Scriptures, in Luther, Calvin, the new Puritan preachers, and other religious writers of the times, all from an Augustinian point of view. These do not prove that

...espeare was in any way a theologian; they prove that ne was an exceptional dramatist who had at his fingertips the religious and theological interests of the times. He could use these interests to draw a character, embellish a scene, and forward the action that was taking place in a Christian context, even a non-Christian context as well. I have chosen seven theological subjects (although there many more) to discuss briefly and show how they appear in some of the plays: God, Man, pride, guilt, mercy, justice, and judgment. They are concepts close to Shakespeare's interests and of course integral to the doctrines of redemption and salvation.

References to God, the gods, and derivative or compound words fill twelve columns in Bartlett's "Complete Concordance of Shakespeare." Most are cliches or conventional expletives. Others however have more depth as when Claudius acknowledges justice is defined by God in heaven rather than by man: "on whom it will, it will; On whom it will not, so; yet still 'tis just." And Hamlet, preparing for the coming match with Laertes sees God's providence in the daily rescues and continuous care of man: "there's a special providence in the fall of a sparrow. If it be now, 'tis not to come; if it be not to come, it will be now; if it be not now, yet it will come: the readiness is all." Readiness is essentially and explicitly Christian, and Hamlet is in a Christian society. References like these remind us that Shakespeare's characters live in a Christian society and think within the framework of Christian meaning. But nowhere does Shakespeare provide a comprehensive understanding of God. References to God contribute to the development of character and action within particular dramatic situations.

For example, throughout Claudius' soliloquy on prayer there is much what many critics would maintain as a valid understanding of God, but the scene attempts to characterize not God; it is to characterize the guilty king. What is fascinating is how often these references occur and how they show just how much the Christian experience infiltrated the very air the characters breathed. When the just Banquo declares "In the great hand of God I stand" we see what a great faith he has in the protection of God to whom he has professed great loyalty.

But all in all Shakespeare is careful, indeed cautious, in his use of God. Many of the plays have the action take place in a pre-Christian setting and he adjusts his god to that particular context: "As flies to wanton boys, are we to th' gods. / They kill us for their sport." (King Lear). And again in the plays that have a Christian setting, his references to God are commonplace and not all that plentiful. One would think that references to God would be many where death occurs, and death occurs often. But it is not the case. References to heaven are not only rare but they are brief. There is Warwick's "Warwick bids you all farewell, to meet in heaven." (3 Henry VI) And King Edward's expectation of an embassage "From my Redeemer to redeem me hence" (Richard III), while even Richard II says only: "Mount, mount, my soul! thy seat is up on high; / Whilst my gross flesh sinks downward, here to die." Such expressions are commonplaces and give a poetic grace to that which is platitude. The same can be said for Horatio's famous address to the dead Hamlet: "Good night, sweet prince, / And flights of angels sing thee to thy rest!" The "Good night" refers to the conception that death is but a sleep, a concept Shakespeare used in one of his sonnets, as did John Donne in his more famous one. "The flights of angels sing thee to thy rest" is from the centuries old Latin burial service still in use in the sixteenth century Catholic funeral service and used at the burial of Henry VIII. The Biblical references to angelic choirs and angels accompanying Lazarus to the bosom of Abraham were familiar to Englishmen. The liturgical text read: "May the angels lead thee into Paradise.... May the choir of angels receive thee and with Lazarus, once a beggar, mayest thou have eternal rest."

Man in the 16th and 17th centuries was still the center of the universe, maybe not as much as he was in the age of Chaucer, but certainly still a creature created in the image and likeness of God. In this God-like quality we recognize the examplar of human dignity. This is evident in King Edward's rebuke of the murder committed by certain of his subjects in "Richard III" " . . . your waiting vassals / Have done a drunken slaughter and defac'd / the precious image of our dear Redeemer." Man's basic worth and dignity consists in the fact that he is created in the image of God and it is because of original sin that he is unwilling to remain content with his inherent dignity, and overreaches himself. Thus Wolsey advises Cromwell: "Cromwell, I charge thee, fling away ambition! / by that sin fell the angels. How can man then / (The image of his Maker) hope to win by it?" (Henry VIII). In the Augustinian view, man, lusting for power and authority in Paradise, desired to be like God at the instigation of the devil. His salvation now is in shearing away all pretenses, stripping himself of all his ambitions in order to see himself simply as a man. Lear acknowledges this truth when he sees naked Tom: "Thou art the thing itself; unaccomodated man is no more but such a poor, bare, forked animal as thou art." Lear recognizing his own condition tears at his clothes, which is probably the most dramatic moment in the whole play. Lear had to be brought to this condition by suffering (certainly not a Christian concept alone, it is at the heart of Oedipus), an understanding Henry V said of himself as king, that "his ceremonies laid by, at his nakedness he appears but a man." Hamlet, in one of his less vengeful moments, says "What is a man, / If his chief good and market of his time / Be but to sleep and feed? A beast, no more, / Sure he that made us with such large discourse, / Looking before and after, gave us not / That capability and godlike reason / To fust in us unus'd?" It must be pointed out that theologians at the time made a commonplace of the fact that man differs from the lower animals in that he was created in the image of God and has been endowed with "discourse of reason."

God's justice operates in a number of ways for the punishment of sin, and the sense of guilt is one of these ways. But God's mercy is always present to assuage the pain of guilt and it becomes one with justice. Even Richard III suffers from the affliction of guilt: "O no! Alas, I rather hate myself / For hateful deeds committed by myself." Hamlet who is torn by the fact that he sees no sense of guilt in his mother is warned by the Ghost to do nothing to Gertrude, "Leave her to heaven, / And to those thorns that in her bosom lodge / to prick and sting her." Of course we know that Hamlet does not follow the advice of the Ghost and forces Gertrude to see herself as in a mirror. Claudius expresses his experience of guilt in "The Harlot's cheek, beautied with plast'ring art, / Is not more ugly to the thing that helps it / Than is my deed to my most painted word. / O heavy burden!" Of course the closing scenes of the play are filled with guilt and terror. Gertrude concludes, "To my sick soul (as sin's true nature is) / Each toy seems prologue to some great amiss, / So full of artless jealousy is guilt / It spills itself in fearing to be spilt." The most striking image of guilt is Macbeth's "O, full of scorpions is my mind, dear wife," The Augustinian sense of guilt that permeates the early part of the "Confessions" is based on the fact that to gain possession of everything desired does not bring contentment. Lady Macbeth expresses this reality when she says, "our desire is got without content." And she further laments, "Tis safer to be that which we destroy." And Macbeth himself declares it is better to "be with the dead" than to continue in such "doubtful joy" and "restless ecstasy."

Pride has traditionally been placed at the top of the seven deadly sins. Augustine used pride as the basis for the fall of the angels and the sixteenth century religious writers were well aware that it was one of the greatest sins and perhaps even as the basis of all sin. But pride is not just a Christian thing. The Greek attitude toward hubris was very well known and despite the Greek and Christian concepts of pride differing significantly in many ways, it was repudiated by both in the same way. For the average reader the overlapping of pagan and Christian pride is taken for granted and is seldom interpreted as one or the other. In the Roman play "Coriolanus" it is remarked that the protagonist "wants nothing of a god but eternity and a heaven to throne in." and that he acts as though he "were a god to punish, not A man of their infirmity." while it is said of Julius Caesar that "this man Is now become a god." In "Julius Caesar" Cassius charges that Caesar wants to be a god with all men below him, just as Caesar declares that Cassius is unwilling to be a man with other men above him: "Such men as he be never at heart's ease / Whiles they behold a greater than themselves." Both men are accusing the other of secular pride,

In "Timon of Athens" we see another form of pride: pride with hypocrisy. Having fled to the wilderness to live as a misanthropic hermit, he is sought out by Apremantus, who accuses Timon of not castigating his pride but actually feeding on it with the affectation of humility. "If thou didst put this sour cold habit on / to castigate thy pride, 'twere well; but thou / Dost it enforcedly. Thou'dst courtier again, / Wert thou not beggar."

In "Hamlet" we see the pride of heroic achievement expressed by Hamlet himself, with a possible touch of envy. In Fontinbras he sees "a delicate and tender prince, / Whose spirit, with divine ambition puff'd, / Makes mouths at the invisible event, / Exposing what Is mortal and unsure / To all that fortune, death, and danger dare, / Even for an eggshell. Rightly to be great / Is not to stir without great argument, / But greatly to find quarrel in a straw / When honor's at stake."

Of course there are so many examples of pride in Shakespeare: the Capulets and Montagues, Lear's division of his kingdom for protestations of love which is not only prideful but foolish; there is the pride of Angelo and the pride of the calculating Shylock, and the mean-spirited pride of Portia.

Justice and judgment occur often in the plays. Evildoers cannot escape the justice of God, as Henry V tells the soldier Williams: "If these men have defeated the law and outrun native punishment, though they can outstrip men, they have no wings to fly from God." God's judgment will come in the end but also can come in this life through calamity, anguish, and guilt. The timing of such divine judgment cannot be predicted by man. "The powers, delaying (not forgetting)" as Ariel tells the "three men of sin" in "The Tempest"will nonetheless certainly visit retribution for evil. That there is earthly and heavenly justice is seen in Claudius' soliloquy: "In the corrupted currents of this world / Offence's gilded hand may show by justice, / And oft 'tis seen the wicked prize itself / Buys out the law; but 'tis not so above." And Claudius continues: "There is no shuffling; there the action lies / In his true nature, and we ourselves compell'd, / Even to the teeth and forehead of our faults, / To give in evidence."

Mercy is referred to often in Shakespeare and is seen in virtuous heathens as well as Christians. Isabella speaks of the value of mercy: "No ceremony that to great ones 'longs, / Not the king's crown nor the deputed sword, / the marshall's truncheon nor the judge's robe, / Become them with one half so good a grace / As mercy does." But invariably mercy is always tied up with justice and justice alone, without mercy, is not enough for salvation. Portia says to Shylock: "Though justice be thy plea, consider this—/ that, in the course of justice, none of us / Should see salvation." The discourse continues with Shylock relying on the Old Law. In repudiating all pleas for mercy, he says, "I stand for judgment," and "I stand here for law." When the Duke asks, "How shalt thou hope for mercy, rend'ring none?" Shylock counters with another question, "What judgment shall I dread, doing no wrong?"

Of course Shylock's characterization is developed in terms of the Old Testament legalism which the New Law repudiated. Consequently we have the conflict between the letter of the law and the spirit of the law. At this moment Shylock will have no part of the spirit of mercy. Isabella in appealing to Angelo calls upon the New Law understanding of Mercy when she says: "How would you be, / If he which is the top of judgment should / But judge you as you are? O, think on that! / And mercy then will breathe within your lips, / Like man new made."

Portia, in appealing to Shylock for mercy, is subtly calling upon the Lord's Prayer (which of course Shylock would not be praying) "forgive us our trespasses as we forgive those who trespass against us." She says, ""We do pray for mercy / And that same prayer doth teach us all to render / The deeds of mercy." Portia's last appeal to Shylock "Then must the Jew be merciful" which is countered by Shylock with "On what compulsion must I? Tell me that," ushers in one of the most famous of Shakespeare's set pieces: "The quality of mercy is not strain'd; / It droppeth as the gentle rain from heaven / Upon the place beneath." But throughout in Shakespeare the Christian teaching that justice must be tempered with mercy, so brilliantly articulated by God in Book III of "Paradise Lost", is even spoken by the hypocrite Angelo when Isabella appeals for mercy. He says. "I show it most when I show justice; / For then I pity those I do not know, / Which a dismiss'd offence would after gall, / And do him right that, answering one foul wrong, / Lives not to act another." The gentle Escalus declares the same position when he says, "Mercy is not itself that oft looks so, /Pardon is still the nurse of second woe."

Conclusion

Along with references to Shakespeare in London go others relating to his family and to his home town. In August

1596 his only son died and was buried there. It is not sure if Shakespeare was in Stratford to attend the burial. Communication was slow and he was heavily scheduled in London with the theater. Two months later John Shakespeare was granted a coat of arms which gave him the status of gentleman, and eventually to his son. In 1597 Will bought a substantial piece of property, New Place, the second largest house in Stratford. He was indeed a prosperous man. Obviously this was to be the home of his family. All his working life was not in Stratford but in London, yet there is no evidence that he had a permanent residence in London. In typical London fashion, he probably rented here and there. We can assume that he would return on occasion to his home in New Place for time with the family, rest, and peacefully work on a particular play. There were no more children with Anne; his elder daughter had one child and the younger had three. Contrary to idle talk, there is no evidence that there was a marital breakdown. There are some documents of dealings, loans, purchases in Stratford that tell us that he kept in close touch with his home.

Study of the records of Will's life show that he was a well-educated, well-read, enterprising man who knew how to manage his business affairs and could pursue financial transactions as a professional. He was a deeply caring man for his family and he was willing to make sacrifices to support them in a career that he obviously loved very much, the theater. To write so much while he was away from Stratford and yet run the family interests in Stratford tells us that he was not only an ambitious man but also a well-organized and disciplined one. He was an energetic man and a prosperous one who left his family comfortable for their future. Obviously he was not garrulous because we do not have any record of personal utterances as we do of others of the time, say Ben Jonson.

The fact that we do not have as much information about his life, personality, and interests, the way we do about John

Milton, is not all that important. The empathy he shows for his characters in his plays and the emotions revealed in the sonnets, the most personal of all forms of writing, speak volumes about this most creative of all Englishmen.

Shakespeare's Plays

Richard III (1591)
King John (in the 1590s)
The Comedy of Errors (1590)
The Taming of the Shrew (1592)
The Two Gentlemen of Verona (1592-3)
Titus Andronicus (1590)
Romeo and Juliet (1595)
Love's Labour's Lost (1595)
A Midsummer Night's Dream (1596)
The Merchant of Venice (between 1596 and 1598)
Richard II (1595)
Henry IV, Part I (1597)
Henry IV, Part II (1597)
Henry V (1599)
The Merry Wives of Windsor (1597)
Much Ado About Nothing (1598-9)
As You Like It (earlier than 1599)
Julius Caesar (1599)
Twelfth Night (1601)
Troilus and Cressida (1602)
All's Well that Ends Well (1603-4)
Hamlet (1599, completed 1601)
Measure for Measure (1604)
Othello (between 1602 and 1604)
King Lear (1604-5)

Macbeth (1606)
Antony and Cleopatra (1606-7)
Coriolanus (1608)
Timon of Athens (1607)
Pericles, Prince of Tyre (between 1606 and 1608)
Henry VIII (before 1613)
Cymbeline (1609-10)
The Winter's Tale (1610 or 1611)
The Tempest (1611)

AUGUSTINE OF HIPPO

One of publishing's most valuable success stories in the past ten years is the Penguin Lives Series under the general editorship of James Atlas. Garry Wills' "St. Augustine" is undoubtedly the finest study in the series. The book is a gem, beautifully and lucidly written for the general reader. In fewer than 150 pages Wills has compressed Augustine's strange life and major works into a readable and accurate tract on the Father's enormous contribution to philosophical and theological thinking. I am especially grateful for Wills' study since some twenty years ago I did a book, "Milton and Augustine" (Penn State University Press), in which I establish the fact that in Milton's Adam and Eve in "Paradise Lost," their sexuality and their love scenes in the garden, are very much indebted to Augustine's "De Civitate Dei" (chapter 14). I am comforted by the fact that my understanding of Augustine's teaching on sexuality in an unfallen state is consonant with Wills'.

Unfortunately, Augustine has had a bad press down through the centuries because of his teaching on human sexuality and man's human nature. I have always shared with my students the theory that the third/fourth century Church Father, because of his conversion and his writings on original sin, human nature, and redemption and salvation, is fundamentally a disciple of hope. My writings on Milton and Augustine make the point that Adam and Eve's expulsion from the Garden of Eden, though 'saddened and tearful,' now have "a paradise within happier far." Actually they are beginning a journey to the future, "the World was all before them ... and Providence thir guide," much like Augustine himself with his conversion, and the basic optimism of "Paradise Lost" is due largely to the poet's use of Augustinian theology.

The sermons, too, of John Donne, macabre in imagery and beautiful in message, are so Augustinian in their 'converted sinner' theme and tone and reflect the Father's theological optimism. But studies continue to come out attributing all mankind's ills to Augustine. David Friedman's "A Mind of Its Own" (2001), spends so much time blaming Augustinian teaching for mankind's dysfunctional sexuality. John Boswell's book "Christianity Social Tolerance and Homosexuality" does much the same. (1981).

I think that Augustine's involvement in Manicheism and his subsequent refutation of the sect, accounts for much of his reputation of pessimism. Unlike his treatment of Donatism and Pelagianism, which he refuted and then moved on, Augustine's continuous refutation of the sect right to the end of his life, with all the business of the evil principle overtaking the good principle, provided scholars much evidence from the numerous tracts for seeing him as a precursor of old time Calvinism. It is only when the Manichean tracts are put in perspective, and the whole body of his works is studied and evaluated, that we can make an accurate judgment.

Life

Despite the fact that there are many fine biographies written of Augustine, books 1 through 9 of his "Confessions" certainly provide us the most accurate and definitive source for his life story.

Augustine was born on November 13, 354 A.D., at Thagaste, at that time a small free city of Numidia, in Algeria, North Africa, forty-two years after Constantine's conversion and twenty-four years after the seat of the empire was transferred from Rome to Constantinople.

Thagaste was comfortably Catholic. His father, Patricius, a city official, was a pagan of modest means, loose morals, and a disposition easily aroused to anger. His mother, Monica, was a well-educated Christian whose admirable qualities have caused the Church to regard her as a model of Christian motherhood. His father taught him to admire the Latin classics (his knowledge of Greek, the language of the international community, was always limited) and fired in him a strong spirit of patriotism. His mother was the initial inspiration for his moral ideal and sensitivity, and much later, for his understanding of the Church as a universal authority.

Owing to the influence and insistence of his mother, Augustine completed his elementary studies as a Christian catechumen but was not baptized. The practice of the time was to reserve baptism for adulthood. He had a least one brother and one sister.

Augustine proved to be a brilliant student at the schools of Thagaste and neighboring Madauros where he got his elementary and secondary education. As a result, his father decided to send him to Carthage, the great seat of learning and which is now the Bay of Tunis in Tunisia, to study rhetoric and prepare for a legal career. Unfortunately, the lack of necessary funds forced Augustine to spend a year at home in idleness and worldly pursuits. About the same time, 370 A.D., his father died after receiving Baptism.

While studying rhetoric at Carthage, Augustine admits to having learned very little from his teachers but was, however, deeply affected by a reading of Cicero's "Hortensius," a work now lost. The work kindled in him a burning love for wisdom. He soon, however, gave up the thought of law as a vocation and abandoned a socially admirable academic career that could have led him to an important post in higher academic circles. Instead, he devoted himself to the pursuit of pleasure and licentiousness. Accordingly, as we read in the "Confessions," he engaged in an illicit relationship with an unnamed woman who bore him a son, Adeodatus (given by God). During all this time he repeatedly scorned the religion of his mother and eventually came under the influence of the sect of the Manicheans.

Manicheism and the dualist understanding of the nature of things deeply impressed Augustine. The Manichean account of the cosmic battle in the beginning, in which particles of the good principle became captive in the power of the evil principle, provided him with an answer to the question of the origin of good and evil. The doctrine comforted him in getting him to believe that it was not he himself who committed sin, but the evil principle within him. He said, "I still thought that it was not we who sin, but that some other nature sins in us, and it pleased my pride to be above all guilt." For nine years (373 to 382), he was a strong supporter of this line of thought but then through his dear friend, Nebridius, he began to question the teaching. Nebridius explained that if the evil principle could injure God, the good principle, which the Manicheans taught, then God must be violable and corruptible. Augustine saw this as absurd. His friend explained also that if the Manicheans contend that God is incorruptible, their whole myth is false. And if they say God is corruptible, this too is false.

After completing his studies at Carthage, Augustine opened a school of rhetoric, first at his native Thagaste and then at Carthage. Near the end of his stay in Carthage, Augustine, still attached but ambivalent about the Manichean sect, visited and questioned the celebrated Manichean bishop, Faustus of Mileve, who, instead of strengthening Augustine's belief in the doctrine, left him completely disillusioned, and as a result he abandoned that sect.

Convinced of the errors of Manicheism, he began to write a series of tracts refuting it. He continued these refutations for the rest of his life. Augustine's writings against the Manichees emphasized the goodness of creation and the freedom of the will. His arguments were quasi-philosophical but mostly biblical. For him the bible was a special form of revelation that provided answers that reason and philosophy could not. Faith in Christ was the necessary condition for understanding the world and man's position in it. This premise is the basis of all his later philosophical and theological works.

In the year 384, Augustine closed his school of rhetoric at Carthage and sailed for Rome. After a brief stay there, through the efforts of Symmachus, the prefect of Rome, he obtained the post of professor of rhetoric at Milan. During the course of this teaching assignment in Milan, Augustine listened to the sermons of St. Ambrose. At the beginning he attended these sermons because he admired Ambrose's use of the classical rhetorical form.

However, as time went on, his avid study of Neo-Platonist works, which refined his concept of God, together with the sermons of Ambrose, inspired him to a greater love for the Scriptures and a genuine love for Christ. After dismissing his companion of fifteen years and through the influence of Bishop Ambrose, Augustine plunged more deeply into Platonic thought. But even Platonism did not provide him the personalism that would explain the implication of the Word made flesh, that "He who was God was made human to make gods those who were humans." For him the God of the classical tradition was too impersonal, too distant, whereby the threefold Christian God was creative love, making and remaking humans and inviting their choice to love in return. This reality, actually the reality of the Incarnation, is recalled very beautifully years later in the "Confessions" when Augustine laments, "How long, how long shall I go on saying tomorrow and again tomorrow? Why not now, why not have an end to my uncleaness this very hour," an existential anguish about the human condition that would plague many young thinkers like Gilbert Keith Chesterton, John Henry Newman, Gerard Manley Hopkins, Francis Thompson and thousands more down through the centuries.

In September of 386 when he was thirty-two, Augustine retired to a country house at Cassiacum, near Milan, with his mother and his fifteen year old son who would die not long afterewards. It was here that he heard in the garden of the house the words, "Take up and read." He picked up a copy of St. Paul's Letter to the Romans and a passage (13: 13-14) there served as the decisive moment that led him to become a Christian. He devoted himself to prayer and preparation for a new life. The "Confessions" recount, "I have loved you too late, Beauty so ancient and so new. I have loved you too late. You were with me but I was not with you. I was away from you, running after the beauties which you have made. The things which exist only through you kept me far away from you. You have called, cried out and pierced my deafness. You have enlightened me, and my blindness is banished by your brightness. I have tasted you and I am hungry for you. You have touched me and I am on fire with longing to embrace you."

At this time Augustine abandoned his post as professor of rhetoric and requested that he be baptized. Accordingly, on Holy Saturday in 387, together with his son Adeodatus, Augustine received Baptism at the hands of St. Ambrose. A few months later, her work on earth accomplished, Monica died peacefully in the arms of Augustine. He then returned to Rome.

After the death of his mother, Augustine remained in Rome for another year, occupying himself in writing. Finally, returning to Africa, he began an ascetic life in company with a group of his friends. However his reputation for holiness and the fame he achieved as the result of his doctrinal teachings became so great that, in 391, Valerius, the Bishop of Hippo in North Africa, asked him to become coadjutor, a decision that was enthusiastically received by the faithful of his diocese. A short time afterward, Augustine was ordained a priest, and he immediately began preaching to the faithful of Hippo.

In 396, Valerius consecrated Augustine a bishop, and when Valerius died, Augustine succeeded him as Bishop of Hippo. As a priest, so now as a bishop, Augustine continued to lead a monastic life together with his priests. He was indefatigable in preaching to the poor and doing whatever he could to alleviate their wretched condition.

However, it was as an apologist and defender of the Faith against the principal heresies and schisms of the time that he achieved his greatest renown and provided inestimable help to the Church. His activities in this endeavor were divided in three directions—the Manichean heresy, the Donatist schism, and the Pelagian heresy.

Augustine continued the controversies with the Manichees that he initiated at Rome. He probably never felt that he had written convincingly enough about the Manichean heresy; it is one of the subjects that dominates his writings right into his later life. Then by preaching and writing he fought against the Donatist schism that held sway over the African Church throughout the fourth century. The Donatist controversy centered about the validity of the sacraments conferred by the clergy who were allegedly guilty of sin. Augustine insisted against the Donatists that the Catholic Church is spread throughout the whole world, as Scripture had promised. It is Christ who baptizes, not the human minister, so that the validity of a sacrament does not depend upon the holiness of the minister. It is interesting to see how Graham Greene fictionally incorporates this profound teaching in his "The Power and the Glory," wonderfully dramatized in the confrontational scene between the police lieutenant and the whisky priest. (See the chapter on Graham Greene in this book.)

Also, Donatism held that Baptism had to be administered a second time to those who had left the

Church and then returned. Augustine opposed this strongly. The repetition of the rite of Baptism, he insisted, subjects the standard of Christ the King to the insult of exorcism. He defended the uniqueness and unity of the Roman Catholic Church whose members were joined together by Christ himself and the sacraments. At this time, he took a very hard line against heretics and schismatics and supported anti-heretical legislation by the State which, he believed, should be an executive arm of the Church, a position that would outrage modern-day society.

It would be unfair to consider Augustine heartless because of his Church/State position, but this was a time of petty wars and invasions, social conflicts, and so much political wealth for the few which only inflicted much suffering on the poor. He was an active and caring bishop whose main concern was the impoverished and unfortunate. It was not beyond him to direct church finances to help the poor. After exhausting his own personal inheritance, he drew on church revenues to relieve the suffering of the destitute. He insisted that the more affluent flock of the diocese should clothe and feed the poor, and share their excess wealth with the unfortunate. Indeed Augustine's position anticipated the Church's present-day position found in Pope Pius XI's encyclical letter "Quadragesimo Anno" (May 15, 1931) which taught that the supreme criterion in economic matters must not be the special interests of individuals. On the contrary, all forms of economic enterprise must be governed by the principle of social justice and charity.

At a solemn religious conference at Carthage in 411, attended by 286 Catholic bishops and 279 Donatist bishops, Augustine as the spokesman of the Catholic bishops scored a glorious victory over the Donatists. He upheld the thesis that the Catholic Church can tolerate sinners for the purpose of converting them without losing its mark of holiness.

Augustine's tenure as bishop continued to be plagued

with heresies. Pelagius, a monk and theologian, probably from Britain, arrived in Rome and became the spiritual guide to many clerics and lay persons. He denied the doctrine of original sin. He came to North Africa with the teaching that humans could reach perfection by freedom of choice, that salvation is possible through human effort alone, by will power and without grace. Augustine refuted this by saying that it was rather freedom to understand and search for God and perfection under God's supernatural grace, with great emphasis on grace, that defined and opened up the road to effective liberty. This defense merited him the title of "Doctor of Grace."

Augustine's constant defense of man's free will makes him the greatest apostle of hope in the Catholic Church. In refuting Manicheism, he fights for man's free will against those who teach that man is predetermined to evil and sin and has no freedom to do otherwise. In refuting the Pelagians who argued that man could be saved simply by freely willing it, he argues that man indeed has free will but needs grace from God, with which man freely cooperates, to achieve eternal salvation. This balanced position on free will represents Augustine's position on all issues and represents Church teaching in general.

Augustine founded a religious order and his Rule of St. Augustine is the basis for religious living for the Augustinians today. He was a brilliant preacher, passionate, witty, learned and profound. His homilies on the Gospels and psalms could bring listeners to gales of laughter or to tears. His subtle insights into the gospel texts astounded his listeners. Yet with all the notoriety he never forgot his sinful past and the suffering of a sinner. Like Christ who ate with tax collectors and prostitutes, Augustine frequently had pagans at his dinner table. He advised numerous people, and his counseling was always based on the words of Christ.

Toward the end of Augustine's life, the Vandals invaded the African provinces, plundering, slaughtering, and burning churches. Augustine died in 430 during the Vandals' fourteen-month-long siege of Hippo; he was seventy-six years old. Augustine is at the forefront of the Doctors of the Church. In the year 700, his remains were placed in the church of St. Pietro in Ciel d'Oro, in Pavia, Italy. He has been proclaimed the patron saint of theologians.

The Confessions

The "Confessions" of St. Augustine, his most popular and best-known work, is not only a narration of biographical events but is a testimony of a soul imbued with the workings of Almighty God, so much so that it can never escape from its creator no matter how desperately it tries. Augustine was a tireless seeker, never satisfied. It explains his love for Aeneas, the hero of his favorite poem, who sails forever toward ever-receding shores. In "De.Trinitate" he says "The impulse present in our seeking goes out beyond the seeker, and hovers as it were, unable to rest in any other goal until what is sought has been found and the seeker is united with it." This restlessness is what Augustine calls "the unstable heart," a restlessness that drives humans toward what they want, without knowing what it is.

The paradox of the pursuer, seeking the lover (the pursued), and actually finding himself being pursued, has populated literature from the time of Augustine. It is impossible to enumerate the hundreds of literary works down through the centuries that have fallen under the influence of this masterpiece. One thinks immediately of Francis Thompson's "The Hound of Heaven," Victor Hugo's "Les Miserables," and Graham Greene's "The Power and the Glory"; and on a more trendy level the famous TV series and eventual award-winning film "The Fugitive."

"The Confessions" was completed about 397 and the title calls attention to the form of the book, which is Augustine's personal address to God. In the presence of God,

Augustine finds his own human personality. Any number of events in Augustine's life are omitted and many events are included that are not biography. Gary Wills calls the book "Testimony" and this is significant because the events that are included are a testimony to God's grace pursuing the sinner. The important thing is that Augustine's personality is delineated through those events where we see God's grace at work. So it is a true spiritual autobiography.

The reader is carried through the changing scenes of his life: Thagaste, Carthage, Rome, Milan: the wanderings among faiths and philosophies up to his baptism into Catholic Christianity; his continued adventures into Manicheanism, Platonism, skepticism, and finally the truth of Christianity. And all through this early journey we see Augustine giving his frustrated love to objects short of God, an inordinate love of finite goods. This frustrated search for love and then to be loved in return only caused him confusion and depression.

Book 1 begins with the stormy dialog with God with Augustine quoting the Psalms 145 and 147: "Great art thou, O Lord and greatly to be praised; great is thy power, and infinite is thy wisdom" which elicits from Augustine the response that "You have made us for yourself, O God, and our hearts are restless until they rest in You." The question of how the finite mind can contain the infinite God, a question that followed Augustine throughout his life, is stated here and it is resolved through a paradoxically articulated divine grace and human faith. In his effort to comprehend the infinite mind he catalogs God's attributes: immensity, omnipotence, mercy, justice, beauty, strength, ubiquitousness, unchangeableness, and all loving. He prays fervently to be absorbed into all of these attributes and be one with God.

In this very early chapter, Augustine discusses infant behavior in a very interesting fashion. He speaks of infant behavior, that is, greed, anger, jealousy, which he vaguely recalls in himself and which he sees in his own son, as sinful. He sees in this behavior traces of primordial evil. The propensity to turn away from good is inherent in human nature, indeed the marks of original sin. One would suspect that Chesterton had this in mind when he said that the reality of original sin was for him observed when on a lovely, summer afternoon he saw bored children torturing a cat.

Furthermore, Augustine sees his childhood bursts of rage, his strong will, stubbornness, love of plays, the entertainment of adults, his hatred of study, cheating at games, gluttony, stealing from parents as sins. Even his preference for Aeneas over the Homeric heroes, and his rejection of the classics, which were forced upon him by his teachers, he sees as sinful since they took him away from God. It must be remembered here that these are the recollections of a penitent experiencing great relief because of his conversion, but is also suffering from intense guilt, indeed hatred, for everything from his past. There is a certain rigorousness here, a rigidity, that loses sight of the fact that these are, for the most part, pranks of a child growing up. Augustine comes down hard on all this and the reader can likely conclude that the convert has become a pretty scrupulous, indeed negative, personality, a reputation that followed Augustine down through the generations.

But Augustine assures the reader that at the moment of birth it is God who nurtures the child through the human agents of mothers and nurses, and it is the mother who trains and instructs the infant in curbing these desires resulting from original sin, a point he will develop in great detail later in the work about the instrumentation of his own mother Monica in his conversion.

I point out this observation of Augustine's, cited so early in the book, because it brings home how prominent Genesis, the Garden, and original sin are in Augustine's thought. Original sin and the consequent Incarnation and Redemption dominate Augustine's theology.

Book II recounts the familiar instance of his childhood prank, that of stealing pears from a neighbor's tree. The second book also describes his growing up with an almost uncontrollable drive for sexual lust, which he ascribes to his studies in pagan education and the recalcitrance of his pagan teachers who failed to develop in him a sense of control as they were refining his intellect.

He speaks of going to the baths, during this interrupted year of studies, with his father and how his father sees in him the potential for fatherhood. Monica worries about the direction that his young life is taking and admonishes him. He admits that often he exaggerated and lied about his conquests to his friends (as a sixteen year old will do) and regrets now his being an occasion of sin for others.

The opening of this book is filled with examples of carnal lust couched in detailed sensual language. Phrases like "consumed in my fornications," "aimlessly driven by my burning lust," and "the muddy concupiscence of the flesh" describe this period of his life. Then suddenly he elaborates on the adolescent prank of stealing from the pear tree. Quite obviously the incident reminds us of the Garden of Eden where original sin took place. Mary A. Reichardt in her wonderful book "Exploring Catholic Literature" points out that such an innocent prank as the stealing of the pears (he didn't even want the fruit; there was plenty back home; he did it simply because it was forbidden) in such close proximity to the incidents of carnal lust again tell the reader that, like the infant sin, there is a propensity in everyeone to defy and turn away from God. "I committed it (the theft), not for want or need, but because I loathed to be honest, and longed to sin." He admits that if he were alone he would not have stolen the pears but did so to impress his friends, which, of course, is pride. The book ends with Augustine warning against "dangerous friendships." Augustine concludes that all sin, be it lust or stealing pears, is a result of original sin which was motivated by pride. Again we see dwelling on original sin and the Garden of Eden as a favorite theme of Augustine. The last two books of the Confessions are given completely to the book of Genesis. And some of his most brilliant theological insights are found in his many treatises on Genesis, the Heptateuch, and the Hexamera.

In Book III, Augustine speaks of his student days at Carthage, "a cauldron of unholy loves was seething and bubbling around me," as he continues his journey of seeking for something, yet rejecting the answer. As a university student would do, he attends a good deal of theater and his responses to the performances and the productions are interesting. He identifies with the plays' characters, especially those who are tragic and suffer and he simply grieves for them, but does not learn from their anguish. His promiscuous life style, he concludes, prevented him from having any aesthetic responses with depth. He speaks of 'subverters,' those who lead others into sin and develops a great hatred for them, only to see later that he too was a subverter and that he was hating himself. Then he encountered Cicero's "Hortensius" which praises the beauty of contemplation of wisdom and exhorts the reader to search for truth. Augustine is nineteen years old now and seems quite ready to seek a higher purpose in life.

In seeking this higher purpose he comes upon the teaching of the Manichees and is impressed with their devotion to truth, their use of 'Christ,' 'Spirit,' and 'Paraclete' in their writings. He finds the style of the Scriptures too simple but the style of the Manichees more like Cicero.

Book IV continues with his delving into the writings of the Manichees, which he later admitted was a mis-direction. Their sophisticated rhetoric had a great appeal to him. And although he had many reservations about the Manichees' cosmology, he remained with this sect for nine years, which was a period of restless soul searching and skepticism. He realizes that he had been seduced by the world, theater, arts, and false religions. He regrets his life of teaching young students the art of 'deceitful' rhetoric. He enters into a relationship with a concubine, to whom he is faithful, yet continues his search for meaning by having lengthy discussions with doctors, mathematicians, and astrologers.

The death of an unnamed friend only contributed to his listlessness for now he had to confront the mystery of death. Augustine spends four chapters in Book IV on this unnamed friend, and despite extremist Oedipal theories of the psychiatrists Charles Klingerman, R. Brandle and W. Neidhart on this friendship, nonetheless the "Confessions' do suggest something homosexual about the relationship. Augustine knew the man as a young boy, but it is scarcely a year that it has become an intimate relationship. Even though it was so brief, Augustine says "my soul could not endure being without him." Throughout the friend's sickness (the sweats and coma suggest pneumonia), Augustine never left his side. And after his death, Augustine is distraught, seeing him in all the familiar places, expecting him to come in a door, only to be left frustrated.

Augustine says that like Orestes and Pylades they resolved "to die for each other, or at least together, for them it was worse than death not to live together." He says he considered his friend "one-half of my soul. I considered that my soul and his were but one soul in two bodies, and hence I loathed life, unwilling to live simply as a half. Therefore, perhaps I was afraid to die, lest he whom I had loved so much would die completely." In this inconsolable state Augustine found no solace in plays, music, banquets, books, poems, sex ("the pleasure of the bed") since "whatever was not he I found loathsome and hateful." It was only through time, the consolation of new friends, and eventually divine love that he was able to go on in life.

In deference to the theory that it was a homosexual relationship, one could conclude that all the allusions point to that, the intense passion, the emotions spent on each other, and the pain of separation. Also this was when Augustine was living most promiscuously with his concubine and for variety's sake he may have been testing new waters. Yet, on the other hand, there is no evidence that the relationship between Orestes and Pylades was a homosexual one, but simply a platonic friendship endemic to the Greeks of Sophocles' time. Also the "one soul in two bodies," imagery, later to be called the 'microcosm conceit' and used by John Donne in his 17th century love poem "The Good Morrow," is definitely a description of spiritual love, devoid of anything physical. The evidence then seems to lean toward this latter theory. It must be remembered that Augustine was a very passionate man not only in terms of sexuality but also in other emotional matters, such as defending the Church against heretics and schismatics. Even in his treatise "De Musica" some of his teachings on music are emotionally charged and couched in fever-pitched imagery. Passion dominated his personality and it is with great passion that he recalls this relationship.

Book V describes his continued struggle with conversion. He is twenty-nine years old now and comes to terms with his disenchantment with the Manichees. The visit with Faustus finalizes his resolve to renounce the sect. He takes a teaching position in Rome because of the better discipline of the Roman students, the students at Carthage having become intolerable. He moves on to Milan for a better teaching position. He also saw this as an opportunity to get away from his mother who he felt had become overbearing about his personal life. Here he meets Ambrose who is so kind to him.

Books VI begins with the lines that express his frustration with this period of his life. He says, "O God, my hope from my youth, where were you then, or where did you withdraw yourself? Was it not you who had made me and distinguished me from the four-footed beasts and the birds of the air? You had made me wiser than they and I was walking in darkness and upon slippery paths, and was seeking you abroad in things outside of me but I did not find you, the God of my heart." The early part of the book then speaks of his mother, her great charity, virtue, and humanitarian efforts. He speaks of his admiration for Ambrose but is confounded by his celibacy. He sees a beggar, drunk, yet full of mirth while he himself, full of learning and doubts, has no where that temporal joy. It perplexes him, but he does not want the beggar's joy, for it is so temporal, even painful.

He goes on to speak of Alypius, his old virtuous friend from his youth, who was led astray by the circus. Many years later Alypius comes upon Augustine while he is teaching a class of students. Augustine sees him and uses the example of the circus in the lecture, which amazes Alypius and he begins to change his ways. He speaks of himself, Alypius, and Nebridius and the attempt to begin a society. His mother finally prevails upon him and he severs the relationship with the concubine.

Book VII recounts his evaluation of the doctrinal errors of his life. Now into his full manhood he examines his knowledge of the nature of God, the origin of evil which he will develop more fully in his metaphysics found in the "De Civitate Dei," his understanding of the Platonists, his study of the Sacred Scriptures, and his difficulty with the Incarnation. The book reads like an examination of doctrinal conscience.

Augustine's attendance at a lecture of Ambrose, at the instigation of his mother and only for the purpose of observing Ambrose's rhetorical style, is probably the most influential step in his journey to conversion. Here he became exposed to the Neoplatonists teaching that God is pure spirit (unlike the teaching of the Manichees) and that evil is nothing, that is, not a substance but a privation of good, a turning away of the free will from God (see Augustine's metaphysics later in this chapter). It seems that at this point in his life the influence of Ambrose, the teachings of the Platonists, and the reality of being a fully grown mature person prepared him for a resolution to his intellectual dilemma, that is, conversion to Catholicism. But there was still the problem of lust. And the will's cry for "Just a little longer, please.".

Book VIII begins relating his going to Simplicianus, the spiritual father of Ambrose, the Bishop, who tells him of the conversion of Victorinus who was once a worshipper of idols. He then investigates the conversion of many famous men. The problem for Augustine at this point, so well delineated in this book, was that he still felt that he could come to conversion on his own terms. He had yet to come to the realization that it is total dependence on God, that is, the acceptance of God's transforming grace that will bring him to conversion and true peace of mind. And that realization came in the garden in Milan when convulsed with tears, he heard the child's voice saying "tolle, lege; tolle, lege" ("pick up and read"). With that he read Paul's Romans 13:13-14. "Let us conduct ourselves properly as in the day, not in orgies and drunkeness, not in promiscuity and licentiousness, not in rivalry and jealousy. But put on the Lord Jesus Christ, and make no provision for the desires of the flesh." The passage struck him in somewhat the same fashion as the lightening struck Paul on the road to Damascus. He says, "I would read no further, nor was there any need for me to do so. For with the conclusion of this sentence, it was as if a light of confidence and security had streamed into my heart, and all the darkness of my former hesitation was dispelled." Divine grace did for him what he could not do for himself. It must be observed here that Augustine's embracing of the celibate life was in no way a denunciation of human sexuality. Chapter fourteen of "The City of God" is a brilliant discourse on the beauty of sexual expression and the joy of the married state as a sacrament. For him it was not a negative renunciation but a positive orientation toward a higher good. It gave him the freedom to concentrate totally on the things of God without the cares of the domestic life.

In Book IX Augustine recounts the vivid and personal communion he has with his mother who is approaching death, their conversations on life and death, her heart at peace now that her son has converted, and the near mystical experience of a lifelong relation of a mother and son.

And it is so interesting to observe how Augustine sees his conversion as a return to Mother Church which in large measure was due to the prayers of his own mother whom he acknowledges so beautifully after his conversion. The interplay of the infant/mother given us by God to direct us from our infant sins as seen in the beginning of the "Confessions," then his mother's prayers directing him to his conversion, and finally conversion as a return to Holy Mother Church bring the whole Augustinian experience full circle.

In retrospect then, Augustine sees all these ostensibly unrelated events in his life as God's grace in operation. His pagan teachers, his never ending struggle with the heresy of Manicheism, his lustful conduct, his introduction to Ambrose and Neoplatonism, his ignoring, even disrespect, for his mother whom he complained of as being a meddler, all the periods of frustration, restlessness, disorientation, and the dissatisfaction with orgasmic release, are all part of God's chasing the soul down the byways of life until the soul is captured. With Book IX and the conversion we can safely say that the spiritual autobiography ends. Books X to XIII deal with the issue of memory and his favorite intellectual challenge, the Book of Genesis.

The "Confessions" is a triumphant expression of joy on the part of a lonely and lost lover finding the lover whom he has been pursuing, and almost lost many times, the lover who has been pursuing him as well through life, the lover who will satisfy all the yearnings of the human heart,.

The City of God

Augustine's greatest work "The City of God" (De Civitate Dei) was written over a fifteen year period from 411-26. It discusses the two societies, Jerusalem and Babylon, the eternal city of God and the pagan empire of this earth. The remarkable work has for its basic premise that humanity is directed to the heavenly city, yet is bound by original sin. This tug-of-war of good and evil in the world is at the heart of all Augustine's writings and centuries of scholars and thinkers have attempted to clarify the Father's teaching on the human condition.

Augustine begins with his most famous distinction: the City of God has a temporal abode here below where pilgrims journey among sinners, and an eternal home in heaven where souls will find eternal peace as their goal. All cities are dominated by a passion for power, and those who are power obsessed are the enemies of the city of God. The unjust, however successful on earth, will not participate in the joys of the world prepared by Divine Providence but the just, even though unsuccessful here on earth, will. Hardships and trouble improve the just, whereas adversity beats, crushes, and washes away the unjust.

Every person has some temporal affliction, no matter how good he/she has been, and they will be rewarded eternal life. The fact that the good often fail to speak out against evil is due to the fact that they might lose some temporal advantages. So the just like the unjust are attached to an earthly life. As God tested Job so the just must stand some adversity as a test of their mettle and their love of God. Augustine assures the reader that whatever good men lose in this life, it is always possible for them to preserve their faith and the joys of the interior life. In the midst of adversity, the good will always have much more than those who are evil.

The earthly life is a school where the just are trained for the eternal life; they are trained to refuse being enslaved by temporal goods. Yet on this earth there are those who appear to be the just; even some notorious adversaries of justice appear to be just (Augustine's gentle way of speaking of hypocrites), but eternal life with the saints will not be theirs. The final separation will come with the Last Judgment.

After these clear yet ponderous introductory statements on the just and unjust, Augustine goes on at length to challenge the view that it was the Christians who brought about the barbarian sack of Rome and the war which desolated the world. And in keeping with his thoughts in the introduction, he shows how it is possible that good things come to the impious and the thankless while devastation can come to the good and faithful. He argues that the sack of Rome was due to internal reasons, its corruption and immorality.

But the reader must not forget that God's providential plan is at work here. Providence, of course, is one of Augustine's major themes. Whatever the apparent present destruction, absolutely nothing occurs outside God's ordaining power. And a final good will always come out victorious. Those who are members of God's City gain more than just the assurance of God's providence; they gain the total remission of sin. And Augustine goes on to analyze a number of historical events that have as their final result the manifestation of God's Providence, good coming out of evil. The whole discussion resonates with Paul's words to the Romans, "Where sin abounded, grace did more abound."

Then Augustine embarks on a lengthy discussion of the divine permission of oppression. He states that a good man, though a slave, is free, and a wicked man, though a king, is a slave. John Donne's beautiful sonnet "Batter My Heart" is a haunting seventeenth-century expression of this Christian paradox. Augustine says that happiness is actually a gift from God, and man should pursue that happiness by worshiping that God. But that God is one of foreknowledge, One who knows that pitiful state of the good man enslaved. Such a condition exists because oftentimes the human will of unjust men prevails—although the power which permits this is God's. In his strong defense for divine determinism, Augustine questions: can anyone believe that the laws which govern the rise and fall of political societies are exempt from the laws of God's providence? The Father concludes that such an assumption is ridiculous. The affairs of the earthly and divine cities are equally foreknown by God in his eternal plan. God governs and rules all things and even though his reason may be hidden, the Kingdom of Heaven is given only to those who believe in him. So the good man who is enslaved, but free, inherits Heaven, the wicked man who is king, but a slave, will not. It is interesting to note that hundreds of seventeenth-century century Puritan preachers used this book from Augustine in their sermons on predestination. Puritan theology was basically Calvinistic and the Puritans were able to read, and often extrapolate, Calvinistic teaching on predestination from the works of Augustine.

Books One through Seven of "The City of God" are largely Church apologetics, defining the Church in relation to the world and justifying its presence here. In Book Eight Augustine turns to philosophical and theological issues and then presents a very enlightening discourse on Platonism and how the Platonists doctrines come closer to Christianity than any other school.

From book Eleven to the end, Augustine discusses the origin and destiny of the two cities which are at present inextricably intermingled with each other. For communication between God and the members of His city, the mind of man is the means, being the most excellent part of man. By the mind, man comes closer to God than by any other means. From here Augustine goes on to discuss the important questions of good and evil, the fall of the angels, the fall of Adam and Eve, God and the Trinity, and the dogmas Incarnation, Redemption, and Salvation.

Augustine begins his treatment of good and evil with a discussion of the terms substance, essence, form, and nature. He teaches that God is the one supreme nature, the creator of all natures, and since he is the creator of all nature, all nature is metaphysically good. Even that material which is absolutely formless and without quality cannot be called evil for it possesses the capacity for form, and is consequently a potential good. Concerning evil in relationship to nature, Augustine argues that evil is not a nature, but it is nothing. Evil is present in nature not as something but as a lack of something which that nature must have. One might say that the presence of evil in a nature is really an absence, a privation of being. Willing evilly is a lapse, a failure to act rather than an act, since action proceeds from being and to be is to be in order. No nature, then, that is positive reality, is evil.

But, although for Augustine all nature is good, all natures are not equally good. The things which God has created are all good, and their goodness lies in their participation in God's goodness, yet not equally so. Some natures are more excellent than others, and yet all, from the highest to the lowest order, are good. All is a scale or hierarchy of natures. After asserting that all nature is good and that without nature evil could not exist, Augustine ventures to apply this to human nature, which he always vigorously maintains is weakened by the fatal flaw. But regardless of this original taint, human nature is not evil—it is simply vitiated. Evil and vice, he insists, only prove that nature is good: the vices themselves are testimonials to the fact that nature is good, for were it not good, vices could not hurt it. Indeed, evil could never have existed had not good nature, though mutable, brought evil upon itself. And this very sin itself is evidence that its nature was originally good. For, just as blindness is a vice of the eye, the very fact indicating that originally the eye was made to see the light, so vices in man indicate that his nature was originally good.

Augustine's position on the basic goodness of nature and the fundamental goodness of all that God has created receives further development where he teaches that even in hell over which Satan rules God's goodness is manifesed. The very existence of hell is a good since it manifests the Creator's justice. And Satan's very existence praises God. Even the demons acknowledge God by their very opposition to him. So do heretics. Man's whole life, whether he knows it or not, testifies to God, as do inanimate things—"Their beauty is their confession of him." This teaching will be further developed when he discusses the Incarnation, Redemption, and the doctrine of the fortunate fall.

Upon this conception that nature retains its original goodness at all costs, Augustine constructs a whole theory on the possibility of spirit transgression. Augustine teaches that a spirit has no ignorance, has no weakness of mind; his nature is so perfect that there is nothing for which he can wish or to which he can aspire. Though he is finite, he is complete in his sphere; and because of his perfection, it is impossible for him to transgress in that sphere. Therefore the only possible explanation for the fall of the spirits must be that they transgressed in another sphere. If a spirit is taken, so to speak, out of his natural order and placed in another, higher order—the supernatural order—there is the possibility of refusal. The spirit may refuse to accept or to hold something that is above his order; he may in fact, rebel against that order. The natural goodness is a singular perfection which is without rival, but to choose supernatural goodness would have been far superior.

Augustine maintains that the angels, from their creation, did not have true and complete beatitude; so their trial must have been one whereby they had a choice to acquire it. Obviously they chose their own natural glory, in its isolation, rather than the community of the supernatural glory. The Incarnation was revealed to the spirits and their unwillingness to adore the God-man was their fall. The angels fell through a deliberate opposition to the supernatural, the Incarnation being the highest phase of the supernatural realm and one of which Lucifer and his followers would have no part. Consequently, the repudiation of the Incarnation on the part of Lucifer and his followers was actually a desire for their own natures in preference to a higher perfection. For Augustine this was the fall of the angels.

Augustine continues his concentration on the three main doctrines inherent in the Fall of Man: paradisal life (preternatural world), which was lost (Original Sin), and finally recovered (Redemption). This threefold pattern of separation, initiation, and return, following a cyclical or spiral path, characterizies all mythical thinking, and Augustine's formula clearly shows the way in which, in the Christian version of the monomyth, all slighter cycles in the history of human endeavor melted into a single gigantic circle comprising the whole of human time. In the Augustinian version of the myth, the brief idyll in the Garden was the first stage in the Christian drama of salvation, the exile of our life occasioned by the Fall was the second, and the recovery of lost paradise was the third.

Concerning the brief idyll in the Garden, Augustine taught that the progenitors of the human race were endowed with remarkable gifts: they did not have to die, they did not have pain, they had superior knowledge, they had total control over their sexual activity, and they had divine grace. All these gifts, save divine grace, have come to be referred to as preternatural by later theologians, which term implies that these qualities did not belong to Adam and Eve as a necessary part of their human nature but were given them as part of God's goodness over and above their purely human faculties and capacities These gifts did not, like grace, put them into a higher order of existence. So typical of Augustine, these gifts did not raise them above their humanity; they simply secured them in it.

Adam and Eve were created such that they could live on forever. It was a privilege over and above their humanity. Augustine insists that it is one thing not to be able to die, as is the case with the angels whom God created: and it is another thing to be able not to die, which was the way Adam and Eve were immortal. Adam was immortal not because he could not die (non posse mori) but simply because it was not necessary that he should die (posse non mori), and the condition was contingent upon the observance of the prohibition of eating of the tree. Immortalization was the reward of faithfulness.

Closely related to the gift of immortalization is their freedom from pain. Augustine's treatment of this gift is considerably free of the exaggerations of the other Church Fathers. For him, all this gift means is that they were free from those pains and evils that are the consequence of sin, that is, guilt, shame, sadness, pains of growing old (they were immortal), decrepitude, all those forerunners of death. He cautions against the errors of other Fathers who taught they were totally immune or wholly incapable of feeling pain. Augustine is careful to add that Adam and Eve would have known hunger and thirst if they did not eat or drink since their bodies were human not spiritual.

Concerning Adam and Eve's superior knowledge, Augustine is cautious, and at times silent about this prerogative. He cautions against the exaggerations of some of the Fathers who taught that Adam's knowledge was close to that of God's. Augustine maintains that at the moment of creation, God infused into Adam and Eve's minds the knowledge which was necessary to enable them to lead a properly ordered human life. They were created adults and they were given all that one accumulates in the growth years. They were given excellent mental faculties and powers of observation so that Adam could name the animals and birds when he saw them. Although they did not have a knowledge of the supernatural, they certainly had a knowledge of what is right and wrong, that to eat of the tree would end it all. If they did not know that taking the fruit was wrong, there would have been no sin.

Augustine's candid treatment of the gift of Adam and Eve's sexuality, so aptly handled by Garry Wills in his book, is a very detailed examination of preternatural sensuality and provides the basis for Christian teaching on sex in the state of innocence. Augustine maintains that all the faculties of man, even those called the lower faculties or appetites, are from God and by their nature tend to find satisfaction in their appropriate acts, which is good. Above these sensitive faculties however are man's reason and will, the higher faculties, which govern and direct all these actions.

Augustine avoids the errors of other Fathers who insisted that the gift of integrity denied Adam and Eve all the pleasures of the sensitive life. Most of the Fathers felt that the sex act did not take place in Eden. Augustine nowhere says that Adam and Eve consummated their marriage; he does say however that they would have had conjugal relations perfectly subject to the will and reason. He says, "It is quite clear they were created male and female, with bodies of different sexes, for the purpose of begetting offspring, to increase and multiply and replenish the earth, and to deny this is a great absurdity." As a matter of fact, he suggests, and later theologians developed the idea, that Adam and Eve enjoyed the pleasures of sex and other pleasures of sense even more than post-lapsarian man, since their natural faculties were purer and therefore keener.

Augustine discusses at great length sex and the married state and maintains that, just as the other of man's members obediently served the will, so also Adam and Eve's organs of generation would have been used for the begetting of offspring under the complete control of their wills. But with the fall, all this control is gone. The shame and the covering of the sex organs by Adam and Eve is very significant for Augustine; he sees in this behavior that man's disobedience to himself is what he merits for his disobedience to God. The body is by nature subject to the mind, but, by the inversion of the hierarchy, it becomes the master of the mind. Augustine further asserts that, before the transgression, it is not that there was no movement of the sexual members; it is that there was no movement without the will's consent. But after the transgression there is an embarrassing example of involuntary bodily movement, and that is why Adam and Eve covered their sex organs.

Since the first disobedience, the motion sometimes importunes the will in spite of itself; and other times the motion fails when there is the desire to feel it, so that, though lust rages in the mind, it does not stir the body. In this failure of response, whether positive or negative, in this insubordination of the body to the mind, Augustine sees the marks of disobedience. And further, he insists that, because this insubordination of the body did not exist before the Fall, we cannot presume that marriage and sexual reproduction, then, are consequences of sin. Marriage was instituted by God in Paradise, and Adam and Eve were to be one, even in the physical sense. The procreation of children belongs to the glory of marriage and not to the punishment of sin, and he who feels that there would be no copulation or procreation but for sin makes sin the origin of the holy number of saints and men. Bodily fecundity, subject to the reason and the will, had its role in the first Paradise; and Aquinas was later to presume that its pleasure was greater in Paradise, owing to the fineness of the human body before sin.

The most important gift given to Adam and Eve was divine grace. This gift was unique because, unlike any of the others, it placed them in a special relationship with God. It completely transcended Adam and Eve's nature, it exceeded the demands and powers of their given nature, and it was one that was completely undue their created state. The gift elevated Adam and Eve to a higher and nobler dignity; it placed them in a real relationship with God, and gave them the pledge of eternal happiness. In a number of the works of Augustine, the word "justice" is used to signify all the gifts given to Adam and Eve; yet in those works where the Father is discussing grace as a unique gift, we find him equating justice with the theological concept of divine grace. Most commentators on Augustine's works agree, however, that grace is practically synonymous with justice. Since the Genesis narrative indicated that Adam and Eve were created in the image and likeness of God, this interior life is a sharing in God's nature and image. Adam and Eve, then, because of divine grace inherent in their souls, are a reflection of the divine image. The loss of this supernatural gift, not the preternatural gifts, changed the whole of the history of mankind. To retrieve this gift, the Almighty in the grand design of things had to ordain an Incarnation, Redemption, and Satisfaction in order that the world might have Salvation.

Concerning Original Sin Augustine is within the mainstream of Christian theology when he specifies that two conditions were necessary for the occurence of transgression in the first place: a command given by God who has supreme authority to make a command and a deliberate and conscious transgression by the one who is bound by the command.

Augustine emphasizes the lightness of the command and the ease with which it might have been observed. It was no mere disobedience of a moral precept; it was a grave sin because of the circumstances surrounding its committal. Adam had been explicitly commanded and he had been warned from the moment of his creation as to consequences of the transgression. There could be no plea of lack of knowledge. Moreover, the act of disobedience, performed by one in such a singularly privileged supernatural and preternatural state whereby nothing was wanting, must have been sheer rebellion of the mind and will against the ultimate supernatural claims and rights of God. Augustine claims the command enjoining abstinence from one kind of food in the midst of a great abundance of other kinds was an extremely light one and required very little effort to observe. Therefore, the iniquity of violating it was all the greater in proportion to the ease with which it might have been kept.

Considering the privileged status of the progenitors and the enormous consequences involved, Augustine, like so many of the other Fathers, catalogs the offenses. "There is in it pride, because man chose to be under the dominion of God; and sacrilege, because he did not believe in God; and murder, because he brought death upon himself; and spiritual fornication, because the purity of the human mind was corrupted by the seducing blandishments of the serpent; and theft, for man turned to his use food he had been forbidden to touch; and avarice, for he had a craving for more than should have been sufficient for him, and whatever other sin that can be discovered upon careful reflection to be involved in this one admitted sin."

The immediate effect produced in Adam and Eve by sin was that they lost their gifts of divine grace, freedom from physical death, exemption from pain, and control of sexual activity. And the issue that arises from this fact is (an issue that has perplexed theologians down through the centuries): what is the state of man's human nature now that it has been attacked by original sin and has experienced the loss of the gifts. If the prerogatives of immortality, impassibility, integrity, and the supernatural gift of sanctifying grace were a constitutive part of Adam's created nature, then with the loss of these endowments, Adam's human nature, and consequently ours as well, would be vitiated because it is deprived of some elements proper and integral to it. If, on the other hand, the endowments were over and above all that went to make up Adam's full manhood, truly gifts that are not necessarily integral to his created human nature, then it follows that with the loss of the endowments Adam's human nature, and consequently ours as well, remains unimpaired by original sin. Human nature then is whole and good in itself.

It was later medieval commentators on Augustine who saw him as a spokesman for the corruption of man's human nature, based on his statement that "the greatness of their crime depraved their nature." But one must consider that Augustine's intellectual life was a dynamic one and to understand a particular teaching one must take an inclusive view of his whole range of mental development.

Augustine considered man's human nature to include essence and accidents. In discussing original sin and human nature, he uses the terms "vitium" and "vitiatum," terms he often used synonymously, but not so when treating Original Sin and its effects. Here in this context they become two different concepts. Vitium is that which is evil; vitiatum is that which is faulty and impaired. He insisted that human nature is not a "vitium" but a "vitiatum," that is, human nature is diminished by a blemish or a defect because of the first disobedience. Consequently he feels that the supernatural and preternatural endowments were not so much a part of a person's nature as to render that person evil because of their loss. The loss renders the person weak and vulnerable, the nature diminished in strength and beauty, but not totally corrupted by the Fall. The nature of somethiing can be considered "depraved" because its accidents have been injured; the essence however remains intact.

Before entering into Augustine's teaching on the final phase of the economy of salvation, that is, Incarnation, Redemption, and Salvation, consideration must be given to Augustine's understanding of God, the creator of all things, and the Trinity.

For Augustine, God is the source of everything other than himself, originally making heaven and earth out of nothing, not out of his own substance, freely, not from any necessity, by his eternal Word, not by any external instrument. Even if God made something from something else that something else was itself made by God. Hence if he made heaven and earth out of unformed matter, he, of course, made the matter out of which he formed the world. Since time is a creature, there was no time before God created heaven and earth. God made everything with measure, number, and order. He made each thing good, and all things together are not merely good, but very good. By their changing, creatures cry out that they have been made; by their beauty, goodness, and wisdom, they testify to the beauty, goodness, and wisdom of their Creator. This Creator then is Being itself, the Truth, absolute, immutable, eternal, omnipresent, and yet a personal God who said to Moses, "I am" And according to Augustine, since Moses did not understand the moment, God went on to explain that "I am the God of Abraham, the God of Isaac, and the God of Jacob."

In his great work, "De Trinitate," Augustine advances the teaching that nothing can be said of God without relation, that is, the Father must be said to be in relation to the Son, and the Son is said to be in relation to the Father, just as the Holy Spirit is said to be in relation to the Father and the Son. Hence whatever is said properly of the individual persons in the Trinity is not said absolutely, but relatively to one another. The Father, Son, and Holy Spirit are consubstantial or of one substance, and "the force of 'the same substance' in the Father, Son, and Holy Spirit is so great that whatever is said of them non-relatively, is not said in the plural, but in the singular."

The final phase in the Augustinian threefold pattern of separation, initiation, and return is the Redemption which includes the Incarnation. The Father's teaching on this phase is the foundation for Catholic teaching on Redemption and Salvation which is continued by Thomas, Bonaventure, and innumerable orthodox theologians down through the centuries.

The Incarnation is the act whereby the Divine Word, the only-begotten Son of God, took to himself a true human nature. This is defined as a mutual hypostatic union of two natures, human and divine. The union of the two natures was such that each remained distinct from the other in the person of Christ. And through the merits of Christ, the race of man would be raised from the state of fallen nature, and, being placed into a state of repaired nature, was capable of being admitted after death to the enjoyment of the supernatural life. In typical Platonic language, Augustine says "out of a certain compassion for the masses God most high bent down and subjected the authority of the divine intellect even to the human body itself" to recall "to the intelligible world souls blinded by the darkness of error and befouled by the slime of the body." And as if to remind the reader of the consubstantiality of the Father and Son, Augustine speaks of Christ as the great intellect that abides in the Father and emphasizes the great mercy and humility involved in the fact that "so great a God has on our account deigned to assume and move about a body of our kind." The Incarnation, then, was the means whereby the Redemption was to be fulfilled.

Concerning Mediation, Augustine says, "(Christ) is the Mediator between God and man because He is God with the Father, and man with man. A mere man could not be Mediator between God and man; nor could a mere God. Divinity without humanity cannot be mediator, nor humanity without divinity, but the human divinity and the divine humanity of Christ is the sole mediator between divinity and humanity." This led Augustine to assert that when God came on earth in the person of Christ, God did not leave heaven. Likewise when Christ ascended into heaven after his earthly mission, he did not leave earth. In the person of the Holy Spirit, God is present on earth in the person of suffering humanity.

Augustine attributes to this Mediator the three offices of prophet, priest, and king. As prophet he will educate his church in heavenly truth and teach the whole will of the Father. As priest he will offer himself as a sacrifice for sinners, the suffering priest. And as king he will rule and preserve the Church and crush its enemies.

Augustine defines Redemption as the act by which Christ, sent in the fulness of time, redeemed all believers at the price of his own blood, which he paid voluntarily in accordance with the eternal plan and grace of God the Father. The perfection of the Redemption is adaquate, that is, the sacrifice made by Christ counterbalanced the evil of the sin; it is universal, that is, if all men fell in Adam, it is the mind of God that all men should rise in Christ; and it is superabundant, that is, the redemptive act was meritorious far in excess of the sins of a human for which it was made. This latter is based on Paul's "Where sin abounded, grace did more abound" (Rom. V.20).

This latter quality stimulated Augustine to proclaim his most beautiful teaching on the "felix culpa" or the happy fault. The joy inherent in the felix culpa is certanly not for the sin committed, but for the superabundant merit derived from the act of Redemption. It recognizes that God knows how to bring good out of evil, an old and familiar Augustinian teaching. If man had not fallen and if God deigned to become a human to live in and among a sinless humanity thereby completing and crowning the work of creation, this would have been a work of infinite love beyond comprehension. But that did not happen. That God took upon himself humanity and suffered, and exhausted all manner of suffering, in order to redeem mankind for his sin, this stupendous revelation of God's love it is that makes the Christian tradition exult, "O felix culpa."

So far as forgiveness of sin is concerned, God could have absolved man from it without taking upon our humanity. God is God. It is in the mercifulness of this remedial character of the Incarnation occasioned by Adam's fall that the tradition rejoices. "O felix culpa." No praise of the sin of Adam is implied in this doctrine; sin is accepted as a consequence of man's freedom. Its meaning is that the Divine Wisdom knows how to draw good out of evil. The Fall becomes fortunate, post factum, because of the Incarnation, and thus creates something of a paradox. Though heartbroken from sorrow for sin, mankind's joy is even greater at the Divine forgiveness. This is Augustine's reasoning behind the happy fault. The grief for sin is there, but now the rejoicing is that God, who had no part in the sin, took occasion from it more wondrously to manifest his mercy, power, and wisdom.

Conclusion

It would be impossible to cover the complete philosophical and theological output of this very prolific Father in an essay of this type. His literary output is staggering. He wrote some ninety-three books. There are about three hundred of his letters and over four hundred sermons that are printed. It is estimated that he preached eight thousand times. The full range of issues he wrote about is astounding. He even expounded on music, military morality where he opposes the death penalty, health issues, aesthetics, marriage, symbolic interpretation of the Scriptures, the hierarchy of being and order in the universe, nutrition, deception in politics and religion, and so much more.

It is unfortunate that posterity has not always been fair in judging Augustine. He has been tainted with the reputation that his philosophical and theological outlook is pessimistic. This is based partially on his unfortunate use of the word "depraved" in reference to human nature, which often has been cited out of context. His teaching of "vitium" and "vitiatum" clearly explains his position. Nature for him has become blemished and weakened by original sin—but not corrupted.

Of course Augustine was a very passionate preacher and writer. In attacking the heresies and in defending the Church's position, he had a tendency to come down pretty heavily on an opponent. Words could have been better chosen. Then he wrote so much that proof for any position can be found somewhere in Augustine, sounding at times as if he were contradicting himself. As we all know, one can find quotes even from the Bible to support any opposing or contradictory position.

But the allegation of pessimism fails when we consider his metaphysics, his teaching that all nature manifests the goodness of God, and that even Satan in hell praises his creator. His compassion is highlighted in his treatment of two homosexual monks in the monastery whose sin, he teaches, is a sin of frailty as contrasted with another monk whose sin was a deliberate manipulation. This latter teaching could very well have been the inspiration for Dante's placing Francesca and Paolo among the less culpable of the lustful in Canto V of the "Inferno." But the beauty of Augustine's journey upward in the "Confessions," his poetic cry "You have made us for yourself, O God, and our hearts are restless until they rest in you," and the hope and optimism in his teaching on the 'fortunate fall' should convince readers that this most prominent of all Church Fathers was in every way an apostle of hope.

Selected Works of Augustine

De Ordine (On Order) 386
De immortalitate animae
(On the Immortality of the Soul) 387
De Musica (On Music) 387
De Libero arbitrio (On freedom of the Will) 388
De Doctrine Christiana (On Christian Doctrine) 396
Confessiones (Confessions) 397-400
De Genesi ad litteram
(Literal Commentary on Genesis) 402-413
De Trinitate (the Trinity) 413-416
De Civitate Dei (the City of God) 413-426
De natura et gratia (Nature and Grace) 415
Enchiridion ad Laurentium (Handbook on
Faith, Hope, and Love) 423
Retractiones (Reconsiderations) 427

JOHN HENRY NEWMAN

The Second Vatican Council of 1962-1965, devoted to aggiornamento, or updating, was said to be Cardinal Newman's Council because of his ideas about the Church in the modern world. His teaching on conscience, the development of doctrine, the possible reconciliation of Anglicanism and Catholicism, the issue of separation of church and state, and the role of the laity and the bishops affected the Council's deliberations profoundly.

Pope John XXIII cited Newman's "Letters on Certain Difficulties Felt by Anglicans in Submitting to the Catholic Church" in calling the Council. Pope Paul VI praised Newman's life as "an itinerary, the most toilsome, but also the greatest, the most meaningful, the most conclusive, that human thought ever traveled during the last century, indeed one might say during the modern era, to arrive at the fullness of wisdom and peace."

With such glowing praise from Pope Paul VI, one wonders why Newman has been so neglected in the late twentieth and early twenty-first centuries (the period after Vatican II) by scholars and professors alike in the academic and theological community. I hope that the following essay might re-introduce readers to this prolific writer, staunch churchman, and brilliant mind.

John Henry Newman was born at 80 Old Broad Street in London on February 21, 1801, the eldest of six children of John Newman, a banker, who was broadminded in religion, but intolerant of Evangelicalism and Jemima Fourdrinier, who was of a Huguenot family driven from France, and who taught her children 'Bible Religion.' John's younger brother, Francis William, became a well-known English free-thinker and socialist, and in later years became professor of Latin at the University of London. Two of his sisters married into the Mozley family and a niece, Anne Mozley, became John's first biographer. His youngest sister, Mary, died at the age of 19, a loss that Newman felt for the rest of his life.

It was a very close-knit family. Newman often alluded to his happy childhood in later life. His father was a loving and tolerant man, and his mother, affectionate and beautiful. The children were lively, garrulous, and outspoken about politics, traits that were cultivated by their learned parents. They were fond of play-going and play-acting. They grew up in solid comfort and their literary, musical, and artistic talents were given every encouragement. No matter how many questions they might have had about religion, however, their loyalty as a family to Anglicanism was resolute.

Newman, not unlike the young Milton, felt in his growing years that he was somehow to do God's work. He was not sure what path this would take, but he knew that it involved a celibate life. "It would be the will of God that I should lead a single life," he says in his autobiographical "Apologia Pre Vita Sua." He loved reading the Bible and he never really had any serious doubt about his Anglicanism. As a matter of fact, one of the singular aspects of Newman's youth, one that distinguishes him from so many later English converts to Catholicism—Chesterton, Knox, Hopkins, and Waugh—was that he did not feel any restlessness, any angst that went with searching for something that would give his life meaning. He was considerably comfortable in his Anglicanism; apparently in his youth the Church provided him all the answers to any church-related questions he might have.

When John was seven he went to a large private boarding school founded at Ealing in the seventeenth century, of which Dr. George Nicholas was owner and headmaster. It had much higher standards than the public schools of the time and was quite progressive. It taught dancing, music was encouraged (Newman learned to play the violin), and a play by Terence or Plautus was done in Latin each year. Charles Francis Adams, son and grandson of Presidents of the United States, was sent there by his father, then American minister in London. It is clear from the way Newman later criticized the standards of Oxford that the foundations of his scholarship were laid at the Ealing school.

Even though he had a youthful fascination with the literature of skepticism, he was never doubtful about the Anglican Church. When he was a student at Ealing he read Thomas Paine's tracts against the Old Testament and enjoyed Paine's objections about the Scriptures. He relished David Hume's "Of Miracles" and enjoyed following the author's logic that such alleged supernatural occurrences were simply ridiculous. Quite obviously, and probably unaware of it, Newman was sharpening his mental faculties in the art of argument and debate. He was very tolerant of these opinions, but he was ever ready to attack what he considered their illogical conclusions.

At this time in Newman's life, he felt that a far more serious issue was that the whole of Christianity of the day was under attack by intimidating philosophical opponents whose arguments for secularism and disbelief could bring the Church down. The "ignorant armies" that "clash by night" of Matthew Arnold's "Dover Beach" certainly make us aware that the best poets and dramatists of the time were every bit as concerned as were the churchmen. "The Sea of Faith" for Arnold was now only a "melancholy, long, withdrawing roar." (This sentiment of Matthew Arnold is so similar to Newman's in "The Second Spring.")

When Newman was 15 and finishing his studies at Ealing, he fell into a Calvinist and Fundamentalist period for about ten years. Although he later threw off the doctrine of predestination as being unacceptable, the Calvinist influence stayed with him for the rest of his life. Like Augustine, the rebelliousness of a wounded human nature was something he had to struggle with. He loved ecclesiastical history and this brought him to a reading of Augustine, Ambrose, and the other church fathers. From this he began to sense a dilemma of faith and ideology. Here he admired the Fathers of the Roman Catholic Church while at the same time, as a Protestant, he was being made to believe that the Catholic Church was in error and the Pope was the Antichrist.

Until the age of 14, Anglicanism was just a label for the young Newman. In a private notebook he says that when he turned 15 "I recollect (in 1815 I believe) thinking I should like to be virtuous, but not religious. There was something in the latter idea I did not like. Nor did I see the *meaning* of loving God." But then a turning point came in his life, mentioned in a score of places in his writings, a first conversion. "When I was fifteen (in the autumn of 1816) a great change of thought took place in me. I fell under the influence of a definite Creed, and received into my intellect impressions of dogma, which through God's mercy, have never been effaced or obscured." Adversity prepared the way for this 'great change of thought'. His father lost whatever fortunes the family had and Newman came down with a serious illness "that made me a Christian—with experiences before and after, awful and known only to God."

He was accepted at Oxford and took up residency at Trinity College in June of 1817 and graduated with a B. A. in 1820, not yet 20 years of age. One would suspect that, since he writes so little of his undergraduate days in his autobiography, he was not particularly happy there. Again like Milton at Christ's College, Cambridge some 200 years before, Newman felt that at Trinity there was too much idleness, a lack of discipline, and a shoddy intellectual life. At Trinity every undergraduate had to subscribe to the Thirty-nine Articles, the accepted summary of Church of England doctrine, so that only Anglicans could be admitted to it. Most of the Fellows of the College were required to take Orders if they wished to retain their Fellowships, and they had to relinquish them on marriage. A very large proportion of graduates entered the Anglican ministry more than any other profession. Newman lived a life of prayer, recollection, and hard work, but Trinity had very little influence on his religious development. He really did not fulfill his potential. He remained at Oxford taking in students on private tuition while at the same time aspiring for a fellowship at Oriel, certainly the most prestigious and most intellectually vigorous college at the university. He won the fellowship and considered this a major moment in his academic career.

Being a fellow at Oriel, he was brought into contact with ideas and personalities that gave direction and purpose to the rest of his life. Richard Whately, another fellow at Oriel, exercised an enormous influence on Newman, such that Newman understandably would consider this the turning point in his life. Whately and his colleagues directed him away from rigid Calvinism, convinced him that total reliance on the Bible was not the way to go, and impressed upon him that the historical Church must be a guiding light. Another fellow, William James, called his attention to the Anglican teaching on apostolic succession, a traditional part of the Anglican creed, which immediately stimulated Newman to analyze all its implications.

Whately was an avid opponent of Erastianism, named for Thomas Erastus, a Swiss theologian who taught that the Church was to be merely an arm of the State. Whately's teaching on Church and State, that each is to be totally independent of the other, deeply affected Newman's mind. Whately said that Church interference in State affairs, and the State's interference into Church affairs was a "profanation of Christ's kingdom," and clergy were never to be hired servants of the Civil Magistrate. Whately's strong position and James's addressing the issue of apostolic succession became the foundation of the Oxford Movement which Newman was to lead some fourteen years later.

On Trinity Sunday, 13 June 1824, Newman was ordained a deacon in the Anglican Church and became curate at St. Clement's Church, Oxford. He threw himself into ministry with abandon, organizing worship, fund-raising, visiting the sick, and preaching. One year later he advanced to the priesthood. He then was given the vicarage of St. Mary's, the university church, and he served as the university select preacher for a year.

In the meantime he continued his intellectual work as a fellow at Oriel and did some writing to supplement his meager salary. His appointment as tutor at Oriel gave him some financial security and a sense of accomplishment. Most significantly, he was becoming a well-known preacher.

His association with John Keble began at this time and Keble's ideas on Church and State, in concert with Whately's, strongly influenced Newman. Keble had his eye on the United States as a place to have a branch of the Anglican Church completely independent of the State. His major concern was about the spiritual authority of the Anglican Church and its autonomy when so completely dependant and subjected to the State. Keble had been a brilliant student and tutor at Oriel. His superior intellect was in no way a threat to his devotional life. He was far more content to be a simple country priest. His publication "The Christian Year" was a collection of short poems intended to inculcate a religious sense into the everyday of the reader's year. It was enormously popular and its influence was felt outside Oxford. I personally think that the tradition of placing the name of a saint's day in the upper right hand corner of a letter, along with or instead of the date, still very popular with the British, is a result of Keble's book. Habits die hard with the British.

Keble's and Whately's position on separation of Church and State and Whateley's ideas of abandoning, to a certain degree, the Scriptures in favor of more expansive influences like the importance of the historical church which Newman came to call the "doctrine of Tradition," shaped for him at this time, now thirty years old, a solid theological and ecclesiastical position. Foremost in his mind now was the business of apostolic succession and the position that the Church is a corporation with its own powers, works, and need of self-governance. In Newman's words, "Keble struck an original note and woke up in the hearts of thousands a new music, the music of a school, long unknown in England." And Newman liked the "new music."

Newman's first full-length book, "The Arians of the Fourth Century" came out in 1833 and is a significant statement of his mind in this early part of his journey to conversion and the Oxford Movement. He tells the story of Arius and his followers who denied the divinity of Christ and were condemned by the Nicene Council in 325 A.D. The book gives a fine picture of the early Christian Church, the heretical doctrines that were springing up, the absolute need for a first ecumenical council, the condemnation of Arius, and the promulgation of the Nicene Creed which was a definitive statement of the Christian Church on the doctrine of the Trinity.

The findings in his research for this book were very important for Newman. First, it showed him how the Church tolerates diverse ideas up to a point at which they began to create a crisis; only then does the Church formulate a creed. Second, the Arian controversy brought home to him the dangers of the Protestant principle of everyone reading and interpreting the Scriptures for himself; an authoritative interpretation is needed. Third, the controversy showed him that secular powers participating with religious figures in defining something so crucial to the Church is a dangerous way to go. The Church is properly itself, a corporate body and independent of the state, and its permanency is secured by the doctrine of apostolic succession. He writes "The grant of permanency was made in the beginning, not to the mere doctrine of the Gospel, but to the Association itself built upon the doctrine." And he refers to the Petrine text, Matthew 16: "Thus the Ecclesiastical Body is a divinely appointed means, towards realizing the great evangelical blessings."

Then in dealing with the question of Roman Catholicism he says, "The glory of the English Church is that it has taken the Via Media, as it has been called. It lies between the (so called) Reformers and the Romanists." (Tracts, 38, 40, 71). He asserts that the English Church was not set up at the Reformation. Indeed, it holds "the doctrines which the Apostles spoke in Scripture and impressed upon the early Church. But now it has fallen away and is in need of a second reformation. There is a danger that people whose devotional feelings were not satisfied in the Church of England would go to Rome, but truth must come before holiness. As long as Rome taught error there could be no union with her." The errors Newman mentions are chiefly practical ones, ideas about the Mass, the refusal of the cup to the laity, compulsory confession, indulgences, Purgatory, the invocation of saints, and images. The work is especially interesting because it reveals, at this early stage in his career, Newman's fear that many of the tenets of the Church of Rome were attracting a number of Englishmen to its persuasion.

Then the Catholic Emancipation Act of 1829 which granted Roman Catholics specifically the right to sit in Parliament, provided they took an oath barring the Pope from interfering in British public affairs, only seemed to compound the threat for him. This was a terrible nightmare for Newman, Keble, and their followers. Immediately they felt that an established Church with the King as its head and governed by Parliament could easily become governed by an non-Anglican ruling the Church who would be elected to Parliament. This could mean there was the possibility of one day a non-Anglican ruling the Church, even a politician of a different faith. Of course, they were thinking of the Irish and, as well, the Pope and this would be an outrage and a blatant violation of the separation of Church and State. For Newman, the threat of Roman Catholicism was escalating.

John Keble on Sunday, 14 July 1833 preached his famous sermon at Oxford entitled "National Apostasy." It was here the Oxford Movement was born. Keble clearly made the point that the nation was denying the faith of its own Church, whose origin was supernatural and whose historical development was apostolic, by allowing its secular Parliament to rule that Church.

Newman, so in advance of his times, felt that the Anglican clergy and laymen had to be made aware of what was going on and this was to be done not by small group discussions in private quarters but by tracts discussing the issues and distributing these tracts to everyone. This, of course, was a giant step toward collegiality and laity involvement in the Church. These tracts had the general title "Tracts for the Times," and were published periodically for eight years from 1833 to 1841 and gave the Oxford Movement its other name, The Tractarian Movement. In all there were 90 tracts with Newman authoring 30 altogether.

Although these tracts were intended to respond and address Parliamentary actions, a real movement was afoot gathering many followers who were more intent on the revitalization of the Anglican Church. This small, zealous group of Oxford thinkers felt that the church was threatened by secularism, atheism, and the growing movement in science. Newman felt there was "a need for a second reformation" and this could only be accomplished by returning to the authority and truth of the Apostolic Church.

Tracts continued to be published and they could be found in bookstores, churches, and university centers. They were popular, very inexpensive, and became the source of much arguing in the newspapers and periodicals. When Edward Bouverie Pusey, then canon of Christ's Church, Oxford, and Regis professor of Hebrew at the University, wrote his tract on fasting and self-denial as staples of the Anglican persuasion, the movement had its first major ecclesiastical figure, along with Keble, on board. The movement was for a time called Puseyism.

Newman at this time became truly convinced that what was needed was an Anglican Church that was a true 'via media,' that is, a middle road between Protestantism and the Roman Church. This was, of course, a very revolutionary idea, but Newman was convinced that Luther, Calvin, and others had broken away from the original, catholic or universal, Church of Christ by denying tradition and relying too much on Scripture and on 'justification by faith." The Roman Church, he felt, had, on the other hand, added too much in the way of doctrine and practice to the primitive church. It was the Anglican Church that should be the compromise. Although Newman eventually abandoned this position, at the time it was the source of much divisiveness.

But as much as the tracts gave life and force to the movement, it was Newman's four o'clock sermons at St. Mary's Church, the university church, that resounded through the corridors of the university, the rest of the churches in the kingdom, and throughout the realm.

Sermons were still being published and widely read, as in the past with the seventeenth century Puritans. The subjects for the sermons were for the most part issues that were raised in the tracts. Newman's style was subdued and sincere, but the force of his charismatic personality and his perfect choice of words and images enchanted his audiences from every walk of life. Great literary figures, such as Matthew Arnold, George Eliot, William Makepeace Thackery, were enthralled with what they heard and read. There are a total of nine volumes of his sermons delivered during his Anglican period.

For Newman, religion was a matter of dogmatic truth, and being a Christian meant, among other things, knowing and professing the creed of the Church. It meant that the visible church, with its sacraments giving invisible grace, was a corporate institution not subject to any state, secular power, parliament, or king. This was indeed the very seed out of which blossomed the Oxford Movement. And for Newman true religion meant genuine opposition to the Roman Church. Newman was far more intolerant of the Roman Church than his colleague Keble, and he was adamant in his conviction that any revitalization of the Anglican Church would succeed only in its separation from Rome.

But the more he researched ancient documents as far back as the Apostolic Church for his sermons and tracts, the more one sees that Newman begins to soften this latter position. He felt very strongly that he had to buttress the cause of the Anglican Church in his sermons and tracts for the sake of his colleagues in the movement who were somewhat sympathetic to Rome. Keble exhorted him to go easy on the dissident Catholicism. In defending so strongly the anti-Rome position, Newman gradually began to feel that in the final analysis, the Anglican Church was the Church in schism.

The bishops throughout the kingdom were not happy with the Tractarian Movement. Even though the last tract, the 90th of the "Tracts for the Times," was an impassioned plea for the members to keep within the Anglican fold, Newman was censured by the Bishop of Oxford in March 1841. He resigned from the Movement, left Oxford, and took up residence in the town of Littlemore, a few miles from Oxford. He continued ministry there but became convinced, with the bitter end of his experience with the Oxford Movement, that there was no room for him in the Anglican priesthood. In 1843 he resigned his orders and delivered his last Anglican sermon, "The Parting of Friends," which is still held up as one of his most beautiful sermons, not to mention one of the greatest pieces of Victorian prose.

In "The Parting of Friends," Newman reminds his listener that when Christ had to bid farewell to his disciples at the last meal, there was "nothing gloomy, churlish, violent or selfish in his grief; it is tender, affectionate, social." And his departure must be the same. He is grateful for all he has been given. The fertile ground, the shining sun was all provided by God, but just as God gives, so too God takes away. And he quotes Ecclesiastes, "To every thing there is a season, and a time to every purpose under heaven; a time to be born and a time to die; a time to plant and a time to pluck up that which is planted; a time to kill and a time to heal; a time to break down and a time to build up . . ." So too, he says, one generation passes away and another comes and all must be accepted as instruments of God's grace. He is grateful for all the times together with his friends and he hopes there are no hard feelings. Newman proceeds to show that the Scriptures are filled with people who had to go forth to fulfill God's will, Jacob, Ishmael, Naomi, Orpah, David, and, of course, the great disciple Paul who bid farewell to many churches. In all these there was sorrow but resignation to the will of God. "And what are all these instances but memorials and tokens of the Son of Man, when His work and His labour were coming to an end?" And he ends the sermon with the thought that if ever he has been a joy or an instrument of God's grace in their lives, always remember him for that and pray for him. The sermon is a magnificent farewell, a wonderful synthesis of brilliant scholarship and heartfelt emotion.

For years the major intellectual dilemma for Newman about the Church of Rome was the additions of doctrines and practices that it imposed on the primitive, apostolic church. Some of these were the veneration of the Virgin Mary, the doctrine of transubstantiation, the supremacy of the Pope, the doctrine of purgatory, the doctrine of penances, and others. It was so drilled into him that the Anglican Church was the true Church of Christ, because of its fidelity to the creed and ritual of the apostolic church the Church of Rome had fallen into error because of its accretions. In an effort to resolve this conflict he embarked on the writing of one of his greatest works, "An Essay on the Development of Christian Doctrine."

In the early part of this work, Newman grapples with the idea of doctrinal development. Much like the present Pontiff, John Paul II, he was never comfortable with the concept that Christian doctrine had developed over the centuries and would continue to develop. But now he begins to understand that the Church of Rome's additions were not necessarily corruptions but actually developments and that the development of doctrine is no more than a gradual unfolding and elucidation of what was received at the beginning.

Many of the practices and doctrines that he saw as corruptions were actually logical sequences of the original doctrine established by Christ from the beginning. After much investigation and analysis, he concludes that the Catholic Church, which claims to be a divine commission, which is well-organized and well-disciplined, which binds together all its members who are spread over the known world, has as a whole, with its doctrines and practices, preserved the true Church of Christ.

Probably the most touching moment in this remarkable work is when Newman resolves for himself the ticklish issue of apostolic succession. In the section entitled "Papal Supremacy," he sets out to examine the Papacy, that institution that the Anglican communion so adamantly rejected. After examining the Fathers, that is, Clement, Ignatius of Antioch, and Ireneaus and with some honest logic which penetrates the whole work (one would think that he was a professional logician), Newman concludes that it is a true development because it preserves the type of the original Christian community. When Jesus lived on earth, He was the infallible source of revealed truth, and when he died, his apostles became that source. So long as the apostles lived, Christians knew, because Christ implored them so many times in his last days that they should be one, that they had to live in unity and they were in unity. With the Christian community growing in numbers and spread all over the globe, divergent courses had to be reconciled. When people disagreed, they consulted their priest, when priests disagreed, they deferred to their bishops, when bishops disagreed, they deferred to the Bishop of Rome, the successor of St. Peter. It was a natural succession, one that persisted for eighteen centuries. The development was a natural one, a logical one, and a true one since it reverted right back to Christ and his public ministry. "If the whole of Christendom is from one kingdom, then one head is essential," Newman wrote.

Interestingly enough, then, this very controversial stand on the development of church doctrine, and his consequent conversion to Catholicism, had for its source Newman's resolution of the problem with "Papal Supremacy." With this problem resolved he was then able to move on further in his theory of doctrinal development. The theory of development was "an hypothesis to account for a difficulty," the difference between the teaching of the primitive and the nineteenth-century Church. The difference was the same as the difference between the boy and the grown man.

He set up seven pragmatic tests for distinguishing legitimate developments from corruptions: fidelity to the original idea, continuity of principles, power to assimilate ideas from outside, early anticipations of later teaching, logical sequence discernible when developments were examined, preservation of earlier teaching, and continuance in a state of chronic vigor. He observes that when "a system is really corrupt, powerful agents, when applied to it, do but develop that corruption, and bring it more speedily to an end. They stimulate it preternaturally; it puts forth its strength, and dies in some memorable act. Very different has been the history of Catholicism, when it had committed itself to such formidable influences. It has borne, and can bear, principles or doctrines, which in other systems of religion quickly degenerate into fanaticism and infidelity. This might be shown at length in the history of Aristotelic philosophy within and without the Church; or in the history of Monachism, or of Mysticism—not that there has not been at first a conflict between these powerful and unruly elements and the Divine System into which they were entering, but that it ended in the victory of Catholicism."

Newman goes on to assert that consistency is the mark of truth, and the coherent development of Christian thought was a remarkable philosophical phenomenon that in no way threatened that consistency. The Essay shows his amazing sense of history, and his theory was the result of a critical study of Patristic writings—"My bulwark was the Fathers." The theory was something almost entirely new, although he had hinted at it in his "Arians of the Fourth Century," where it was accepted with no difficulty in Catholic theology. Charles Dessain observes that Darwin's "Origin of Species" came out fourteen years later and Newman found no difficulty in accepting the idea of evolution as long as it was theistic. The theistic quality gives Christianity the power to assimilate ideas from outside.

Dessain also asserts that Newman had often developed the theory of 'salvation history.' God had 'made history to be doctrine.' The Christian Revelation was not a series of propositions, but historical events, with the Incarnation at the center. So the way to Christ lay through the Living Church. The Revelation of God given in history, however, required a living authority in every age, guaranteed to keep it immune from error. Newman says, "Some authority there must be if there is a revelation, and other authority there is none but the Church which the Scripture expressly calls the pillar and ground of Truth.... if Christianity is both social and dogmatic, and intended for all ages, it must, humanly speaking, have an infallible expounder."

In the "Apologia Pro Vita Sua," he says, "As I advanced, my difficulties so cleared away that I ceased to speak of 'the Roman Catholics,' and boldly called them Catholics. Before I got to the end, I resolved to be received, and the book remains in the state in which it was then, unfinished." He resigned his position at Oriel and on October 9, 1845, at the age of forty-five, he was received into the Roman Catholic Church by Fr. Dominic Barberi of the Passionist Order.

Newman's conversion created a sensation in England. Many of his friends who were stunned by the event eventually followed him into the Catholic Church. John Henry Newman, distinguished Oxford professor, brilliant preacher, leader of the Oxford Movement, and leading spokesman for the Anglican Church, a convert to Rome! The Oxford Movement was now over and conversion was on the lips of all of England. To this very day, faculty and students at Oxford, Cambridge, and London speak of this astounding event. And of course the event was a coup for Roman Catholics in England.

A year later Newman went to Rome and after a period of study and training, he was ordained a priest on 30 May 1847. He received a commission from Pope Pius IX to introduce into England the institution of the Oratory. He returned to England on Christmas Eve of 1847 and began a fifteen year period of loneliness and rejection from both sides; he claimed that they were the most difficult years of his life.

For many Englishmen and colleagues, what he had done was a betrayal of a nation and its Church. For Catholics, although it was a 'catch,' there was an element of distrust in the whole event. Laity actually spoke of his turncoat act and if a person betrays once, then what is to stop him from doing so again. In his letters, he repeatedly spoke of the sense of rejection he felt because of his conversion and the distrust it generated. He cites examples of his visiting Catholic clergy rectories, and of priests straining to be hospitable to him. It was a difficult time.

It was the Oratory in Birmingham, which he founded in February of 1848, that gave him great comfort and spiritual solice. Aside from a brief period as Rector of the Catholic University in Ireland, Newman's life was spent in service here. The Oratory was a small group of secular priests, Newman felt 12 was an ideal number, living under a rule of life developed by themselves and living in community with a number of brothers and novices. The Oratorians heard confessions, celebrated mass, carried out pastoral duties, studied and wrote, and, in many instances, taught in the schools attached to the Oratory. A year later the London Oratory was founded with F. W. Faber, a friend of Newman's, as its head. One of Newman's most comforting ministries at the Oratory was preaching and instructing the factory workers of Birmingham.

Several projects fell through for Newman in these early days at the Oratory. A new translation of the Bible was aborted because of lack of funds. Then there was his involvement in a trial for libel. In the fifth lecture of his "Lectures on the Present Position of Catholics," he had denounced the ex-Dominican Giacinto Achilli who was attracting audiences with his accounts of the corruptions of Rome and his own sufferings for his beliefs at the hands of Church authorities. He was sponsored by The Evangelical Alliance, which had been founded in London in 1846 "to associate and concentrate the strength of an enlightened Protestantism against encroachments of Popery and Puseyism, and to promote the interests of a Scriptural Christianity." In fact Achilli had been in trouble for a series of crimes of seduction. Cardinal Wiseman had already exposed him in the "Dublin Review" and had documentary proof of the often very scandalous crimes.

Relying on this, and in order to undermine his reliability as a witness, Newman denounced Achilli, who had already lectured in Birmingham and had impressed even Catholics by what appeared to be the testimony of actual experience. Unfortunately Wiseman failed to produce the vital documents, which might have staved off a trial, and Newman spent a stressful eighteen months under the threat of a term of imprisonment. He was able to bring to England as witnesses some of Achilli's victims, respectable married women, and secured a moral victory. But, since he could not substantiate every charge, he was found guilty of libel, and fined one hundred pounds. Judges and jury were biased, and it was recognized that Protestant prejudice had led to a miscarriage of justice. Newman's expenses, over twelve thousand pounds, were paid by Catholics from all over the world, but in the eyes of the English public he was somewhat disgraced.

Yet Newman's program of public lectures in 1850 and 1851 was very successful. He addresses his fellow Tractarians who did not make the transition with him and exhorts them to stop the hesitations and the lingering. He speaks of the Anglican Church as a function and operation of the state and reminds them that a Church cannot be a champion of orthodoxy if it is a functionary of Parliament. The lectures, which were put out in book form, are filled with biting phrases, irony, and wit. They are brilliant, aggressive, and often humorous. They had a tremendous response from the London audiences where some of them were delivered, not only from Catholics but from many Protestant dissenters who had their own disagreement with the Anglican Church. A number of important conversions followed and in August of 1850, Rome conferred upon Newman the honorary degree of Doctor of Divinity.

One month later the Pope restored the Roman Catholic hierarchy in England. This was seen as a legitimate return of Roman Catholicism to the country and the country exploded. Chaos ensued with protests all over the land, the Pope being burned in effigy, windows broken in Catholic chapels, and priests publicly harassed. Newman, in the summer of 1851, delivered a series of "Lectures on the Present Position of Catholics in England" as a response to the outcry and reveals just how deep-seated the prejudice and hatred were of the Protestant Englishman against the Roman Catholic Church. But his most beautiful and most compelling sermon on the return of Catholicism to England was his "The Second Spring," a work that alone would qualify him as one of the greatest writers of prose in the Victorian era.

"The Second Spring" was preached on July 13, 1852, in St. Mary's College, Oscott, in the First Provincial Synod of Westminster, before Cardinal Wiseman and the Bishops of England. Newman begins the sermon quoting from *The Song of Songs*, "Arise, make haste, my love, my dove, my beautiful one, and come. For the winter is now past, the rain is over and gone. The flowers have appeared in our land." The quotation sets the tone for the whole sermon.

Newman introduces the thought that despite changes in our transitory world, order and the law of permanence bind the whole natural world together. Though the world is ever dying, it is ever coming to life again. We experience daily "the order, the constancy, the perpetual renovation of the material world which surrounds us." Reminiscent of the seventeenth-century Robert Herrick he says, "We mourn over the blossoms of May, because they are to wither; but we know, withal, that May is one day to have its revenge upon November, by the revolution of that solemn circle which never stops."

So, too, man. Man, the greatest work of God's hands under the sun, in all the manifestations of his complex being, is born to die. Yet he lives on in his children, he lives on in his name, and he lives on in his works. All his efforts of genius, his conquests, the doctrines he has originated, the nations he has civilized, the state he has created, all outlive him by many centuries, but they too end and that end is dissolution.

Man and all his works are mortal; they die and have no power of renovation. But not the Church of Rome which now experiences a renovation with the restoration of the Roman Catholic hierarchy to England. That church has that order and constancy of the solemn circle; like the death of the blossom in May it will have its revenge upon November. It is a restoration in the moral world, such as that which yearly takes place in the physical world. It is the coming of a Second Spring.

Newman then enumerates the past glories of England, the saints, the archbishops, the illustrious hierarchy of the Roman Catholic Church that "stood in this land in pride of place." There was never a more glorious time in all of Christendom. Roman Catholicism was England's greatness. He mourns that miserable day that saw the martyrdom of Truth, "hacked piecemeal, and every limb and organ carried off, and burned in the fire, or cast into the deep! . . . Truth was disposed of, and shoveled away . . ."

Newman reminds his listener that this great event of restoration of the hierarchy might bring on the blood of martyrs. Just as Christianity rose from the blood of the early martyrs, and just as many faithful Englishmen died for the faith three centuries ago, so, too, now martyrs might be called upon to "re-consecrate the soil of God." And in a true spirit of resolve, he says, "One thing alone I know-that according to our need, so will be our strength. One thing I am sure of, that the more the enemy rages against us, so much the more will the Saints in Heaven plead for us; the more fearful are our trials from the world, the more present to us will be our Mother Mary, and our good Patrons, and Angel Guardians; the more malicious are the devices of men against us, the louder cry of supplication will ascend from the bosom of the whole Church to God for us. We shall not be left orphans." And all of this is not to be done violently, or with unseemly struggle, but calmly, sweetly, joyously "as on the rush of Angel's wings."

The imagery of the sermon is magnificent, all functioning to establish a tone of renewal and rebirth. The fig tree, the vine, the blossom, the bright sun, (O stella matutina), the spring time, the May morning all suggesting growth, newness, and rebirth. It is no wonder that the Second Vatican council is so often referred to as "the Cardinal Newman Council."

Newman in these defensive lectures addresses each individual objection of the Anglicans against the Catholics, that is, miracles, relics, papacy, statues, and devotion to saints. He claims that the objections are so deep-rooted in the tradition (and, he reminds the reader, the English are a very tradition-loving people) that it has blinded them of any common sense, any intellectual honesty. Again all of this is done with such cool detachment and good logic. The bottom line to Newman's arguments is that prejudice is ignorance and such prejudice is going to be around for a long time because the very law of the land perpetuates this ignorance. It is tradition!

The only way for things to improve is for Catholics to have a better knowledge of their faith and to increase the general understanding of the faith among the Protestants. Catholics needed their own center of learning. Oxford and Cambridge were Protestant, London University was secular; there was nowhere for a Catholic to go. At the invitation of Archbishop Paul Cullen, primate of Ireland, Newman went to Dublin to design and lead an institution to be called the Catholic University of Ireland. For several years he gave it his best shot but the whole project came to nothing. English Catholics simply did not want to go to Dublin and conditions were pretty bad, mostly due to lack of finances. (The experience of Hopkins going there as a professor is very telling. See my chapter on Hopkins in "Personal Journeys" pp. 104-21 [2001]). Newman resigned in 1858. But the experience was an invaluable one because out of Newman's tenure there came a series of lectures on the nature and purposes of liberal education entitled "The Idea of a University Defined and Illustrated."

But for Newman, the 1850s was a period of frustration. Many of the projects he engaged in came to nothing: the translation of the Bible, the work on the Lives of the Saints, the creation of a university. And then Newman missed his old Anglican friends, and as temptation will have it, he sometimes felt that maybe his conversion was too precipitous. Even an article of his on laity consultation in matters of doctrine that appeared in the "Rambler" did not sit well with Rome, although nothing came of it. (Yet some years later at the Second Vatican Council, Newman's ideas on laity consultation became one of the major issues in the Council's deliberations.)

In 1848, the "Rambler" was founded as a literary magazine for educated Catholics, and as one that would present the Catholic case among educated people generally. For a decade it had set a standard never surpassed since among English Catholics, but it aroused the ire of Cardinal Wiseman and the bishops, mostly because of the tone of its theological criticism. Newman, at the request of Cardinal Wiseman, was asked to take on the editorship of the magazine, and after much prayer, he accepted with the intention of furthering the education of the thinking laity.

Newman already had objected to the tone, not to the principles, of the "Rambler." In an early article on laity consultation in matters of doctrine, he states, "we do unfeignedly believe ... that their Lordships (the Bishops) really desire to know the opinion of the laity on subjects in which the laity are especially concerned. If even in the preparation of a dogmatic definition the faithful are consulted, as lately in the instance of the Immaculate Conception, it is at least as natural to anticipate such an act of kind feeling and sympathy in great practical questions, out of the condescension which belong to those who are 'forma facti gregis ex animo.' If our words or tone were disrespectful, we deeply grieve and apologize for such a fault; but surely we are not disrespectful in thinking, and in having thought, that the Bishops would like to know the sentiments of an influential portion of the laity before they took any step which perhaps they could not recall."

It became obvious that this line of thought would not do with the hierarchy and he resigned his editorship. He had accepted the position reluctantly as the will of God and now resigned for the same reason. In the famous article "On Consulting the Faithful in Matters of Doctrine," he shows how the examination of the beliefs of the ordinary faithful was one of the ways of discovering what the truths were that had been revealed: "the tradition of the Apostles, committed to the whole Church . . . manifests itself variously at various times: sometimes by the mouth of the episcopacy, sometimes by the doctors, sometimes by the people." None of these channels of tradition was to be neglected and Newman laid great stress on the 'consent of the people.' This was something he learned when he studied the Fathers, thirty years before; it underlay his theory of development, the unfolding of what was implicitly held. He asked "by what channels had the divine philosophy descended down from the Great Teacher through three centuries of persecution?" And he replied, "In the earliest age, it was simply the living spirit of the myriads of the faithful, none of them known to fame, who received from the disciples of our Lord, and husbanded so well . . ."

The Church was a Communion, with a common

conscience, that of all its members, and was not to be looked on as a mere juridical entity, ruled by officers. Bishops, priests, and laity formed one body, and there must be consultation and trust, for the laity was an essential part of the Church. (This teaching was to be incorporated in the Conciliar Decree on the Church at the Second Vatican Council.) There was no serious condemnation of Newman from the Vatican but the cloud of heresy hung over his head for some ten years after the "Rambler" incident.

It was in the early 1860s that Newman entered into a controversy with Charles Kingsley, chaplain to the Queen, a professor at Cambridge and the well-known novelist. The controversy centered about truth and Newman's definition of it and his use of it. Newman handled it all with his usual aplomb. There was an exchange of pamphlets and the press made quite a sensation of the exchange. Newman came out the better of it, in clarity, in logic. It was generally agreed that Kingsley should go back to ministering to the Queen and writing novels. Fortunately, out of this came Newman's great work, "Apologia Pro Vita Sua."

The publication of his beautiful poem, "The Dream of Gerontius" further advanced his reputation. With the "Apologia" and this poem he was becoming very well known as the spokesman for English Catholicism. "The Dream of Gerontius," which was later set to music by Elgar, is a vision of a just soul leaving the body at death with angelic choruses accompanying it. The vision, half dream, half inspiration, of the beginnings of the world beyond this life, is his most direct appeal to the reader. Swinburne recognized "the force, the fervour, the terse energy" in its verse. Immediately it had a great attraction for the unlearned and the scholar alike. There are immortal lines in it such as "Praise to the Holiest," which like his "Lead kindly Light" have never been forgotten.

There was some correspondence, and even a pamphlet, with his old friend, Dr. Pusey, who had implied that there might be the possibility for a reconciliation of Anglicans and Catholics, but Newman responded that there was still too much of the old Protestant prejudice about the Church of Rome and that it did not seem likely for a long time.

Newman's next project was a work entitled "An Essay in Aid of a Grammar of Assent," a difficult and controversial work in which he addresses the fundamental religious issue of the age, that is, of belief in God. Against those who taught that people's assent to religious truth is 'notional," that is, inferential, intellectual, and abstract, Newman objects by teaching that real assent in man comes from ordinary man's experience of Conscience. Newman suggests that conscience is the voice of God in man; it is the creative principle of religion.

To a friend he wrote that "the object of the book is twofold. In the first part it shows that you can believe what you cannot understand. In the second part that you can believe what you cannot absolutely prove." The first part is not concerned directly with the problem of certitude but with showing the importance and value of doctrinal statements in religion. Newman takes up the defense of theology and shows that so far from being antagonistic to vital religion, there can be no sound Christianity without it. It is an abstract, logical science, but it makes clear for us the truths on which our religion must rest. It can be merely an intellectual science without the life of religion, but it need not be. Its formulas elucidate for the worshiper the object on which his imagination and affections rest. Devotion is protected by dogma. On the other hand, what is real is particular, and theology deals with general notions. It merely holds a truth in the intellect, whereas faith gives a real assent to a concrete reality, which is appropriated by the imagination and the heart. Newman then proceeds to show how, leaving aside Revelation, we can give a vivid assent to the being of God far stronger than we give to a mere notion of the intellect. He argues from one sense of moral obligation and shows how conscience is the connecting principle between the creature and his Creator. It brings us into His presence as a Living Person.

These pages in the "Grammar" are Newman's clearest exposition of this fundamental theme: how, by means of our conscience, we come to hold as a great religious fact or reality that there is One Personal and Present God. He insists that the proposition "'There is a God', when really apprehended, is the object of a strong energetic adhesion, which works a revolution in the mind; but when held merely as a notion, it requires but a cold and ineffective acceptance, though it be held ever so unconditionally." In a similar way, he maintains of the doctrine of the Holy Trinity, professed in the Creeds, that it deals not with abstractions but with realities, and on them our spiritual life is built.

It is in Part II of the "Grammar" that Newman deals with his basic problem, certitude, and above all certitude in matters of religion. His purpose is to show 'that you can believe what you cannot absolutely prove.' Newman was writing to counter rationalism, and to explain how faith, whether in the sphere of religion or of ordinary life, was a reasonable act, even when not based on strictly scientific demonstration. He had in mind two distinct classes of people. First there were the educated, the high-minded Victorian agnostics and rationalists. They were taught, in matters of importance, only to assent after proof, and to regard it as an offense against the truth, to accept more than was demonstrated. The acceptance of beliefs, which could not be demonstrated in proper form, must take rank below convictions established by science. This tension Newman experienced from the beginning of his life, but it was made agonizing for him when he saw it as a living reality in the minds of his friends.

Besides the educated agnostics there was the other category Newman had in mind, the vast majority of mankind, who believed truths which they were quite incapable either of explaining satisfactorily or defending logically. In their case, too, it was necessary to show that they were justified in believing what they could not absolutely prove. The ordinary simple Christian, the day laborer, had, until Newman appeared, found few to defend his right to believe without logical proof. He proposed to defend the mass of the faithful against the accusation that they were fideists. The apologists of the day naively remarked that it was not difficult to understand how learned people could judge with certainty that they ought to believe in the Christian Revelation; the difficulty was to see how the simple and uneducated could do so. Yet we are told that Christ came to preach the Gospel to the poor, and to reveal mysteries that were hidden from the wise and prudent to little ones, and it is usually these who find it easiest to have firm faith.

Newman's aim then was to vindicate the right of the ordinary man, and especially the simple, unlearned one, to assent to and have certitude about truths which he never had, and probably never could demonstrate. This brief outline of Newman's intention in writing the "Grammar" in no way conveys the depth and breath of the arguments and examples used in this most profound of works. Newman was never very pleased with this work and his theory was attacked from both sides of the theological battleground, by Catholics and Protestants.

Then the issue of papal infallibility came to a head. Pius IX called a Vatican Council for 1867 and everyone knew that the issue of infallibility would be a top agenda topic. Newman was invited to attend but could not because of ill health. Of course his opinion was sought and he was very cautious and moderate on this delicate issue. He avoided the extremists who taught that the Pope's infallibility was a direct revelation from God and there was no necessity for consultation with the Church. Newman saw the authority of the Pope in more traditional terms, involving the consultation with the Church, along with examination of Scripture, and apostolic tradition.

But Newman thought that the whole issue was far too precipitous and he told them so. He reminded the fathers of the Council that the Church pondered the doctrine of the Immaculate Conception of Mary for several centuries before defining it. It must be recalled here that Newman was a great supporter of the concept of the development of doctrine in his early career; it was one of the convictions that contributed to his converting to Roman Catholicism. And he reminded the fathers of the Council that any teaching on papal infallibility would not go over well with the Protestant world.

And he was right. William E. Gladstone, former prime minister and leading Anglican layman, attacked the Council by saying that Catholics had lost their freedom to the point that they could no longer be considered trustworthy subjects of the State. Newman responded to this by writing a refutation of Gladstone's position to the Duke of Norfolk; it was titled "Letter addressed to his Grace the Duke of Norfolk" (1875). The Duke was a Catholic, a peer of the realm, a man whose patriotism could hardly be questioned.

Newman argues that conscience is an inalienable thing which cannot be given to another person, even the Pope. It is the voice of God implanted in created man and its authority is supreme. If the word of the Pope comes in conflict with conscience, then conscience must be followed in spite of the Pope's word. Secondly, the conflict can hardly occur since the Pope's infallibility is in the domain of speculative truth and abstract doctrine, whereby the domain of conscience is conduct, action. The Pope's infallibility does not pertain to that "domain" that Gladstone is so spastic about, that of good citizenship. The Pope is not infallible in his laws, commands, his acts of state, his administration, his public policy. Newman argues that the Pope is not infallible in that domain of conduct with which conscience is concerned; so, the dead-lock can hardly take place. With Newman's attack, Gladstone withdrew his charge immediately and withdrew from the controversy in defeat. This was Newman's last controversial work.

Newman was seventy-five now and decided to spend much time in revising and republishing his early works. He was elected the first honorary fellow of Trinity College, his undergraduate school, and this gave him great happiness. He had not set foot there since 1846 and this was a wonderful reunion of old friends. Pope Leo XIII made him a Cardinal and the aged Newman went to Rome for the honor. He returned to London and Birmingham to great jubilation. This was a marvelous honor for him but, more so, for all of England. England had its cardinal again. It can be truly said that England had changed enormously in the last thirty-five years because of Newman's conversion and his writings.

The last decade of his life he lived quietly, continuing his duties at the Birmingham Oratory, the love of his life. He died quietly on 11 August 1890. The words engraved on his memorial stone were of his own choosing: Ex Umbris Et Imaginibus In Veritatem.

All of Newman's works are of exceptional value. They not only give us an insight into the soul of a great clergyman and preacher, but they provide us with the philosophical and theological trends of the Catholic and Anglican Church at that time, not to speak of the political and cultural milieu of the 1800s.

The "Apologia Pro Vita Sua," which started out as a defense against Kingsley's allegations that John Henry Newman did not know what he was about, eventually assumed more and more the shape of a spiritual and intellectual autobiography. The five chapters treat the stages of Newman's life as he recalls them in 1864. Only the introductory and concluding chapters give attention to Kingsley's allegations.

The first chapter treats his early religious opinions. The second and third treat the Oxford Movement, the fourth describes the years at Littlemore, the writing of his essay on the development of Christian Doctrine, and his conversion to Roman Catholicism. The first four chapters are invaluable for the biographical information, always much more reliable when it comes from the pen of the character being portrayed. The prose is clear, direct, and honest. The anecdotes about his colleagues at Oriel, the friends and opponents in the Oxford Movement, are deferential, polite, and often witty. The wonderful part of the work is the gradual and progressive development of his thinking from year to year. We see him developing into maturity while at the same time getting a history of his religious opinions. His intellectual honesty is astounding. So often in controversy he is not afraid to stand corrected or to admit defeat.

The fifth chapter is a strong statement of his fundamental belief. He firmly accepts all the articles of the Christian Creed, whether held by Protestants or Catholics. He admits that he has difficulties with some of them and he cannot resolve these difficulties. But these difficulties, or even doubts, do not weaken his belief. This is rock-bottom faith.

He admits with such integrity that the very "being of God" gives him the most difficulty. The reason for this is what he sees about him, with such distress, in the world of men. He sees no reflection of a Creator in the busy lives in the world. Some fifty-five years later, T.S. Eliot will write of the same distress in his "Wasteland" when paraphrasing Dante "I had not thought death had undone so many." Newman says he sees the many races of men, their anxieties, their alienation, their aimless courses, their lives of disappointments. He sees the defeat of good, the success of evil, the mental anguish, the intensity of sin, the pervading idolatries, the corruption. It is no wonder that for so many there is doubt of the existence of God.

In amazingly Augustinian fashion he says that if there is a God, then a terrible event discarded the world from His presence, some aboriginal calamity has thrown everything out of kilter. Of course: original sin. And he says that the doctrine of what is "theologically called original sin becomes to me almost as certain as that the world exists, and as the existence of God." And the reconciliation of a world in original sin with the existence of God cannot come from reason, which was the recent trend, or education, or Scripture. It comes from the Will of the Creator interfering in human affairs, the Incarnation, and providing to the world the Catholic Church of Christ, founded by God himself, existing in unbroken continuity for 1800 years, and spread throughout the world. Only in this institution will mankind counteract that original sin that deters the world from its Creator.

In reading this amazing account of the progress of Newman's soul, the reader grasps any number of nuances. Newman knew the futility of dealing simply with the particular arguments Kingsley had brought against him. He said it was a "bias of the court" and claimed "that prepossession against me, which takes it for granted that, when my reasoning is convincing it is only ingenious, and that when my statements are unanswerable, there is always something put out of sight or hidden in my sleeve."

For thirty years Newman had been advocating religious beliefs which, to the majority of Englishmen, were admittedly more Romish than Protestant. When at the age of forty-five he joined the Catholic Church, the bitterness knew no limits, the hate brigade came out of the woodwork. There were the all knowing who said, "I told you so!" There were those who saw it all as a Jesuit conspiracy (flogging that old dead horse again) and that Newman had been a Jesuit, secretly assigned to the task of winning converts from within the Anglican Church.

Newman had to insure that the "Apologia" would be

an attempt to persuade people of the genuineness of his profession, the sincerity of his conversion, by recounting the history of his opinions. The book then is, in effect, a spiritual autobiography.

He had to take the reader through his early reading, much of which convinced him that the Pope was the anti-Christ. He had to show that the influences of his life were primarily Protestant and Puritan, and only when he joined Keble and Pusey did he become concerned with the task of recovering for the Anglican Church the marks of the true Church (holiness, apostolicity, and catholicity) which led to the Oxford Movement.

He had to show that his anti-Erastian sentiment "against the profanation of Christ's Kingdom . . . the interference of the Church in temporals, and the state in spirituals," that his acceptance of a sacramental system "that is, the doctrine that the material phenomena are both the types and the instruments of real things unseen," and his mystical belief that the divine presence is "hidden behind the visible things." are all a part of his Anglican experience. He candidly states, "I am not setting myself up as a pattern of good sense or anything else: I am but vindicating myself from the charge of dishonesty." That is why he is writing not a 'confessio' like Augustine who addresses his story to God but an 'apologia' where he addresses his friends, critics, and the English people.

Newman goes on to explain that he had come to a point where Protestant individualism and subjectivism, which tended to make religion purely an affair of a man's inner self did not satisfy him. He needed the more social character of divine revelation as found in sacraments, dogmas, and the discipline of the Church. He rejects the maxim "the Bible and the Bible only is the religion of Protestants" and says that "the sacred text was never intended to teach doctrine, but only to prove it, and that if we would learn doctrine, we must have recourse to the formularies of the

Church." The principle of "private judgment" for him was the beginning of rationalism, liberalism, skepticism, and atheism.

Newman really felt that the Anglican Church could be the true via media (even though it was a persuasion confined to one country) between Protestantism and Roman Catholicism. He felt that the Protestants had cut themselves off from the Apostolic succession and the Catholics were corrupt and idolatrous in their veneration of saints and their subservience to the Pope. But the tracts clearly begin to show that simultaneously with the bishops insisting on ending the writing of tracts, the intellectuals rejecting the via media concept, and the bishops rejecting the Oxford Movement, Newman was becoming less certain that the Catholic Church was reprobate, and more certain that the Anglican Church, like the Lutheran and Calvinistic groups, was schismatic.

Having arrived privately at these conclusions, Newman was understandably embarrassed by his public position. As colleagues were going over to the Church of Rome, he continued to oppose this and advised them to submit to their own Church and pray for one day when the churches would be one. On this last point, Newman gradually becomes silent. He admits that the Anglican Church as being a via media was a position he now regrets holding because he had not read the Church Fathers closely enough. And oddly, Newman held that those who did not adhere assiduously to either the Catholic Church or the Anglican Church, those who drifted to other persuasions or just became free-thinkers, were 'liberals.' In an age which made a fetish of free-thinking and individuality of belief, Newman stressed the need for roots and the importance to the individual of respect for the past and of obedience to authority. Holding this latter view was not for him a commitment to a die hard conservatism. It was a commitment to tradition and Church authority wherein freedom and liberation existed. Newman detested being called a 'conservative.'

The work is an amazing profession of faith; it was a resounding success from the moment of its publication. It won universal praise and brought a wave of conversions to the Church. The work spread through the rest of Europe, America, India, and other lands.

Newman's lectures of 1852, which were the outcome of his experience in founding a Catholic University in Dublin, are a classic statement of the nature and purposes of liberal education. The nine discourses delivered in Dublin are the heart of "The Idea of a University Defined and Illustrated." They appear as Part One of the book "University Teaching"; Part Two entitled "University Subjects" is composed of ten further essays and lectures that came out in 1859. This masterful work may not have had the currency of interest as the theological and philosophical issues had and that Newman was involved in, but it certainly has all the brilliant logic, good common sense, and authority of all his other works. No other work on education is equal to it.

The first four discourses take up the delicate question of the position of theology in the university curriculum. Newman was well aware that some members of his audience supported the secular universities at Cork and Galway, while others meant by the phrase "Catholic University" an institution devoted primarily to religious training. Neither of these, Newman maintained, is a proper university. The latter, which seeks primarily a moral objective, contradicts the basic purpose of a university, which is to foster "the culture of the intellect." The former, the purely secular university having no chair of theology at all, is for Newman an intellectual absurdity because, while professing in its designation "university" to be concerned with universal and total knowledge, it excludes at the outset one branch of knowledge that is as important and as large, and that is theology.

This point that Newman argues out in detail in discourse two under the title "Theology a Branch of Knowledge" is one of the most energetic and challenging of all the lectures. The target here is liberalism in religion, which Newman has always opposed. It is a liberalism that taught that religion was not concerned with knowledge but sentiment and feeling; a liberalism that believes in God but believes that nothing can be known about the origin of the world and the end of Man. Newman maintains that this is nonsense, that theology is knowledge, not mere sentiment, and theology has much to tell about the origin of the world and the destiny of man. He convincingly argues that theology is a branch of knowledge and must be a part of a university curriculum.

If theology is omitted, Newman argues, then other disciplines will usurp its place. Economics or political economy will give us "economic man" and that man will become concerned only with economic issues and nothing else. And this can be applied to Biology, Languages, whatever. No Christian can possibly believe that physical health or economic well-being is the total purpose of man's life. This would be a total neglect of universal truth and theology is essential to universal truth.

Newman implies that theology is the most important branch of knowledge. Theology pertains to the supernatural, while the other branches of knowledge pertain to the natural and despite that they are distinct, it is theology that will keep things in perspective. Newman never feared the many scientific accounts of the natural world that were floating around in this era of ignorant armies clashing by night. His fear was that an education system without theological enquiry will come up only with secular answers and man will be deprived of a whole world of answers that the supernatural can supply.

Having established in the first four discourses the place of theology in a true university, Newman moves on to the overall aim of education in discourse five entitled "Knowledge Its Own End." This work has been read by probably eighty percent of Catholic college graduates in the United States during the last half of the last century. It is the rock of Gibraltar when it comes to liberal education and the culture of the intellect. Now today, with the emphasis on education for career, for jobs and wealth, and for political and personal agendas, this work is hardly ever found on reserve shelves of college libraries.

Newman teaches that the kind of knowledge of concern in a university is not "useful" in the ordinary sense; it is not acquired to be used for some further purpose, but is in itself an end. "Knowledge is capable of being its own end. Such is the constitution of the human mind, that any kind of knowledge, if it really be such, is its own reward." Knowledge "is an object, in its own nature so really and undeniably good, as to be the compensation of a great deal of thought in the compassing, and a great deal of trouble in the attaining." It does not bring wealth or honor with it. Nor does it bring virtue: "Knowledge is one thing, virtue is another." "There is a physical beauty and a moral: there is a beauty of person, there is a beauty of our moral being, which is natural virtue; and in like manner there is beauty, there is perfection, of the intellect." This, and only this, a university seeks to develop.

This ideology that theology is a necessary ingredient in a university system, that education is for the whole person, that knowledge does not guarantee virtue, and that knowledge is its own end was certainly new and provocative. It became the basis for the liberal arts concept.

Newman's intellectual and literary legacy is diverse and rich. His collected "Works" occupy forty volumes, his "Letters and Diaries" an additional thirty-one. His poetry is not of the highest order, but his "Dream of Gerontius" and "Lead kindly Light" are memorable expressions of deep spirituality. His "Apologia Pro Vita Sua" is a great spiritual and autobiographical statement that stands next to the "Confessions" of St. Augustine. His "Essay on the Development of Christian Doctrine" and his "Essay in Aid of a Grammar of Assent" are distinct contributions to theology and religious thought. "The Idea of a University" is an assured classic of educational theory, far outdoing Milton's "Of Studies." Many of his sermons are the finest in the English language, rivaled only by those of John Donne. And his mastery of language, his use of rhetorical and stylistic devices, his choice of words that could express the profoundest emotions made him one of the greatest prose stylists of the Victorian Age.

Newman was a powerful and persuasive defender of religious faith in a period of growing unbelief. His was a voice of hope in an era of pessimism, secularism, skepticism, all brought about by Godless attitudes in scientific enquiry, denial of the supernatural, and a fashionable atheism.

After his conversion in 1845, Newman contributed immeasurably to knowledgeable and sympathetic understanding of the Roman Catholic Church in the English-speaking world. Newman's positions on the role of the laity in the Church, his truly unified and well-articulated theory of the development of doctrine, his strong stand on church-state relationship, his logical position on apostolic succession, his well-balanced and moderate position on papal infallibility, and his via media conviction that would eventually see the unification of the Anglican Church with the Church of Rome, are just a few of the ideas that were to find their way into the Vatican II meetings. But what made him the true precursor of the Second Vatican Council was his spirit of openess, his genuine commitment to aggiornamento, and his belief in a true ecumenical world.

Selected Works of Newman

The Arians of the Fourth Century (1833)
An Essay on the Development of Christian Doctrine (1845)
Lectures on Certain Difficulties Felt by Anglicans in
Submitting to the Catholic Church (1850)
Lectures on the Present Position of Catholics in England (1851)
The Second Spring (1852)
Apologia pro Vita Sua (1864)
The Dream of Gerontius (1865)
An Essay in Aid of a Grammar of Assent (1870)
The Via Media of the Anglican Church
(between 1830 and 1841)
Lead, Kindly Light (1884)
The Idea of the University, Illustrated and
Defined (from 1854 to 1858)

GILBERT KEITH CHESTERTON

Gilbert Keith Chesterton was born on the 29 May 1874 in a house in Sheffield Terrace, a secluded street situated between Holland Park and Kensington Palace Gardens, some four hundred yards from Notting Hill Gate underground station in London. Anyone visiting the birthplace, No. 32, will see a square brass plaque with the giant name of Chesterton backed by garish yellow. The family on his father's side was in real estate for some three generations; the family firm of Chesterton and Son is still one of the largest agents in London.

Chesterton gives very little of the family's early history in his posthumously published "Autobiography." He never took seriously the family claim to be descended from the Lords of the Manor of Chesterton, a small village once on the outskirts of Cambridge but now absorbed by the town. Chesterton's father, Edward, was serious and humorous, a man of many endearing talents. He was a Liberal of the school that existed before the rise of Socialism. He entered the family firm but was not of the best of health and he retired. This allowed him to devote himself to his many pastimes: water-color painting, photography, collecting stained glass, and especially his love for toy theater which his son Gilbert was to inherit. Above all, he was very well read and knew English Literature fluently, passing this love on to his son, Gilbert, who could recite passages from Shakespeare, as early as six years of age, without having any idea of the meaning of the words.

Gilbert's mother, Marie Louise Grosjean, was of Swiss-Scottish descent. She was one of twenty-three children. Her father, a great lover of opera at Covent Garden, was a Wesleyan lay preacher who was involved in the temperance movement. Marie Louise's mother was a member of the Keith family of Aberdeen, hence Gilbert's second Christian name. Gilbert does not give his mother much notice in his autobiography, but by other accounts she was a very clever, witty woman. Gilbert's very sharp wit, for which he was renowned, came from her. She had three children, Beatrice, who died at the age of 8, Gilbert, and Cecil who was born when Gilbert was 5. When Cecil was born, Gilbert was reputed to have said, "that's all right; now I shall have an audience," and in his autobiography, speaking of his much-loved brother, he says, "My brother, Cecil, was born when I was about five years old; and after a brief pause, began to argue. He continued to argue to the end" and despite the fact "that through all those years we never stopped arguing, we never once quarreled."

The Chesterton boys were never known for neatness. They were always unkempt, Gilbert always grubby looking and Cecil always with a running nose. The Chesterton parents believed in complete freedom of thought, never putting any restrictions on their development, both intellectually or spiritually. There was a general distrust of religion, although they did have a flirtation with the Unitarian form of worship. But Gilbert always accepted the supernatural intuitively. In his earliest age, he believed in fairy tales because, he recalled in later life, "Fairyland is nothing but the sunny country of common sense." He always had a sense of wonder. In his autobiography he says, "What was wonderful about childhood is that everything in it was a wonder . . . it was a miraculous world." All biographers are agreed that the sense of wonder remained with Gilbert right to the end.

It is this sense of wonder that led him eventually to embrace Roman Catholicism. The actual move was late in life, but so many traits about him in his early and middle years were those of Victorian Catholics. His child-like qualities, qualities that Catholic priests preached as the essence of humility, were based on his total belief that the Kingdom of Heaven was made of 'these little ones,' his total conviction that the Good News of the gospels is basically hope. The hope and optimism that was part of his public persona made him so beloved by colleagues. His love of St. Francis of Assisi who called his followers *Jongleurs de Dieu* (God's jugglers), allowed him to play the buffoon wearing the renowned loose-fitting Inverness cape, the enormous slouch hat, and the swordstick as a pose. No wonder many of his readers were so surprised when he formally adopted the Roman Catholic faith—they thought he was one all along.

Chesterton's early education was at St. Paul's School. The family had moved to Warwick Gardens by this time, still in Kensington, and within walking distance of the school. He recorded very little about his time at St. Paul's. He was an unusually tall, lanky boy with a brooding face that would erratically explode into laughter. He was absent-minded, still ill-kempt, always sleepy, and obviously very lonely. He sat in the back of the room where he scribbled drawings on his books, an angel with a devil's face, a crucified Christ sketched over incomplete French conjugations, two duelists drawing blood. Nobody could make him out. The other boys in the class, who thought him an oddity, played practical jokes on him, which he always accepted with a vague smile. One of the masters made the scathing remark, "You know, Chesterton, if we could open your head, we should not find any brain but only a lump of white fat!," a great way to destroy a young boy's spirit. Yet Gilbert was known for his generosity. It was not unusual for him to give a fellow student a few shillings so that he could buy some sweets at the shop. He was never good at knowing the value of money, but such generosity of spirit was something that stayed with him his whole life.

The St. Paul experience could have been a total disaster but for the new High Master, Dr. Frederick William Walker, who took notice of Chesterton. Walker was a forceful personality. He knew every boy in the school, he hated pretense of any sort and was insistent that St. Paul's was a day school and would not play the role of a boarding school. Parents and the home were to play an equal part in the development of industrious, morally pure and upright young boys. And Gilbert's father certainly cooperated. He took his son to museums, art galleries, theater productions performed at Warwick Gardens, and extended his knowledge of literature. Of the High Master Walker, Chesterton said, he led me "out of the comfortable and protected atmosphere of obscurity and failure."

Chesterton developed a deep and lasting friendship with Lucian Oldershaw, who would one day become his brother-in-law. At sixteen Gilbert began the Junior Debating Club and it was Oldershaw's powers of organization and highly developed sense that made the Club and its mouthpiece, "The Debater," such a remarkable success. The practical side of producing and distributing the paper was altogether beyond Gilbert's powers and it was best left in the hands of Oldershaw. The magazine contains some startling good work by Gilbert, a boy of sixteen who was, by the way, two years behind his contemporaries in school work. Gilbert's contributions were a foreshadowing of a long journalistic and literary career that would rank him one day with George Bernard Shaw, H.G. Wells, Hilaire Belloc, and Rudyard Kipling.

Gilbert was already the kind of being that he was to remain all his life: absent-minded, good-natured almost to a fault, yet of a rock-like strength in holding and maintaining his ideas. Some of those ideas were inherited: love of freedom, belief in human equality, and in all that is generally known as liberalism; others he was slowly acquiring. As he sat at his desk, a tall, clumsy, unbrushed, untidy hulk of a creature, drawing all over his blotter and his books, his mind was deeply concentrated, not on his lessons, but on the deepest problems of reality. This 'miraculous world' which was the very heart of his optimistic character did not very much reveal itself publicly.

As the months passed, "The Debater" went from strength to strength because of the high standard of contributions. The Junior Debating Club came to be known as "Hence, loathed melancholy," a fitting tribute to St. Paul's most illustrious graduate, John Milton. Eventually in a later issue, the magazine announced "As we go to press we hear the pleasant news that our Chairman, Mr. Chesterton, has gained the Milton Prize for English verse at St. Paul's School, the subject for treatment being St. Francis Xavier, the apostle of the Indies." The prize poem was not up to the level of his prose contributions in the earlier issues, but the honor was all-important. The prize was a great surprise to the school since the Milton Prize had until then always been won by a member of the Eighth form, a student of higher achievement. Gilbert, academically, was never to rise higher than form 6B, two years behind the average achievement of boys his age. But Dr. Walker, quick to curtail some possible tensions, put a notice on the school board that read, "G.K. Chesterton to rank with the Eighth."

Chesterton left St. Paul's at the end of the summer term of 1892. Despite the fact he did so well with "The Debater," he did not have much confidence in his writing. His notebooks gave ample testimony to his skill as a draughtsman, especially to a cartoonist's talent. His father felt that this was the path he should take and arranged for a trip to France to view some art before he would begin his first year at University College, London. Meetings of the Junior Debating Club continued where it was decided to end "The Debater" as a publication. This hurt Chesterton very much. Also, he missed his friends terribly since Oldershaw still had one more year to go before leaving St. Paul's.

Chesterton matriculated at University College on the 6 October, 1893. He had chosen to read Latin, English, French, and Fine Arts. His professor for Latin was A.E. Housman and after a year both agreed that he should give up the subject. He studied English under W.P. Ker. His Fine Arts classes were held at the Slade, a department of University College, which took its name from the philantropist Felix Slade. Chesterton really thought he would do well here but it was not the case. After a year they asked him to leave. Most of the students at Slade felt challenged, but Chesterton found the instruction mediocre and the teachers devoid of any energy or enthusiasm. Yet he admitted in all honesty that he himself was 'a very idle person' at the time.

It was abundantly clear, despite his lack of confidence, that writing, not drawing, was his primary talent. But that he could and still did draw may be seen from his illustrations to Hilaire Belloc's novels: he would often complete the sketches for one of these in a couple of hours: at all times he would draw and paint while he talked or thought. "The Coloured Lands," published in 1938 after his death, contains a fair sample of his work at different periods.

As brilliant as Gilbert's mind was, that mind went through a very bleak and nihilistic period. The problem of sin was often on his mind, he was fascinated with evil and the devil, and he dabbled in spiritualism. He and his brother played with the ouija board but were always aware that this was nonsense. Much of this distress may have been due to his physical problems. He was apparently going through a late puberty. His voice had not changed and his laugh was of a high treble. His strange conduct provoked two of his closest friends to consider him mad or homosexual. All of this made him cynical and depressed, and these fits of depression produced drawings of grotesque and sadistic figures. One drawing in his notebook had a woman in a very lewd and inviting position.

Before returning to College for his second year, he and

some classmates took a trip to Florence, Verona, and Venice which was a needed break in this difficult period. His sense of failure was exacerbated by the fact that his colleagues from St. Paul's were all doing quite well at Oxford and Cambridge. They kept in touch and tried to keep him included, but there was a gradual drifting apart because of distance. But a notebook that Chesterton began at this time shows that with the trip to Italy there came a gradual turning point in his philosophical and spiritual development. He actually speaks of communicating with God, face to face.

Chesterton left University College at the end of the summer term of 1895 without a degree. He took a job at the small publishing house, Redway, where he read manuscripts during the day and did his own writing in the evening. He says, "I solemnly pledge myself to the opinion that there is no work so tiring as writing, that is, not for fun, but for publication." No truer words were ever spoken. After a few months he took a position at Fisher Unwin, a larger and more prosperous publishing firm. By 1901 he was the author of two books of verse and one of essays. Although he was being compensated with amazingly low wages, he moved gradually and fully into journalism. This became his profession, and in later years when his fame was at its height, he would claim no other title than that of journalist.

It was through Oldershaw that Chesterton attended a debate at the home of Frances Blogg in Bedford Park. They fell in love at first sight, but both were so shy that it was months before they spoke to each other on a personal level. Frances was an ardent Anglican, having been educated at a nearby convent, and she was twenty-seven years old, five years older than he. Her family was quite poor and she worked as a secretary for the Parents' National Educational Union. He, although advancing professionally, still had a totally disordered appearance and was of enormous girth.

Both knew from the beginning that parents on both sides would be totally opposed to this union. Their courtship was a long one and their correspondence when they were apart was intimate, humorus, and often very beautiful. She adored his humor. Once when he was on holiday with the family, he wrote her that he was having an idle time and that his body was "absorbing tea, coffee, claret, sea-water, and oxygen, to its own satisfaction. It is happiest swimming, I think, the sea being about a convenient size." Opposition on the part of both families, plus a twenty-five shilling a week salary at Fisher Unwin, made an early marriage an impossibility.

The debates continued at the Blogg house with Oldershaw, brother Cecil, and Chesterton participating. It was here that he would see Frances, but the continental custom of young couples who had a love interest never being left alone existed in England as well.

He continued working daily and his writing continued to improve. The tragedy of Frances' sister, Gertrude, being killed while riding her bicycle left Frances inconsolable. And it is amazing the grief felt by Gilbert himself. His letters of consolation to her are beautiful. She tried to accept her grief in the spirit of the Gospels and wrote to Gilbert that, as God had allowed Gertrude's death, they must say as the disciple on the Mount of Tranfiguration said, "It is good for us to be here." Gilbert's reply was, "It has always been one of my unclerical sermons to myself, that that remark which Peter made on seeing the vision of a single hour, ought to be made by us all, in contemplating every panoramic change in the long Vision we call life."

The liberal magazine, "The Speaker," which had printed several of his poems, was taken over by some Oxford colleagues of Oldershaw. Chesterton saw this as a possibility of his doing more writing and less publishing work. The magazine, which had been moderately liberal, now became anti-imperialistic and unashamedly pro-Boer. Gilbert submitted something and was astounded at being rejected because his hand-writing, according to the editor, was Jewish. The magazine was anti-Jewish since it felt that the Boer War was being fought because of the greed of international bankers, most of whom were foreigners or Jews. This is quite ironic in the light that Chesterton had to live for many years with the reputation of being anti-semitic. But then maybe the rejection and the reason for the rejection only added fuel to an already deep-rooted anti-semitism, something that was endemic to many literary personalities of the times.

But by 1899 he was a regular contributor to "The Speaker" and he now was invited to do some art criticism for the "Bookman," a magazine specializing in art and artists. It is in the submissions to "Bookman" that we see Gilbert's very strong views on Impressionism as a product of the age's skepticism and modern neo-paganism.

Early in April of 1900 Gilbert attended a pro-Boer meeting in Bedford Park at the studio of the artist, Archie MacGregor, and it was the first time he had the chance to meet and hear Hilaire Belloc. He was completely engrossed with Belloc's personality, subject matter, and presentation. MacGregor's studio was to become quite a gathering place for extemporaneous theater presentations in which Chesterton, George Bernard Shaw, and London theater actors would jokingly carouse.

It was in a little Soho restaurant, the Mont Blanc in Gerrard Street, that Chesterton and Belloc would truly meet and begin a friendship that would last the rest of their lives, a literary and ideological friendship that Bernard Shaw coined "Chesterbelloc". That evening both learned that they were pro-Boer and both disliked a lot of people who were pro-Boers. This was a very impressionistic time for Gilbert and just as Frances' Anglicanism did much for Gilbert's religious thinking, Belloc's liberalism did much for his social thinking.

Hilaire Belloc was born outside Paris to a father who was half French and half Irish and a mother who was English, a Roman Catholic from Birmingham. As a young widow Madame Belloc moved to Sussex, consequently Belloc's upbringing and education was English. He had a sound classical education from the Oratory School, Birmingham, and went to Balliol College, Oxford, where he took a First in history and became President of the Union. On one of his trips to America he married an Irish-American girl named Elodie Hogan, who had tried her vocation with the Sisters of Charity. He returned to Oxford with his wife and taught and did some writing for the University Extension. By the time Belloc met Chesterton, he was a successful author and prose satirist.

Despite their close friendship, the two men were temperamentally different. Like most genuine friends, they shared many ideas on major issues, and where they disagreed, they learned from each other. Gilbert was the more imaginative, Hilaire the more real. Gilbert had remarkable insights into literature, Hilaire had an extraordinary range of historical knowledge. It was Belloc's influence on Chesterton that led him to an awareness of the place of the Roman Catholic Church in history.

Chesterton continued to write for "The Speaker" and "Bookman" and by 1901 and the death of Queen Victoria, his journalistic career had so escalated that everyone who did any reading of newspapers knew about G.K.C. As a respite from his journalistic responsibilities, he had written some nonsense poems which were quite popular and enjoyable, but his new association with "The Daily News" (1901) became the 'turning point in his journalistic fate.' His articles would appear in the "News" on a Saturday, and after a time were said to double the paper's circulation on that day. This made him famous and gave him some semblance of regular employment for twelve years. It was during this period that he made his reputation for writing about the Boer War.

The Boer War, or the South African War (1899-1902), an extremely painful situation for England, South Africa, and the world, became a major concern for Chesterton and for his liberal colleagues. With the acquisition of the Cape of Good Hope, the British had gradually increased their territorial possession in South Africa. The Boers (Dutch) who had already settled in some of these areas resented the British advance; more so with the discovery of gold and the British coming to Transvaal. Despite protests by the British, the Boers taxed the newcomers very heavily. The British dispatched troops to protect their rights and the Boers declared war on Oct. 12, 1899. The well-equipped Boers had early victories but the tide turned when heavy British reinforcements arrived. The British occupied the major cities and the Boers resorted to guerilla attacks. The Boers finally accepted the British sovereign in return for a promise of responsible government in the future. The whole debacle was not without its share of bloodshed, suffering, and hunger for women and children, and near starvation for farmers. These latter consequences of British imperialism became a major concern for Gilbert.

During the war, the publication of "The Wild Knight and Other Poems" on 20 November, 1900, financed by his father, was a big event in Chesterton's literary career. It contained some of his already published poems but for the most part the poems were new. It was written over a period of ten years; so, there is an uneven quality to the work. Some critics observed that it had a hit and miss quality. The title poem is a boring thing about a Wild Knight who rides seeking for God and meets his end by making the villainous Lord Orm his God. All the characters in the work make trivial things their life's end and so end tragically. Even Lord Orm says in one place "Evil be my good" (echoes of Milton's

Satan). There is no doubt that Chesterton is teaching here that the resolution to life's crises lies in the facts that truth is bound up with faith, and that good ultimately triumphs over evil. Some years later Gilbert will say it better with "He who does not believe in God will believe in anything." But the volume does contain three of his best poems, "By the Babe Unborn," "The Donkey," and "The Pessimist."

It was at this time that Chesterton's reputation as a "Master of Paradox" began to take hold. He resented it because for so many it meant nonsense through contradiction. For him it meant 'mere restoration of reality.' Serious readers began to see him as a far more serious thinker and not just the writer of nonsense verse. He was serious about reality and common sense. In an article on patriotism that he wrote for "The Daily News," he takes to task the people who protest that they love their country, and yet do not know the real meaning of "the love of country." For them it is comparable to what a child might mean by a love of jam. He says, "It is like saying, 'My Mother, drunk or sober.' No doubt if a decent man's mother took a drink he would share her troubles to the last; but to talk as if he would be in a state of gay indifference as to whether his mother took to drink or not is certainly not the language of men who know the great mystery."

Strangely, it was this type article for "The Daily News" that made him in a sense a spokesman for his country at war. He had sympathy for the Boers and he was opposed to the war because he saw it as British imperialism. He found himself torn by the conflict of patriotism and fierce criticism of the country he so dearly loved. Rightly or wrongly, Gilbert accepted the war because of his patriotism and saw his own unpopularity at being pro-Boer as a consequence of that freedom he so zealously espoused all his life, freedom of political views, and more so, freedom of dissent.

His first novel "The Napoleon of Notting Hill" is a fantastic illustration of his political ideology at the time.

The work is set in a future in which London is plunged into a strange mixture of medieval nostalgia and street warfare. The work develops his political attitudes, glorifying the little man, revering the color and romance of 'Merry England', and goes on to attack big business, technology, and the monolithic state. His attitude on the war and the personal love of his sovereign both belonged to a social and political philosophy that he was slowly working out. He believed in small nations and strict boundaries. Patriotism to him was not akin to imperialism but its very opposite. The patriot loves his own country; the imperialist wants to swallow other countries. He opposed in the Boer War the imperialism of England and was entirely logical in opposing in the First World War the imperialism of Germany. Maisie Ward, who knew him so well, said that he was never a pacifist but always an anti-imperialist.

So from being a daily newspaper writer with a talent for light-weight nonsense poems, he was becoming a noticeably serious fiction writer and a highly respected war time journalist. With the problem of finances resolved, Gilbert and Frances married at St. Mary Abbots, the Kensington parish Anglican church. The Rev. Conrad Noel, an old friend, officiated. They took their honeymoon in Ipswich, Dickens country. After their arrival, Chesterton, with a bit too much wine in him, took a short walk to see some of the Ipswich country, got lost, came back late to what was a disastrous first night.

Quite obviously the marriage was not consummated. Michael Ffinch in his authoritative biography of Chesterton has unearthed a great deal of valuable information on this aspect of Frances' and Gilbert's personal life. Ffinch maintains that when they returned to London and went to live in Battersea, Gilbert confided to his brother Cecil that things did not go right. Cecil was comforting in assuring him that time is an important factor in adapting and to be patient in their marriage. Ada Jones, Cecil's wife, after the death of Gilbert, Frances, and Cecil, published her book, "The Chestertons," in 1941 where she revealed that Gilbert was haunted by the experience of the first night and blamed himself for his brutality. Apparently Gilbert was no lover and Frances had not reconciled herself to the realities of marriage. The first night experience shocked her profoundly. She desired children very much but she shrank from sex. She had never really enjoyed good health; she had a spinal problem all her life and for years had to wear a support belt to relieve pain.

She checked in at the Clinical Medical Unit at St. Thomas Hospital and Dr. Harold Gardner Hill concluded that she had gynecological reasons for not enjoying sex. She underwent surgery for an imperforate hymen to make it possible for her to have children. Unfortunately all attempts to solve the problem proved unsuccessful. Of course this was a great heartbreak for Gilbert and Frances because they wanted very much to have family. Despite the fact that they both felt themselves failures, they did come closer together. For their whole remaining life they considered themselves happily married. Gilbert often wrote of marriage, the sacrifices that must be made, the compromises that are required, the patience needed for compatibility, but he never alluded to his own marriage as an unhappy one. As a matter of fact, he occasionally wrote humorously and in jest about the marriage state. So Gilbert and Frances lived their lives as normal married people, attending the annual dinner of the Junior Debating Club, enjoying the company of many new friends, and relishing in the success of Gilbert in his work as writer and journalist.

Frances was not a luke-warm Anglican; she was a daily communicant. The only contact that Gilbert had with any religion at this time was through her. Occasionally he would attend services with her. He kept his relationship with the priest who married them, Fr. Conrad Noel. Noel was a radical socialist and an active member of the Christian

Social Union. When he went to his next assignment in Essex, he organized a communist crusade. But as it was with so many other things with Chesterton, as with the possibility that his family was aristocracy, he just did not take seriously such matters. And the radical political positions of his colleagues were not to be taken that seriously or personally. Those positions belonged on a debating platform or on an op ed page. They had nothing to do with friendship.

In many of the debates that occurred in "The Daily News," he concerned himself with the issues at hand. He felt that any political party blunders badly when it associated itself with a theological or ecclesiastical persuasion. He always kept a Liberal stand although he insisted that he was not one. (John Henry Newman who so often took conservative stands insisted that he was not one.) Gilbert insisted that the best Liberals he knew were all Anglo-Catholics; so, religion at this time in his life was associated with politics. In his arguments in the "News," there always seemed to be a tendency to favor Anglo-Catholicism. But it was never a deep-rooted commitment as it was with Frances. Until his friendship with Belloc had become so deep and influential, religion for Gilbert was simply an aspect of politics.

During this early period of his marriage, "The Defendant," his book of essays, was published and it did much to enhance his reputation. It got very good reviews. Sir Arthur Quiller-Couch in his review of it in "Bookman" really sums up what Chesterton is all about. He says, "the most ordinary occurrences in the world are marvelous in his eyes, and the optimism proceeds from a blessed contentment with a planet which provides so many daily miracles." In October 1902 a second book of essays, "Twelve Types," came out to generally good reviews. Like "The Defendant," this volume was made up of pieces from "The Daily News" and "The Speaker." The diversity of subjects, 'types,' is significant. The book included Savonarola, Walter Scott, St. Francis of

Assisi, Leo Tolstoy, Charlotte Bronte, William Morris, Lord Byron, Alexander Pope, Edmond Rostand, Charles II, Robert Louis Stevenson, and Thomas Carlyle. Later Gilbert went on to write full-length biographies of some of these individuals.

By the summer of 1903 Chesterton was the toast of Fleet Street. He was a literary personality, a famous journalist whom young writers aspired to meet. Also, he was heavy into wine and beer at his favorite London haunts, El Vino, The George, and The Bodega. With his remarkable powers of concentration he was able to do much writing in smoke filled, noisy pubs. He kept all kinds of hours that displeased Frances. He became very active on the lecture circuit and Frances made it a point to accompany him to these dates. It was at a lecture up north at Keighley that he met a Catholic priest, Fr. John O'Connor, who had written him previously expressing much admiration for his work. It was the beginning of a life-long friendship, one that would culminate in the famous Chesterton Father Brown stories.

During this period Chesterton became embroiled in a controversy with Robert Blatchford, editor of "The Clarion." Blatchford had published a rationalist credo "God and My Neighbor" which elicited a response from Chesterton. For the most part Blatchford's work was an attack on Christianity and Chesterton rose to the occasion by responding to each of Blatchford's positions with good common sense, and in those brilliant parallelisms for which he was so famous.

One of the many assertions that Blatchford made was that poor environment produced bad men, whereas good conditions insure good men. Chesterton found this proposition preposterous and for his response he used the British Isles itself. He said that there was every conceivable degree of luxury and poverty in the land and one cannot possibly conclude that from one or the other of the classes there was a glaring morality or an onslaught of corruption.

At this time, of course, Gilbert and Frances were very heavily involved in social reform and municipal affairs in Battersea. Blatchford's premise hit a sore spot. Working people trying to better their conditions found an ally in the Chestertons. Gilbert often praised the 'eternal heroism of the slums.' Blatchford and Gilbert always remained cordial when they met publicly. The whole event is significant because the debate on Christianity was now to become, whether he was aware of it or not, the central focus of his life, his debating, his writing.

The year of 1905 was one where Chesterton, now a known celebrity, held many parties with famous guests, while taking on many public lectures. Frances always accompanied him on all of these and recorded them in her diary. He met Henry James, Joseph Conrad, Laurence Binyan, Algernon Charles Swinburne, Prime Minister Balfour, J.M. Barrie, George Meredith, and, of course, Bernard Shaw. His mind was as organized as ever and he could debate with the best of them; it was quite a contrast to the disorganization of his life style and his mode of dress. He had become famous for being late for lectures, sometimes arriving after too many wines at the pub. He was becoming more and more eccentric, which worried Frances. His drinking, his laughing raucously on a bus while reading a book, his talking to himself was becoming a familiar sight around London. Gilbert was becoming that familiar stereotype, the English eccentric. In 1905 he accepted the offer to write the 'Our Notebook' column in the "Illustrated London News," which gave him a generous weekly salary for the rest of his life. At the same time his book "Heretics" came out which turned out to be one of his best works.

In "Heretics" (1905) Chesterton, in twenty compact chapters, takes on Bernard Shaw, H.G. Wells, Rudyard Kipling, Henrik Ibsen, Thomas Carlyle, and a host of others who had abandoned institutional Christianity and sought to retain some sort of religious belief. One of his major targets was Darwin's "The Origin of Species" (1859) and Darwin's later treatise "The Descent of Man" (1871). The haunting question of man's identification with the animal kingdom had, according to Gilbert, only isolated Victorian man, alienated him from the community of humans. It was no wonder that pessimism had become the very air man breathed. He argued that many English scientists who were themselves men of strong religious convictions actually damaged the established faith by the impact of their scientific discoveries.

Chesterton's columns in "The Daily News" were concerned with Darwin's theories and his "Origin of Species." In "Heretics" however he concentrated on individuals and their responses to Darwinism. Gilbert felt that the whole approach to evolution taken at the time was de-humanizing and an insult to the common man, always a major concern of his. In the "News" he said, "Mankind is not a tribe of animals to which we owe compassion. Mankind is a club to which we owe a subscription." He insisted that the theory of evolution may have been true as a biological fact, but he insisted that man was a creature of a different order from the beasts, a spiritual creature, who possessed a fallen nature. Man was the only creature subject to evil and the only creature endowed with free will. He said, as a matter of fact, "the less beastly you may grow, the more bad you may grow."

Later in 1925, "The Everlasting Man" was published and in it he developed further and refined all his thoughts on this matter, the evil effect that Darwinism has on faith. In speaking of the impracticality of evolution he said, "Nobody can get an inch nearer to it by explaining how something could turn into something else. It is really far more logical to start by saying 'In the beginning God created heaven and earth' even if you only mean 'In the beginning some unthinkable power began some unthinkable process.' For God is by its nature a name of mystery, and nobody ever supposed that man could imagine how a world was created any more than he could create one. But evolution is mistaken for explanation. It had the fatal quality of leaving in many minds the impression that they do understand it and everything else."

George Bernard Shaw, one of the heretics in the book, and Chesterton began a friendship at this time that kept the Victorian literary establishment highly entertained. Shaw had read a review of Gilbert's of Scott's "Ivanhoe" and wrote Gilbert to compliment him. Gilbert never responded. Shaw who was eighteen years older than Gilbert was interested in directing his literary career and felt that Belloc's relationship with Gilbert was harmful and eventually disastrous. Shaw saw Chesterton as a potential dramatist. Although there were many dramatic moments to their relationship, the genre of drama was hardly the basis for the relationship.

They began debating in columns and on the platforms about everything and the exchanges became some of the most amusing entertainments in London. Shaw considered him "a man of colossal genius," and Chesterton considered him "one of the most brilliant and most honest men alive." Yet they disagreed on everything. Their first encounter was about Shakespeare. Shaw had written an article claiming that Shakespeare had written many inferior plays and had done so to become famous and to make money. Chesterton in his column for three weeks running responded to every objection of Shaw's. This exchange on Shakespeare was the start of a program of debates on everything.

Chesterton's biography of "Charles Dickens" (1906) came out to great notices. T.S. Eliot thought that there was no finer critic of Dickens than Chesterton. Shaw who was a great fan of Dickens read it, wrote Gilbert about some errors, and praised it with reservations. Chesterton's knowledge of Dickens was astounding, knowing all the plots of the novels, all the characters, and quoting from memory many lengthy passages from the works. Dickens, who was popular in his own day, had fallen out of favor at this time and Chesterton's evaluation of him brought about a revival of interest. The most interesting reaction came from Dickens' daughter, Mrs. Perugini, who wrote two enthusiastic letters about the biography. Gilbert and Frances visited her and were very congenial to her corrections; he promised to insert the corrections in future editions.

In January 1908, Chesterton wrote a provocative article entitled "Why I Am Not a Socialist" which, as one would imagine, set off a great controversy which came to be known the "Chesterton-Belloc-Wells-Shaw Controversy." It set off a lot of political sparks and was not without it share of humor. To read it makes one wonder whatever happened to the good-spirited art of disagreement that we see in this exchange without the mud-slinging of the hate brigade that we see today. In any case, the controversy began to solidify Chesterton's social philosophy. Just as he was pro-Boer, yet anti-Boers, so too he was Liberal, yet anti-Liberals. He was a committed Liberal but not a Socialist. Socialism for him was a Johnny-come-lately hanging on to Liberal causes, and useless.

1908 also saw his novel "The Man Who Was Thursday" come out to some fascinating reviews. C. S. Lewis saw in it some Kafka without the pessimism, and Ronald Knox saw it as a 'Pilgrims Progress.' It begins in Saffron Park, a scarcely disguised Bedford Park, where "a man who stepped into its social atmosphere felt as if he had stepped into a written comedy." The story tells how a Christian poet named Gabriel Syme, who also appears to be a Scotland Yard detective, initially led on by Lucian Gregory, an anarchist poet, infiltrates a supposed anarchist plot to destroy the world. The Central Anarchist Council consists of seven members, each known as the name of one of the days of the week, and Syme is given the name of Thursday. In the course of the nightmare, Syme becomes involved with each member of the Council in turn, and he seems to explore an ever-increasing hellishness of both will and intellect. It turns out that at the end of each episode, each member of the Council is also a detective who is sent out to unmask the plot under the orders of the Police Chief, of whom Syme had only seen the huge back.

Only the President of the Council, Sunday, remains elusive and as the six detectives pursue Sunday in the widest chase of all, he uses, in the inconsequential manner of dreams, a cab, a fire-engine, an elephant, and a balloon as a means of escape. At last in Sunday's own back garden, robed in garments denoting the six days of God's Creation, the six of them face Sunday, who turns out to be the Police Chief who had given them their orders. When he is asked who and what he is, he replies without moving, "I am the Sabbath. I am the peace of God." The nightmare ends with the poet Gregory, the only real anarchist, appearing before them all, since 'when the sons of God came to present themselves before the Lord . . . Satan came also among them.' Gregory admits that he would destroy the world if he could. He accuses the seven of having found happiness.

When the vision ended, Syme could only remember that he "had swooned before the face of Sunday," but he could not remember how he came to be there. "Gradually and naturally he knew that he had been walking along a country lane with an easy and conversational companion." He felt as though he were now in possession of some "impossible good news." Critics who for the most part raved about this book were completely at odds on the allegorical meaning of the book's ending.

Certainly the best thing to come out during 1908-09 was his "Orthodoxy." It was called by Chesterton "a sort of slovenly autobiography." It was written in answer to A.G. Street who, having found himself included in Gilbert's list of 'heretics,' challenged Gilbert to stop worrying about others' philosophy and to tell the world something of his own. In the Introduction the author says that many complained about "Heretics" because it concentrated on criticizing current philosophies without offering an alternative philosophy. Of course the alternative is Christianity and in the nine chapters, Gilbert does not pretend to teach how the Christian faith can be believed but, in the spirit of Newman's "Apologia Pro Vita Sua," he tells how he personally came to believe it himself.

Gilbert said that his faith was an attempt to answer a double spiritual need, "the need for that mixture of the familiar and the unfamiliar which Christendom had rightly named romance. For the very word 'romance' has in it the mystery and ancient meaning of Rome." By mentioning Rome here however Gilbert is not implying that orthodoxy was Roman Catholicism, though he later came to see that to all intents and purposes it was. But now Orthodoxy is admitting to the actual fact that the central Christian theology, summarized in the Apostles' Creed, is the best root of energy and sound ethics. As against the various 'prophets' of the period—Ibsen, Shaw, Wells, Kipling, and the rest—each of whom was stressing some sort of cure for the illnesses of the times, Chesterton saw the riddle of a vast variety in the universe and he came to see Christianity as the one answer to the riddle.

Christianity made a new balance that was also a liberation. It teaches moderation when two impetuous emotions clash; it got over the "difficulty of combining furious opposites by keeping them both furious." It taught "terrible ideals and devouring doctrines"; it managed "to make the lion lie down with the lamb and yet keep his royal ferocity." Orthodox Christianity then steered a course between two extremes, although it had so often been accused, at one and the same time, of being too optimistic about the universe and of being too pessimistic about the world.

There are so many ingenious arguments in support of orthodox Christianity in this volume, one is sufficient to represent the whole. To those who argue that Christianity might well have provided answers in the past, that some of her dogmas were credible in the twelfth century, but were totally irrelevant in the twentieth, Gilbert says, "You might as well say that a certain philosophy can be believed on Mondays, but cannot be believed on Tuesdays. You might as well say of a view of the cosmos that it was suitable to half-past three, but not suitable to half-past four. What a man can believe depends upon his philosophy, not upon the clock or the century. If a man believes in unalterable natural law, he cannot believe any miracle in any age. If a man believes in a will behind law, he can believe any miracle in any age."

It is interesting to note that Gilbert does not attach himself to any particular faith in this work. Much of his reasoning is common sense. Basically when he speaks of the 'familiar' and 'unfamiliar' he means the universe, the world we know, and the Maker behind it. He sees in the universe many miracles, even the simple changing of the seasons, and deduces that a miracle worker is behind the universe. So much of the creation is for him magic and the riddle behind the creation is that there must be a magician.

But in the final analysis his argument for Christianity is that it has been around for a very long time, has weathered many a storm, such storms that if it were not supernatural it would never have lasted. Also it has the answers, all the answers. And in concluding the work, he has a lengthy argument that Christianity brings joy to mankind and to an England that at this time is immersed in pessimism.

In 1909 Gilbert and Frances settled in Beaconsfield where she cared for her garden and he commuted to London, some twenty-five miles. They remained there for the rest of their lives. They had a vast living room where they had parties for young and old, played charades, and put on plays in Gilbert's favorite toy theater. He spent much time in painting and cutting out figures and scenery for this theater and in making drawings for guessing games for children. As compensation for having no child of their own, the Chestertons surrounded themselves with nieces, nephews, godchildren and young neighbors. Yet there was no let up on submissions to journals, poetry writing, lectures, and debates. There was never a time when Gilbert was uninvolved.

With all this feverish activity, he continued to be late for lectures, get lost, even deliver the wrong lecture one evening; Frances had to accompany him to be sure he fulfilled his commitments. He was beginning to show that he had his bad days and he had his good days as a lecturer. Evening talks were much better than afternoon ones. At times he gave two a day, and the exhaustion began to show because of travel and, of course, his girth.

"The Innocence of Father Brown," a collection of twelve stories, was published in 1911. This probably was his best known work which he felt was his least important. Critics began to see them as potboilers. "The Invisible Man" was the most popular. Even though Fr. Brown was nothing like Fr. O'Connor who was the priest it was based upon, he was a character like Poirot and Miss Marple to serve a purpose.

Fr. O'Connor, who was not small, portly, nor impish, and who eventually became a Monsignor, was a Yorkshireman to whom Gilbert owes much in terms of what direction his life was taking. Their long walks over the Yorkshire moors helped Gilbert to thrash out ideas that beset him. He confided to O'Connor that he wanted to come into the Catholic Church, but only until he could bring himself to tell Frances. He did not do it for a number of years, but he delivered a lecture at Cambridge where he all but told his audience.

Both O'Connor and Belloc were deeply concerned with the social angle of Christianity's answer to the riddle of the universe. Chesterton's social philosophy was becoming clearer and clearer in focus as he battled against the opposing ideas held by Shaw and others. There were series of lectures with Shaw which were a delight for audiences, Chesterton always favoring orthodoxy and Shaw always favoring materialism. One was on cremation and aside from the interest it provoked, it did bring home how Chesterton often was out of touch with what was going on and what was coming. In 1909, he had published a brilliant sketch of Shaw which elicited the response from Shaw "I liked it very much, especially as it was so completely free from my own influence." This sketch cleared the ground for "What's Wrong with the World?" (1910) much as "Heretics" and the Blatchford controversy cleared it for "Orthodoxy."

Then came "The Ballad of the White Horse," a long King Alfred poem, which seemed an attempt to convince his public he was more profound than a detective story writer. He took Frances for a motor trip to King Arthur country planning his "The Ballad of the White Horse." He kept in close contact with his friends in London. He appeared in pageants as Dr. Johnson and he grew fatter and fatter each year. Describing himself as living in the north, he said "When I sit by the wayside, the villagers look and they take me for one of two things. They either take me for the village idiot or for one of Harrods' delivery vans." He had become more and more a figure of legend, wearing a large flapping hat and a big cloak, carrying a sword-stick and getting lost on every possible and impossible occasion. More than once he had to telegraph his wife, "Where am I supposed to be?"

There was a General Election in 1909 and Gilbert spoke for the Liberal candidate. The listeners were delighted at his carrying on. In responding to a Tory heckling him he said, "What do they mean by being conservatives? They meant that they wanted to keep certain good and valuable things as they were. He should like to be a conservative if he could, because he should like to keep the old English institutions in existence. He liked them, and was fond of them, but they would find that any institution, the boots they wore, their hats, their shirts, however fond of them they were, all had to be constantly revolutionized. If they wanted a white shirt, for instance, they would find it desirable occasionally to have it washed, and even from time to time to replace it. Therefore Liberalism meant the principle of laundry, of washing from time to time of all the institutions of the State."

At this time Chesterton defined, or rather refined, his concept of Liberalism, something that stemmed back to his article "Why I am Not a Socialist" and which provoked the "Chesterton-Belloc-Wells-Shaw Controversy." Liberalism was a philosophy that he had inherited from his family and more than ever he believed in it. "But there was a rosy time of innocence when I believed in Liberals." It seemed to him that while no medical doctor says: "we've had too much scarlet fever, let's try a little measles for a change," that was precisely what the sociological 'doctors' were saying. Capitalism was a failure: he agreed that it was a disease, but when they said "let's try a little socialism for a change", it seems to him that for lack of a clear picture of health one disease was being offered as remedy for another.

His book "What's Wrong With the World?," presents Chesterton's anti-Calvinist social credo and his theory of Distributism. The theory is based on the very nature of man, of sex, of the child and its education. Historically and of his nature man needs the family, for its protection the family needs property which capitalism destroys no less than socialism. He says "It is the negation of property that the Duke of Sutherland should have all the farms in one estate: just as it would be the negation of marriage if he had all our wives in one harem." Property in its true meaning is also a condition for the ordinary man's development: "Property is the art of the democracy." He goes on to define "the functions of the father, mother, and child as such" and to show the limits that a free family would set to the power of the State. For the next fifteen years, Gilbert's essays expressed this same social credo; it was one of his most frequent lecture topics.

World War I came in 1914 and with it came Chesterton's almost mortal illness. He had been over-working, over-eating, and drinking. Frequently friends had observed that while he would be talking excitedly, his plate and glass would be filled and emptied in no time and the plate and glass would be filled and emptied again. The war came as a final blow. The diagnosis was very serious: heart trouble, all gout, and liver gone because of the heavy drinking. They got him a waterbed for comfort and healing. The doctor heard him murmur as he was lifted into the water-bed, "I wonder if this bally ship will ever get to shore." But he slipped into a coma. Francis kept in touch with Fr. O'Connor. She knew that he wanted the last rites because she knew his intentions. Maisie Ward insisted O'Connor go there for the last rites. But when he got there, Frances had become difficult and odd. Gilbert was in a state of unconsciousness for three months, his mind not functioning, and his body pretty much of a mess. He became so small that when he came to America in 1921 the reporters in New York hardly recognized him because they were expecting the former giant. But Frances nursed him devotedly and finally brought him back to full life

From his sick bed and during the recuperation, Chesterton kept up with the war through Belloc's articles. He was very patriotic and almost felt that he was left to live to see England regain her stature in this difficult time. When his health was restored and his wit retrieved, he wrote to Bernard Shaw "I am afraid you must reconcile yourself to the dismal prospect of my being more or less like what I was before; and any resumption of my ordinary habits must necessarily include the habit of disagreeing with you."

It is amazing what happened upon Gilbert's recovery from his near-death illness. It seemed that he burst forth with a new energy and an unbelievable productivity in writing and lecturing.

After "The Ballad of the White Horse" was published in 1911, "Manalive" came out in 1912, which was among the best of Chesterton's fantastic stories, expressing as it does supremely the intense zest which he brought to the business of living. "The Victorian Age in Literature" (1913) showed him still brilliant in the field of pure literature. The same year, goaded by Shaw, he produced a play, "Magic," which despite some admiring reviews, was a stage failure. Then in 1917 appeared his fascinating and inaccurate "Short History of England." It exasperated historians, yet a professor friend said in a wry fashion, "He's got at something we hadn't got." In 1919 came "Irish Impressions" and in 1920 "The New Jerusalem." These books all mark stages in that voyage of discovery that Gilbert, historically and in the contemporary world, was approaching nearer and nearer to the Roman Catholic Church. Externally he was at once urged forward and held back by the circumstances of life.

Cecil Chesterton and Belloc some years earlier had started a newspaper called the "Eye Witness," (1911) and later renamed the "New Witness" (1912) to combat corruption in public life and to uphold and restore the liberties of the poor against a growing bureaucracy. Upon Cecil's joining the army in 1916, Gilbert took over the editorship. Cecil died in France in December 1918 of the effects of the last days of the fighting, and, grief-stricken, Gilbert continued to edit the paper until its termination in 1923. It was revived under his editorship in 1925 as "G.K.C's Weekly," which survived until 1938. This editorship however was beginning to produce again a chronic condition of overwork.

Gilbert and Frances began an agenda of traveling that would give fresh inspiration to his thinking and would strengthen his awareness of the Church's universality. The traveling they did during the rest of their lives would have buried any lesser mortal after a month. All his thinking—directly religious, philosophical, sociological—brought him to the same conclusion. The Church of Rome would be his ultimate liberation, his final resolution.

They went to Ireland as a guest of William Butler Yeats to lecture at the Abbey Theater. Shaw was invited, too, but they did not lecture on the same night. The articles that resulted from this visit were published in "Irish Impressions" where Gilbert shows a real grasp of the Irish Problem. The articles should be reprinted today and should be read by the Irish on both sides of the border.

They then went to the Holy Land in December 1919, for some four months, by way of France, Italy, where they were thrilled by the Roman antiquities, then on to Alexandria, Cairo, and Jerusalem. He lectured all the way. He made every effort to see Zionist sites and wanted to strengthen his ideology on a Zionist state.

On the journey to Jerusalem, Gilbert stopped to deliver lectures at Ismailia, Suez, and Jaffa. In Jerusalen they stayed at the Grand New Hotel where they had beautiful quarters and were treated as special guests for close to two months. He met a number of influential Zionists with whom he had many animated discussions. Dr. Eder, President of the Zionist Commission, introduced him to the famous Zionist Dr. Weizmann who told Gilbert that "he did not think Palestine could ever be a single and simple national territory quite in the sense of France, but he did not see why it should not be a commonwealth of canons after the manner of Switzerland. Some of these could be Jewish canons, others Arab canons, and so on according to the type of population." (Fflynn's "G.K. Chesterton" has a fine discussion of this part of their journey, pp. 259-262.) This idea Chesterton saw clearly involved the abandonment of the solidarity of Palestine and tolerated the idea of groups of Jews being separated from each other by populations of different types.

In his book "The New Jerusalem," where Gilbert at last admits his anti-semitism, he says that a Jewish territorial scheme might really be attempted and might really succeed. He pursues the issue in the book, but not in too much depth. Readers have found that he never really pursues or addresses the con—troversy with his accustomed intensity or fervor. It may be that at the time in Jerusalem, his many visits to any number of Anglican churches, and the resultant disillusionment with the visits, overshadowed all other concerns that he had. He admits that the visits made him more aware that his heart and mind were no longer at peace in the Church of England. His mind had become consumed with Roman Catholicism.

On their return to Italy they stopped at Brindisi and something happened there which confirmed all the more his urge to join the Church of Rome. Here Gilbert came to the conclusion while at Mass that Catholicism was not statues, candles, rosaries, and incense which the Anglicans also had enough of; nor fasts, relics, not even the Pope. It was Our Lady, the Blessed Mother. The idea of Mary as intercessor with her Son completely overtook his mind. The presence of Mary throughout all of Europe in the form of great art or a simple calendar picture in palaces as well as farm houses brought home to him the power the Blessed Mother held on the faith of people.

It is difficult to reconcile Chesterton's deep interest in Jerusalem and his deep-rooted anti-semitism. It does not help to place the blame on his relationship with Belloc, who was indeed anti-semitic. Every man is responsible for his own actions, and Gilbert would be the first to preach that. So often in his lectures and poetry there are stock images of the Jewish money-lender from Shakespeare, offensive allusions to ghetto, the tribe, and any other stereotype. Chesterton had many Jewish friends and the Solomon brothers who were in school with him stayed friends of his for life. Lawrence Solomon even moved his residence to

Beaconsfield to be close to Gilbert and Frances. They were probably like some of my Italian-American colleagues who seem to delight noddingly in "The Sopranos" and the "Godfather" films, the latter being savaged by Mangione's and Morreale's "La Storia: Five Centuries of the Italian American Experience." The authors see "Coppola's comment that mafia is a metaphor of corrupt America is less applicable to America than it is to his and Puzo's compromise with their own principles and aspirations." (Harper Collins, 1992, p. 413).

In denying his anti-semitism and referring to his Zionism, Chesterton said that the Jew must realize he is a separate race, with a history of its own and must "perceive the necessity for a habitat, a centrum, where he can develop what he now lacks, nationality. You see I am not an anti-semite, I am a Zionist." In his early years he hotly denied his anti-semitism because it was something no Christian ought to be. He said, "But every Christian ought to be a Zionist." So much of it is illogical, but then is there ever logic behind bigotry and racism? Maybe he felt that his Distributism was threatened by what Belloc called "an international money power which was largely Jewish and which attempted to control the policies of European nations." That seems to have been the root of the anti-semitism of so many literary people at the time, like T. S. Eliot and Ezra Pound. Hemingway, who had his share of it, in a half-hearted defense of Pound maintained that the only difference between Pound and all the others was that Pound broadcast it. In any case, the facts are there with Chesterton and it is a serious blemish on the character of this brilliant personality.

In late spring of 1920 they were back in England and exhausted. "The New Witness" was in terrible financial state, largely because of its anti-semitism. They set sail for the United States on New Years Day of 1921. His journals have wonderful observations on the Statue of Liberty, New

York City, and Prohibition. He told reporters why he came to America and the line is a classic: "It was a pity to see a people who started out with the Declaration of Independence end up with Prohibition." Of course he thought it was ridiculous. "Our Lord turned water into wine, not into ginger bread." he said. They stayed at the Biltmore where they were treated royally. Reporters were ecstatic and he gave them plenty about which to be excited.

His first lecture at the Times Square Theater on some ridiculous topic was more to amuse than to instruct. He was a great success, but was always tired and Frances was terribly homesick. They then moved on to Boston, Nashville, and up to Canada. Each stop at the major cities had any number of literary people to greet them and wine and dine them, which they hardly needed. John Crowe Ransom was very impressed with him. Gilbert had the wise talent for saying to the people what they wanted to hear. He researched what crisis they were having. In Albany there was a trolley-strike and he said, "I am always unalterably on the side of labor." There were often demonstrations by Jewish groups. There are hundreds of witty observations about Americans, one of which is "There is nothing that an American likes so much as to have a secret society, and to make no secret of it." They returned to England on the Aquitania and Gilbert immediately got down to the business of conversion.

The years 1922-25 are so important. Gilbert wanted so much that Frances come into the church with him. She did not, quite simply and honestly, because as she said she just was not yet prepared. Gilbert's christening took place in the parish church on Sunday, July 30, 1922. He had gone through his Penny Catechism under the direction of Fr. O'Connor. He made his first confession and Frances wept for joy all through the reception ceremony. In his autobiography, Gilbert says, "When people ask me, or indeed anybody else, 'Why did you join the Church of

Rome?' The first essential answer, if it is partly an elliptical answer, is 'to get rid of my sins.' For there is no other religious system that does really profess to get rid of people's sins. It is confirmed by logic, which to many seems startling, by which the Church deduces that sin confessed and adequately repented is actually abolished; and that the sinner does really begin again as if he had never sinned." And later he would be heard to say, "I cannot explain why I am a Catholic; because now that I am a Catholic I cannot imagine myself as anything else." There were many messages of congratulations from throughout the world. Shaw's message to him, "My dear G.K.C., This is going too far." should not be seen as cynicism but as an example of Shavian low key humor.

Books and articles continued to be released. "What I Saw in America," is a series of articles recounting his experience in the United States. Then the book "The Man Who Knew Too Much," a book of short detective stories came out to good reviews but, critics agreed, was not of the stature of the early Fr. Brown stories. The two best works to come after his conversion were "St. Francis of Assisi," a tranquil book which is less a biography and more a meditation, and "The Everlasting Man," a masterpiece of apologetics.

Francis of Assisi had always been a boyhood favorite of Gilbert. He is included in the "Twelve Types" book where he says of him, "If you had taken him to the loneliest star that the madness of the astronomer can conceive, he would have only beheld in it the features of a new friend." Gilbert loved the Troubadour aspect of Francis, a troubadour being a lover. But Francis' love was not only the love of God in an ascetical sense, but a lover of man, a rarer type of mysticism. The book, like Gilbert's "Chaucer" to come in a few years, is not in any sense a true biography. As a matter of fact, Chesterton presumes that the reader has an adequate knowledge of the biographical data and then goes on to use the events of the saint's life for flights of spiritual and religious discourse.

His treatment of the encounter of Francis, who detested lepers as a young rich boy of Assisi, with his first leper is a classic example: "He was riding listlessly in some wayside place, apparently in the open country, when he saw a figure coming along the road towards him and halted; for he saw it was a leper. And he knew instantly that his courage was challenged, not as the world challenges, but as one would challenge who knew the secrets of the heart of a man. What he saw advancing was not the banner and spears of Perugia, from which it never occurred to him to shrink; not the armies that fought for the crown of Sicily, of which he had always thought as a courageous man thinks of mere vulgar danger. Francis Bernardone saw his fear coming along the road towards him; the fear that comes from within and not without; though it stood white and horrible in the sunlight. For once in the long rush of his life his soul stood still. Then he sprang from his horse, knowing nothing between stillness and swiftness, and rushed on the leper and threw his arms around him. It was the beginning of a long vocation of ministry among many lepers, for whom he did many services; to this man he gave what money he could and mounted and rode on. We do not know how far he rode, or with what sense of things around him; but it is said that when he looked back, he could see no figure on the road."

"The Everlasting Man" (1925-27) answers the rationalists' thesis that man as an animal has evolved from primitive life and is not a special creation of God. In "Orthodoxy" Gilbert had traced his own discovery of Christianity, in "The Everlasting Man" he traced rather what that discovery, that revelation, had meant for mankind as a whole. He says, "I do not believe that the best way to produce an outline of history is to rub out the lines." His aim was not merely to draw an outline but to show something that seemed stale, dusty, and old, which it really was, as something fresh and everlastingly new. He asked men to read the Gospels like their daily paper, not merely as good news but as 'news.' "I desire to help the reader to see Christendom from the outside in the sense of seeing it as a whole against the background of other historic things; just as I desire him to see humanity as a whole against the background of natural things. And I say that in both cases when seen thus, they stand out from their background like supernatural things."

Dorothy Collins, an admirer of Gilbert's, joined him and Frances in 1926 as a professional secretary and it made all the difference in their lives for the rest of their time. The services of a professional secretary were crucial. Frances had become ill and could hardly keep up with the pace of their lives, "GKC Weekly" was showing success with Walter de la Mare becoming a major contributor, Distributism was still a major interest in Gilbert's life, so much so, that the "Weekly" had become the mouthpiece for the movement. With Dorothy now on board, plans were being made for further travel.

Gilbert was convinced that Distributism had its roots in Pope Leo XIII's "Rerum Novarum" (1891) and Gilbert insisted that the encyclical had given stature to his movement. The Pope had offered this encyclical as an alternative to both the capitalist system and the emerging socialism, which was unjust because, to quote the Pope' own words, "every man has, by nature, the right to possess property as his own" and it was within man's right to "possess things, not merely for temporary and momentary use, as other living things do, but to hold them in stable and permanent possession." Man, the Pope said, precedes the state. "Prior to the formation of any state, man possesses the right to provide for the sustenance of his body."

The most important day of the year of 1926 was November 1, All Saint's Day, when Frances was received into the Catholic Church, four years after Gilbert's reception. According to all reports a complete change came over her. Very definitely her health improved, her very demeanor exuded tranquil joy. Maisie Ward said she became a different person. Gilbert himself was jubilant as he continued to write about his own conversion. His article called "The New Heresy," (1926) an attack on sexual morality, birth control, and abortion made an enormous impact on people of religion in England. In his own words, he says "the madness of tomorrow is not in Moscow, but much more in Manhattan—most of what was in Broadway is already in Piccadilly."

Poland and her Catholicism had always been on Gilbert's mind even before his conversion. With the professional assistance of Dorothy who made all the arrangements, and with the obvious enthusiasm of Frances since her reception into the Church, and with that inexplicable vigor that always came to Gilbert when there was a new audience, the three of them departed for Warsaw in late 1926. The trip was a great success. Hundreds of people greeted them wherever they went. The Poles saw him as their savior because of his support during their early years of struggle for freedom. His love for the Polish people grew enormously with this visit.

The years 1927 to 1933 were remarkable for people so ill and infirm to do so much traveling and lecturing. Gilbert's life of "St. Thomas Aquinas" comes out, another book which was the result of his conversion. "Do We Agree" a debate between Chesterton and Shaw, which was highly publicized and broadcast on radio, caused a near riot by people who were not able to get into the hall. Chesterton had rejected Socialism fully by now and Shaw, whose position had softened, was more guarded in the debate. Both however continued to agree on the distribution of wealth.

Their travels continued as the three of them went on to Rome for three months. They stayed at the Hotel Hassler at the top of the Piazza de Spagna. Gilbert recorded many of his impressions in his book "The Resurrection of Rome," especially his meeting with Mussolini and his audience with Pius XI.

The next step in their travels was a trip to Canada (1930) which was paid for by the University of Notre Dame where Gilbert lectured for six weeks on Victorian literature. Students adored him and he really enjoyed the idea of staying in one place for lecturing rather than traveling on the circuit. Notre Dame gave him an honorary Doctorate in Letters, one of the many honorary degrees he accumulated during his travels throughout the United States. He really came to love Americans and was invigorated by the American university student. He loved the excitement of the country, the energy. His major criticism was one that he shared with many Europeans then as well as today: people spend so much energy in building up only to tear down in a few years. The pilgrims he felt came here full of ideals of religion. That passionate energy passed away and the people threw their energy into business. It is the worship of activity for its own sake. In England, he felt, the rich classes that worship laziness were as bad. Both are false religions. As for the Puritans, Chesterton felt the English should have instituted a special Thanksgiving Day to celebrate the fact that the Pilgrim Fathers had left England.

Gilbert moved on to California and to Hollywood which he loved. Hollywood producers wanted some of his Father Brown stories for filming and Gilbert and Frances were thrilled about this since Frances had become ill and the bills for her medical treatment were exorbitant. Gilbert traveled up and down the coast lecturing, draining him of whatever energy he had left. They returned to New York for some lectures before embarking for London. Their return to England coincided with the publication of his "Chaucer." It is a wonderful book in the spirit of Saint Francis of Assisi.

Again he asserted that he did not want to be considered a biographer in these things; they are works of reflection.

They then went to Dublin for the Eucharistic Congress to which they had been invited as important guests. Among the many personalities they met at the Congress was John MacCormack, the Irish tenor. MacCormack sang at the solemn Pontifical High Mass and Gilbert wore his scarlet robe, green hood, and black velvet cap of a Doctor of Letters which he had received from the National University of Ireland. The events of the Congress and other reminiscences are recorded in his book "Christendom in Dublin."

Back in London, Gilbert collapsed from total exhaustion. A trip to France had to be canceled. Yet the years 1933-36 are still amazing for activity. The editorials in the "Weekly" were very much concerned with Hitlerism spreading over Europe. He admired some of Hitler's ideas on Distributism but detested Hitler and the Nazi threat. His attitude toward Mussolini was different. Like Ezra Pound, he admired him for his economic savvy and for the alterations he had made in the national administration. But Gilbert was not a Fascist and the allegations that the "Weekly" was being partially funded by the Fascists were absurd. He took upon himself the role of a broadcaster for a short period of time. This was a successful venture because of the volatile situation in Europe and the overall pessimism in Britain. He became the voice of optimism.

Despite the fact that Gilbert and Frances were experiencing a gradual breakdown in health, Dorothy arranged a trip to Florence for the three of them. It was to be part work and part pleasure. He was to lecture in Florence, then go to Rome to receive the honor of the Order of St. Gregory the Great with Belloc. The plan was to continue on to the Holy Land by way of Sicily, but Gilbert collapsed in Syracuse, so they returned immediately to London.

The "Weekly" had become embroiled in the controversy over the Italian campaign in Abyssinia. Gilbert was very sick now and apologized that he did not deal with Abyssinia at length. However he went on to say that England was not in a position to administer a moral rebuke, since she was at present in possession of an empire far bigger than Italy could ever hope to attain, and had acquired it by methods 'which the most hard-boiled Fascist would repudiate with disgust.' England had no right to be self-righteous regarding the aggressions of her neighbors, he believed.

Added to Chesterton's many activities in his last years were several series of radio talks for the British Broadcasting Corporation. Both his own purely literary talks and his contributions to various series on the BBC were received with rare enthusiasm. In these talks and in his writing, right down to the hour of his death, an element was present that has caused the most fundamental disagreement as to Chesterton's character and his place in history. A note of youth, of high spirits, of fooling, present when he entered the career of a young journalist, was as audible in the mature man broadcasting his last message to his countrymen. In refuting the philosophy of T. S. Eliot, a poet whom he admired very much, and who held that the world would go out with a whimper, Gilbert said, "They may go out with a whimper / But I will go out with a bang."

In June of 1936, Gilbert was so sick that he drifted in and out of consciousness. Frances informed close relatives of his condition, but she was very protective about the public knowing anything. She insisted that these last moments remain private. Monsignor Smith, the parish priest, gave Gilbert the last rites and his final Communion on the 12th of June, 1936. Fr. Vincent McNabb came down from London's St. Dominic's Priory to be at his bedside. Seeing Gilbert's pen on the little table by the bed, he picked it up and blessed it. In a brief moment of consciousness, Gilbert said to Frances who was by his bed, "Hallo, my Darling." And then to Dorothy standing nearby, he said "Hallo, my Dear" They were his last words.

The funeral was in St. Teresa's Church in Beaconsfield, after much fuss over the coffin being too big to go down the winding stairs of the house so that a window had to be removed. He was laid to rest in the Catholic cemetery that today is Frances's also, for she survived him for only two years. Belloc wept bitterly.

A memorial service was held in Westminster Cathedral where Ronald Knox spoke his tribute; Cardinal Pacelli, who was later to become Pope Pius XII, cabled of the grief of the Holy Father at the death of a devoted son. After all had settled down, Frances wrote to their old friend Fr. O'Connor, "I find it increasingly difficult to keep going on . . . the feeling that he no longer needs me is almost unbearable. How do lovers love without each other? We were always lovers."

"Chesterton the Child" was the supreme attribute given to Chesterton by Walter de la Mare at the time of his death. But there was nothing childish in Chesterton, nothing callow in his youthful high spirits. Childlike, yes, but not childish. The conception of Chesterton as a Peter Pan who never grew up does not accord well with the books and ideas which led philosophers to welcome him as one of their own caliber, poets to give him front rank among themselves, and men of letters to acclaim his Dickens, his Browning, and his Stevenson as showing the insight of genius.

A high-spirited, combative, opinionated man, he impressed on everything that he wrote a strong, whimsical, humorous personality which marked him out as a genuine and most quotable man-of-letters. Deep scholarship he did not claim; and he was often out of touch with the spirit of an age which counted his colleagues Shaw, Wells, Hardy, and Arnold Bennett among its major prophets. Yet for all his passionate and unashamed championship of dogma, for all his arguing like a professional contrarian, for all his flashy verbal paradox and stylistic virtuosity, his most bitter opponents, infuriated though they may have been by what they considered a false and tortuous philosophy, freely granted him credit for his wit, his gift of prose, his love of liberty, his personal kindliness, his broad humanity.

You cannot ask for more than that out of a life.

Selected Works of Chesterton

The Wild Knight and Other Poems (1900)
Twelve Types (1902)
Robert Louis Stevenson (1902)
Robert Browning (1903)
Leo Tolstoy (1903)
The Napoleon of Notting Hill (1904)
Heretics (1905)
Charles Dickens (1906)
The Man Who Was Thursday (1908)
Orthodoxy (1909)
George Bernard Shaw (1910)
What's Wrong with the World? (1910)
William Blake (1910)
The Innocence of Father Brown (1911)
The Ballad of the White Horse (1911)
The Victorian Age in Literature (1913)
A Short History of England (1917)
Irish Impressions (1919)
The New Jerusalem (1920)
The Man Who Knew Too Much (1922)
St. Francis of Assisi (1923)
The Everlasting Man (1925-27)
The Catholic Church and Conversion (1926)
The Resurrection of Rome (1930)
Chaucer (1932)
St. Thomas Aquinas (1933)

Graham Greene

During the period when Graham Greene's novels were concerned with Catholic interests his fiction was actually a part of the movement in the late forties and early fifties of the last century called the "Catholic Novel Tradition," a tradition that stems from the French Decadence. The operation of God's grace is seen at work in a world of secular and diverse values, a world populated by pimps, whores, whiskey priests, adulterers, crooked politicians, and corrupt secret service men. Where Francois Mauriac introduced this theme in the bleak French provinces, and Evelyn Waugh introduced it into the rich British aristocracy, Greene brought it to life in the worlds of chintzy Brighton, war-torn London, an oppressively persecuted Mexico, and Scobie's Sierra Leone backwater civilization. It was called the "Catholic Novel Tradition" because the theme of the novels was Augustinian ("not yet Lord"); grace is the hound that seeks and chases the sinner through the highways and byways of depraved societies and, ironically and unexpectedly, triumphs in the most sick, hopeless, godless, low-life people, societies, and situations. The literary movement captured the interest of many readers, yet offended others.

Graham Greene was born on October 2, 1904 at Berkhamsted, Hertfordshire, England, to Charles Henry Greene, headmaster of Berkhamsted School, and Marion R. Greene. He was one of six children. The parents were cousins, both born with the family name Greene, and Robert Louis Stevenson was a first cousin of Marion Greene's.

Greene entered Berkhamsted School when he was 11 and left in 1921, when he was 17.

His early life, as a member of a large, provincial, middle-class family at the beginning of the century, was a tranquil one. In his autobiography, "A Sort of Life" (1971), he describes the happy atmosphere of his home, despite a sense of distance he felt from his parents. His mother was remote and indifferent to the affairs of the children; love was there but it was often out of reach. His father, though busy all the time, was always caring.

His childhood innocence was replaced by the unhappy experience of becoming a boarder at Berkhamsted School, of which his father was then headmaster. The hostile environment of boarding school, with its noisy, smelly dormitories, shared lavatories, and total lack of privacy was a profoundly unpleasant experience, one that many of England's writers of middle-class backgrounds had to experience in their youth. These writers wrote with an intense nostalgia for school days which they hated and, therefore, loved to recall.

Greene's experience however was aggravated by the peculiar situation of being the headmaster's son and his home being attached to the school. He never felt he had a happy home to retreat to after a day of academic misery. The school was entered from home through a green baize door in his father's study. This door became a symbol for Greene of the border between innocence and experience, a symbol that will appear in one shape or another in just about all of his fiction.

In the eyes of the young Greene evil was ever present in the school. The dark corridors, the stone stairs, the bells ringing early, the cruelty of the children, all created for him an environment of fear. The adults actually took upon themselves the genuine quality of evil. Hell was all around him and if there was a heaven, it was far from there, or else if heaven was there, it had become totally corrupted. Hell as more prevalent and credible than heaven is another way of saying that corruption had consumed innocence and was now part of the cultural landscape. This too would become a theme that Greene would use for the rest of his career.

A third theme closely related to that of the green baize door with its innocence being introduced to experience and that of innocence being overtaken by corruption is that of the rite of passage that appears early in Greene's work. During his earliest period, Greene dealt often in both his long and his short fiction with the initiation of a young person into the adult world and how this experience can be cruel and disillusioning, and sometimes edifying. Greene wrote volumes of short fiction, but three of the short stories, I think, will serve to show how these three early themes work in his short fiction and how they make their way into his novels. The stories are: "The Basement Room," "The Hint of an Explanation," and "The Destructors."

In "The Basement Room" (1936) the child Philip Lane spends most of his time in the world of the nursery and the world of the basement living room of Philip's idol, the butler Baines, and his acerbic wife. When his parents go on holiday Philip penetrates the green baize door of childhood to find freedom in Baines's quarters, where he lives every word of the butler's totally fabricated stories. This innocent brush with the adult world has serious consequences. Philip is startled, during one of his flights beyond the baize door, to find Baines kissing a girl, Emmy, whom he has introduced as his niece. Philip is present to see a struggle between Baines and his wife which ends with the woman falling down the staircase to her death. The whole grown-up world revolts him and he shuts it out by running away only to be found by a policeman. In his innocence he blurts out, "It was all Emmy's fault!," unknowingly referring to the loss of his innocence as well as the accident.

Philip discovers the realities of the grown-up world: the hatred between Baines and his wife, Baines's desperate bid for happiness with his mistress, Emmy, all the lies involved after Philip has discovered them together, and then the death of Baines' wife; all change his life completely. By penetrating the baize door he became "caught up in other people's darkness" and he can never return to an innocence which has been lost forever. "The whole house had been turned over to the grown-up world . . . their passions had flooded in." Philip retreats into his own world, surrenders all responsibility, and becomes incapable of mature and selfless love. "That was what happened when you loved— you get involved; and Philip extricated himself from life, from love, from Baines."

In 1948, "The Basement Room" became a successful and popular film named "The Fallen Idol" with Carol Reed as director and Greene himself as scenarist. Greene changed the ending of the story by having Baines cleared. I have not been able to find out why. Possibly it was pressure from the studio. But the original ending is vintage Greene. Philip dies sixty years later after the incident, a lonely bitter recluse who has spent his life avoiding all relationships.

In "The Hint of an Explanation" (1948), two strangers on a train get into a conversation about God and the spiritual world. The narrator is an agnostic, the other a Catholic. Their conversation reveals a different situation and outcome of a youth who penetrated the baize door to adulthood. The Catholic traveler explains, the hint of an explanation, to the agnostic stranger that period from his life which 'let the future in' for him as a child. Growing up as a Catholic in a largely Protestant society, he had as a boy felt marginalized and different. People in the town had harassed him, calling him "Popey Martin." Blacker, the town baker and an atheist, has a pathologically deep hatred of Catholicism. He plans to revenge himself on everything he hated, the boy, his father, all Catholics.

Blacker's plan is to 'seduce' Popey, by offering him a toy if in exchange he procures for him a consecrated host when he goes to Mass, which he needs to prove to himself that there is no such thing as transubstantiation. Blacker also threatens the boy's life with a razor if he does not comply with his demand. That Sunday at Mass the boy removes the host from his own mouth and keeps it for the baker. However, as he lies in bed that night, waiting for Blacker's whistle outside his window, Popey begins to realize the diobolical implications of the sacrilege he has been asked to commit and becomes aware, for the first time, of the forces of evil that exist in the world. The whole plan backfires. The boy eats the host on impulse and the atheist begins to cry. Looking back on the moment from his adult point of view, Popey feels that these were the tears of a man whose complete being had been consumed by the forces of hate and evil.

The failure of the forces of evil reaches its fullest moment when, at the very end of the story, the coat of the Catholic stranger falls open and it is revealed that he is wearing the collar of a Roman Catholic priest. The moment in which he had resisted Blacker's plan to corrupt him had "let in" a future of priesthood, service to God, and the forces of good. The paradox of the situation comes in the last line when the priest admits to the agnostic that he in fact owes a lot to the baker: "You see, I am a very happy man."

"The Destructors" (1954) is one of Greene's best stories, certainly his favorite ("I believe I have never written anything better"). Its time and place is the World War II blitzkrieg of London. Trevor, an early teen who goes by the name "T." joins and takes over a street gang, the Wormsley Common Gang, whose intent is to demolish the Common's last standing building, a house and a loo belonging to an elderly man who has offered them chocolates, which they see as a bribe. They name the old householder, "Old Misery" and their plan is to dismantle his house with its 200 year old corkscrew staircase, from the inside, and bring down to their level a building that, to T., is invisibly held up "by opposite forces."

T. and his forces dispossess the old man, but they are not thieves: they burn his seventy bank notes one by one just to see Old Misery's face when they are through, but T. denies hating the old man. "There'd be no fun if I hated him." For T. hate and love are opposing forces but they are a lot of, as he says, "hooey." They put Old Misery in his own loo and lock the door behind him They make sure he has a blanket, buttered buns, and sausage rolls. Then a lorry, having been tied to the strut of the house, completes T.'s insidious demolition, as the lorry driver bursts into hysterical laughter at Old Misery's misery. Again, opposing forces are at work to the end. The fact that the house had escaped the fate of the German bombing only to be eaten away by a gang of boys is seen as funny. "One moment the house had stood there with such dignity between the bombsites like a man in a top hat, and then bang, crash, there wasn't anything left—not anything." The lorry driver calls to Old Misery, "I'm sorry. I can't help it . . . There's nothing personal, but you got to admit that it is funny."

Although there are some interesting parallels between Greene's story and Anthony Burgess's "A Clockwork Orange," which came out some eight years later (1962), the alarming vision of violence, high technology, and authoritarianism in the Burgess work contains little or none of the interplay of innocence and depravity that Greene has in his work. Burgess, brilliant writer that he was, introduces evil as endemic to the nature of the youths in the London street gangs, and consequently they are without hope. It is a darker vision. Greene gives a more balanced view of human nature.

"The Basement Room" and "The Destructors" are about youth in desperate situations and unable to escape. In the first, goodness loses out to forces it cannot understand; in the second, to forces it understands all too well. Innocence and experience conflict with the forces of evil, and evil is victorious. In "The Hint of an Explanation" however the youth is in an impossible situation, but the forces of evil lose out to grace, something about which the boy has no idea until he is a grown man and a priest. The story, written ten years later than "Brighton Rock," supposedly his first Catholic novel, gives us Greene fully immersed in his 'religious experience' period.

The three works, done over a thirty year period, do reveal a familiar pattern in the author's journey. In all three there is the symbol of the baize door, innocence and experience, innocence overcome by corruption, and the concept of grace, accepted or rejected. Also the black humor of "The Destructors" runs throughout almost all of Greene's short stories and he delights in irony, absurdity and quirky, even fantastic twists of fate, which often give his stories an unexpected ending, as seen in "The Hint of an Explanation." In each the young man being initiated into the adult world is not so consciously reluctant as in all the later works because of the fact that he is so young. But the devices used in these three works will be fully developed in the later novels.

After graduation from Berkhamsted School, Greene went on to Balliol College, Oxford to read modern history. While there he joined the Communist party as a dues-paying member for about five weeks, paying about twenty-eight cents. This would come back to haunt him thirty years later. He was a life long socialist and pro-Marxist, supporting Charlie Chaplin and favoring Fidel Castro. He once said that he would prefer, if the choice were given him, to live in the Soviet Union rather than in America. His later friendship with the eccentric, ultra-conservative Evelyn Waugh was founded on their shared Catholicism and of course fiction and the art of fiction. Waugh considered socialism as one of the great evils of modern society, and

Greene resented the rigidity of Catholic practice and custom. Both however were in total agreement on what Newman termed man's 'aboriginal calamity', the doctrine of the fall.

Greene took a second-class degree at Oxford in 1925 and in that year his first book was published, a book of poetry, "Babbling April," which was a disaster. He was converted to Roman Catholicism in 1926 and then married in the following year the Catholic Vivien Dayrell-Browning, a marriage that was not a very happy one. In the decade following his conversion he worked as a literary journalist and then as an editor on the Times. In 1929 his first novel was published.

"The Man Within" is a distressingly complex and confusing narrative from the pen of a young novelist who shows a great deal of promise. But it is a hard read. Andrews is a young man plagued by recollections of an unhappy childhood and a brutal father. The father is a smuggler and the son inherits the same kind of work. To bring vengeance on his father for his own lost innocence, Andrews informs on the smugglers. They are tried and set free and in turn they revenge themselves on the woman Andrews loves. She commits suicide and Andrews gives himself up to the police as her murderer. If nothing, the novel contains more of Greene's themes in rudimentary form that he would later develop to perfection: betrayal upon betrayal, the protagonist's sense of failure, loyalty and honor, God as silent and indifferent. The success of the novel brought Greene an advance of six hundred pounds from Doubleday for three years in return for three novels. He was to become a professional novelist.

"Stamboul Train" (1932), published in the United States as "Orient Express," marks the beginning of Greene's debut as a writer of contemporary thrillers, the genre in which he was to achieve his best work over the next ten years. The main function of the train journey is a structural one. The action follows the Orient Express as it leaves Ostend and crosses Europe on its way to Istanbul. The novel is segmented into five parts, each a major station on the route and each propelling the action forward. For the most part, the action is confined to the closed setting of the train. The closed setting, a technique favored later by Katherine Anne Porter in "Ship of Fools" and John Steinbeck in "Wayward Bus," and many others, allows Greene to isolate his characters in order to let them interact in a confined space independent of an ouisde world, with the actual setting becoming a microcosm of that world. The journey, a technique that goes back to Chaucer and Boccaccio, indeed, to the Gospel of Luke, provides an opportunity to bring together in a capricious fashion a broad range of characters who will illustrate Greene's view and impressions of contemporary society.

The passengers are made up of stock Greene characters: a waif-like young girl (Coral), a second-rate novelist (Savory), an inadequate priest (Opie), a journalist with little interest in the truth (Mabel Warren), a Communist facing disillusion (Dr. Czinner). All reveal their inner conflicts and any number of sub-plots are introduced. The main action centers on Dr. Czinner, an exiled communist revolutionary who is returning to his native Belgrade to lead an uprising. As a young doctor in Belgrade, Czinner had become frustrated in his attempts to help his people, the poor, because he was unable to cure them of their main ailment: poverty.

Having once been brought to trial as a revolutionary, Czinner had escaped and lived as an exile in England, working as a schoolmaster. The planned uprising gives him new hope and even when it is revealed on the train that the revolutionary plan has backfired and that the revolution has already failed, he decides to persevere and stand trial with the other conspirators, for at least the trial will give recognition to the world of the cause. The trial, a secret and unconstitutional military affair, is a travesty and Czinner too is a humiliating failure.

The novel, devoid of any of the religious themes that are seen in the future novels, is what Greene called one of his 'entertainments'; most critics saw it as a potboiler. It contains all the ingredients of the train books and films of the time: murder, revolution, love, political intrigue, sex, all on the Orient Express which suggests luxury, romance, and mystery. Also it introduces readers to one of Greene's interests in later novels, the protagonist functioning on an international scene. Greene always wanted to write a book that would be made into a film (train films were very popular in the 30s), and, much to his distress, this one was. He considered it a turkey. A BBC television production came out in 1962; it was worse.

Like many young intellectuals of the 1930s, Greene was drawn to the Left in politics, particularly in those areas concerning social justice. In "It's a Battlefield" (1934), the most overtly political of his early novels, he paints a broad and graphic picture of injustice and inequality in contemporary society, taking up the cause endured by the millions of low paid and unemployed workers in the Depression. Jim Drover, a bus driver and a Communist, has hit and accidentally killed a policeman who he thought was going to strike his wife, Milly, during a political demonstration in Hyde Park. Jim is found guilty of murder and sentenced to death. The novel, which is an account of his plea for justice and clemency, exposes a justice system that ignores the appeal of the innocent comman man and protects the vested interests of the wealthy. Jim's fate is seen ultimately to rest not on his innocence or guilt, but on the warped public opinion, shared by an unscrupulous media, and on the unethical manipulation of politicians for their own careers.

The injustice Greene is attacking in "It's a Battlefield" is not just the injustice which can condemn an innocent man to death out of political expediency, but the wider injustice of a society in which wealth and power are so unevenly distributed. It is an activist book and one that did not come as a surprise to many young liberals in London in the 1930s. The book had great appeal to young readers caught up in the liberal political ideology of the time. It has its mark as a Greene piece: innocence and corruption, a silent God, the left-wing politics, the little man overpowered by bureaucracy, e.g., the bad men are wealthy armament manufacturers, and the good men are usually Communists.

"England Made Me" (1935) begins with Anthony, a listless individual in his thirties who has drifted from one failure to another since he left school. He is helped by his twin sister, Kate, who through a certain ruthlessness has become the mistress of Krogh, a powerful figure in the Krogh empire in Stockholm. Krogh might be modeled on Krupp, the industrial complex that was feeding Hitler's armies with munitions. She persuades Krogh to hire Anthony as his personal bodyguard, thus keeping her brother close to her. There are suggestions here of an incestuous relationship.

The novel is more about social conditioning than was "It's a Battlefield." It paints an even more vivid and distressing picture of individuals at the mercy of a dysfunctional society and incapable of extricating themselves. Krogh represents the new rootless civilization of the twentieth century while Anthony, and a journalist down and out expatriate friend of his, Minty, represent old-fashioned moral values. They have been paralyzed intellectually by the English public school system (like Greene) but they still adhere to the values that were instilled in them by their parents and their schoolmasters. When Krogh enters into an unscrupulous and illegal deal, the weak Anthony takes a moral stand. This moral triumph shows that he never unlearned the strict moral lessons beaten into him at school. Krogh, who has no scruples or allegiance, thinks he has escaped and has been liberated from everything of the past but in fact has only imprisoned himself in the present.

In Greene's later novels religious belief is always there as a sense of enlarging life, but that is not here, except in the person of Minty, who simply has a nodding allegiance to Anglo-Catholicism. It is not enough to offer him hope. The end is significant where Minty keeps a spider trapped under his toothglass. This represents the deterministic view of life, in which man cannot rise and exercise his free will. All the characters are trapped, even Krogh, who is trapped behind the glass and steel of his empire, and no one can break away. The depressing conclusion, that man is a trapped creature, was a frequent motif in much of the poetry and fiction of the times.

With an advance of three hundred fifty pounds from Doubleday, Greene traveled through the jungles of Liberia which provided him material for his first travel book, "Journey Without Maps." This was to be a new endeavor for him. Upon return to London he continued with his writing of novels, 'entertainments' which were for the most part thrillers and which were distinguishable from his more serious novels.

"A Gun for Sale" (1936), published in the United States as "This Gun for Hire," is a neatly arranged plot about Sir Marcus, a millionaire armaments manufacturer, who hires Raven, a ruthless criminal to murder the War Minister of a foreign government. The assassination brings Europe to the brink of war and raises the consumption of munitions, thus making magnificent profits for Marcus. Raven is not an evil man but a victim of sociological and psychological forces. Marcus represents unscrupulous capitalism, the ultimate evil, and Raven, is his victim, especially so since Marcus pays him with stolen bank notes (his passing these on attracts the attention of the police). Furious at this, Raven, who is being pursued by the police, is in pursuit of personal justice, that is, hunting down Marcus. Mather is the detective in pursuit of Raven and Raven, ironically, kidnaps Anne, the detective's girlfriend, to help him escape. In the end, Anne who has become sympathetic to his plight, is ultimately responsible for his arrest.

The novel is fast-paced and suspenseful, having all the Greene touches of chase, confession, and betrayal, which he will use brilliantly in his later fiction. Raven becomes a classic figure in modern fiction, a typical Graham Greene protagonist, the man who is not a hateful person but is engaged to commit hateful deeds by a corrupt society. The book is imbued by a sense of the immorality of international capitalism and the plight of the exploited. Raven's victim, the minister, is "said to love humanity" and is thus a victim of the greed of those advancing a war. Part of the action takes place at Christmas and Raven looking at the '"swaddled child" in a crib calls him "the little bastard" and sees himself an outcast with "no room at the inn." He with his twisted bitterness, his hare-lip and disturbed childhood, has a certain honor, "I don't go back on a fellow who treats me right" and his warped moral code is, "It's not the killing I mind, it's the double-crossing." But being betrayed by Anne, the only person he ever trusted in life, he remains to his death bitter and a nonbeliever. The religious note seen in Greene's later novels, although slightly suggested here in the Augustinian 'the pursued and the pursuer' motif, is no where to be found here and in the early entertainments.

"The Confidential Agent" (1939) is concerned with trust and loyalty in the extreme situation of war. The agent of the title is D, who comes to England to purchase essential supplies of coal for his government which is engaged in a bitter civil war. The reader is sure it is the Spanish Civil War, although never named. The opposition also send an agent to buy the same supply of coal, and whoever obtains the coal will gain a decisive advantage over the other side.

But D. is an agent whose government does not really

have much confidence in him and he does not have confidence in himself. He is one the period's 'hollow men' and having come from a war zone, he finds in England a calmness and peace among people who have no awareness of the war that he is bringing to their shore. But he soon realizes that beneath this mask of tranquility is a far more tragic situation, a nation of people struggling with life in a world without God, a world that Eliot would observe, paraphrasing Dante, "I had not thought death had undone so many." This struggle is an integral part of the human condition throughout the world, thus the use of initials for keeping the characters anonymous and for emphasizing the universality of this spiritual wasteland.

D., an old French scholar with a sense of failure who has found an unheroic earlier version of the Roland and Oliver story, is out of his depth in England and his own malaise gets him involved in the treachery of the situation. The most effective element in the narrative is the sharp reversal of interest when, in the second part, D., the pursued, becomes in turn the revenging pursuer, the old Augustinian motif.

It is appropriate to consider here, in mentioning the chase and pursuit motif, Greene's "The Third Man." A popular story which was never intended to be anything more than a movie script, it was written at the suggestion of Alexander Korda as a basis for a film by Carol Reed, and a very popular film it became indeed (1949). Rollo Martin goes to Vienna immediately after the war at the invitation of Harry Lime, the friend whom he had admired from schooldays. He arrives only to find that his friend has died mysteriously and Rollo attends the funeral. In trying to track down Harry Lime's murderer he comes to realize that the funeral was a fake and that he is in pursuit of Harry himself who had been prominent in black-market dealing in adulterated penicillin, which can kill or maim. In a classic chase through the sewers of the city, Rollo shoots Harry.

Greene insisted that this work was never meant to be

anything more than the raw material for a movie. But many themes to be developed elsewhere are present: the total corruption of an intelligent and humorous man by power and money; the betrayal of the betrayer by a decent ordinary friend who is driven to take a stand to be seen again in one of Greene's most mature works, "The Quiet American." As literature "The Third Man" is a pretty unexciting, barren piece of writing. It is probably the best known of all Greene's thrillers and it plays on the national loyalties during the Cold War. Harry Lime was played by Orson Welles and Rollo Martin by Joseph Cotton. Through the brilliant cinematography, chilling music, the devices of film noir, and the remarkable editing and pacing for suspense, the story came vividly to life in the cinema, becoming one of the most popular and successful films of all times.

"The Ministry of Fear" (1943) is set against the dramatic background of the London blitz and tells the story of Rowe, who becomes involved in a sinister underworld when he innocently gives a secret password—by guessing the correct weight of a cake at a charity fete. The mysterious organization wants to retrieve the cake, which contains a secret (never revealed to Rowe or the reader). He fights them off but is knocked unconscious by a bomb hitting his house; he ends up in a nursing home with amnesia. In the clinic is a green baize door leading to the sick bay. Its barred windows and high walls keep the patients in fear if they do not cooperate. Rowe doubts if anyone is in the sick bay but this soon changes when a Major Stone, a fellow patient, is taken there. Rowe fears the same fate. He goes through the door of the clinic (like Greene's experience of the door in his father's study) into a world of bewilderment. Before his loss of memory he suffered from terrible guilt for his wife whom he assisted in death out of great pity. It is a mysterious story, often leaving the reader bewildered, but it has Greene's familiar themes. Rowe's going to the fete in the first place was out of the curiosity of what was on the other side of the baize door, from innocence into the adult and corrupt world. Also there is the element of pity, so much a part of his later fiction.

"Brighton Rock" (1938) was the first of Greene's novels to have a clear, popular success. It was begun as an 'entertainment,' but it grew naturally into its religious dimension and marks the beginning of that phase of Greene's work in which he clearly presents himself as a Roman Catholic novelist.

The novel is set on Bank holiday in the seedy area of the Brighton seaside, a world of gang warfare and protection rackets. It focuses on Pinkie Brown, who was brought up as a Roman Catholic, and is now involved in the gangsterism of the 1930s Brighton. It begins where Hale, a lightweight journalist who has double-crossed Pinkie's gang, has thrown in his lot with Colleoni's gang. It is for this that Pinkie and his rival mob are seeking to kill him. Hale has betrayed Kite, the leader of Pinkie's gang, to Colleoni, and Pinkie is seeking revenge for Kite's murder in order to prove himself, at seventeen, a worthy successor. It is, in fact, Raven, the central figure of "A Gun for Sale" who has killed Kite.

Knowing that a witness is his only means of safety, Hale picks up Ida Arnold, a big friendly woman. But he becomes Pinkie's victim anyway because he is slain while waiting for Ida on the oceanfront to come out of the lavatory. Ida, who refuses to accept the cause of her friend's death as natural, determines to track down his murderer. Her unremitting pursuit of Pinkie provides a motif dear to Greene's heart: the chase. In her relentless pursuit of Pinkie, he, the pursued, is driven to kill others.

Pinkie, who is often referred to as the Boy, finds himself obliged to marry a sixteen year old waitress named Rose, whom he detests and whom he knows is the only one who can turn evidence against him. Rose, like Pinkie, is a slum-born Roman Catholic. She is genuinely sincere, and she loves and protects Pinkie. Even though she is aware of his low-life dealings, the protection racket, she is not aware of his series of killings. Pinkie, in order to insure that she will not report him, insists that they marry, even though they are underage. He also insists on a grisly suicide pact that he has no intention of observing. He actually intends that Rose will go through with the suicide and he will back out and go free.

Pinkie's gang begins to break up, his world begins to fall apart, and Ida, in her intense search for Pinkie, catches up with him on the cliffs. Thinking that Rose has betrayed him, in a fit of rage, Pinkie takes vitriol which he always carried with him and throws it at her face. It blows back on to his and in screaming agony Pinkie throws himself over the cliff. The conclusion comes when the pregnant Rose goes to confession. The priest comforts her, telling her that her love may have redeemed her, that in the strange mercy of God even Pinkie may be saved, and that she should pray that her child will become a saint.

She leaves the confessional to play the recorded message which Pinkie had given her as a wedding present and which she had never heard. The message was: "God damn you, you little bitch, why can't you go home forever and let me be?" The last words of the novel are, "She walked rapidly in the thin June sunlight toward the worst horror of all."

In the Greene credo, Pinkie and Rose, with their distinctiveness of being Roman Catholic, are far more prone to salvation or damnation than Ida who is simple, vigorous, and fun-loving. Pinkie is pure evil and Rose is pure innocence and they are pronounced human beings. They represent Greene's pervasive theme of the coexistence of corruption and innocence. Ida, on the other hand, represents a kind of innocuous common decency and her lack of religion makes her somehow a less defined person than even the evil Pinkie. Many critics have observed Greene's lack of sympathy for her. It is not a fair criticism.

Greene here is dealing with the injunction from Revelation, 3:15-16 "You are neither cold or hot. I wish you were one or the other, but since you are neither, but only lukewarm, I will spit you out of my mouth." She is dull because she does not possess a pronounced goodness or evil, just a lukewarm decency. Evelyn Waugh saw Pinkie as "completely damnable" and Sean O'Casey saw Pinkie and Rose as the most stupid and evil mortals that a man's mind could ever conceive.

The novel makes a strong case in Pinkie's defense because of his social background. This is not unusual for Greene in this phase of his career; his treatment of Raven is much the same. The misery and deprivation are largely responsible for Pinkie's later delinquency. He speaks at times of having been an altar server and he even considered becoming a priest. Greene himself admits, in his "The Other Man," that Pinkie is not guilty of mortal sin "because his actions were not committed in defiance of God, but arose out of the conditions to which he had been born." More than any other adjective, Greene uses the word 'sick' in reference to Pinkie, while he uses 'healthy' in reference to Ida. She is one of the holiday people on the Brighton front, having a good time, and with a moral code that stands for nothing. Sin and repentance are simply not of the real world for her. "Believe me. It's the world we got to deal with," she says. She lacks a religious dimension and therefore lacks importance. Her actions do not have the supernatural importance of Pinkie's. T.S. Eliot's essay on Baudelaire sums up the paradox of Greene's "Brighton Rock": "So far as we are human, what we do must be either evil or good; so as far as we do evil or good we are human; and it is better, in a paradoxical way, to do evil, than to do nothing: at least we exist."

It should be noted that Greene does not write from within the Catholic faith, nor does he review his characters from its perspective. Pinkie and Rose are of an alienated world where, for most, God is dead and the sinner who is conscious of his sin is a holy sinner. Pinkie bears the scars of a deprived childhood in the wretched slums of Kemp Town. He is divided not only from decent people but from big-time gangsters. People are better dressed and better washed than he is. The police inspector treats him like a child, telling him he is too young to be running a racket. People tease him over his marriage to Rose and the attendant at the shooting-gallery insults him. When he was a child sleeping on the couch, he could hear his parents love making and the sounds, especially from his mother, were undignified, indeed, gross. It influenced the way he treated Rose and other women; it contributed to his being a sexual failure. The force of social determinism and the 'aboriginal calamity' produced a very sad person.

Greene went to Mexico in the late winter of 1937-1938. He had been commissioned by his London publisher, Longmans, Green, to study the plight of the Mexican Catholic church, which had for over a decade been engaged in a running feud with the revolutionary government. In his preface to the Viking Critical Edition of "The Power and the Glory" he asserts that the last thing on his mind was to write a novel about the situation. But when he was in Villahermosa by accident he came upon an idea for a principal character.

A villager told him about the last priest in the state. The priest had baptized the villager's son, giving him a girl's name, for he was so drunk he could hardly stand for the ceremony, let alone remember a name. Afterwards he disappeared in the same mountains on the borders of Chiapas which Greene himself, astride a mule, rode that winter on his way to Las Casas, where the churches were still standing but where priests were prohibited. The world was on the threshold of World War II, the Pope was dying, and Greene was suffering from dysentery. A libel action had been brought against him by Shirley Temple for remarks he had made in a film review that appeared in "Night and Day." The case was settled but he still feared that he might be arrested on his return to England. He stayed two months longer, at which time he accumulated material for this fascinating novel, one of his finest achievements.

"The Power and the Glory" (1940) is a simple drama in which two human beings, with wholly different aims, confront each other: the whisky priest (unnamed) and the police lieutenant (also unnamed). The book's American title was "The Labyrinthine Ways," a phrase from Francis Thompson's well-known poem "The Hound of Heaven," which dramatizes the relentless hunt of Christ for the renegade sinner. The novel is one of pursuit, escape, and finally capture and death.

The priest, conscious that he is in mortal sin for having fathered a child, continues as best he can as the only surviving minister of the Church in the churchless state of Tabasco to hear confessions, to baptize, and even to say Mass. The lieutenant is dedicated to wiping out what he regards as ignorance, superstition, and exploitation. The priest in his flight meets peons, policemen, children, the English dentist, the little girl of the English owner of a banana plantation, a good-hearted American Lutheran couple, the Lehrs, and people in prison. These encounters do not affect his life in any way. He persists in his determination to bring the sacraments to the oppressed people, even though he is in the state of mortal sin.

The narrative begins with the priest waiting to go aboard the steamer which leaves for Vera Cruz every few weeks. He is in a shabby suit and he has discarded his altarstone. He is sheltered in a banana shed by Coral Fellows, the twelve-year old daughter of the plantation manager. Meanwhile the lieutenant of police plans to hunt him down and obtains permission from his chief to take a hostage from each village and shoot them if his whereabouts are not disclosed.

The priest revisits the village where the woman lives

who has borne his daughter. He sees the daughter, a pathetic little creature, too old for her years and in danger of early corruption. The lieutenant and soldiers arrive after he has said Mass but the villagers do not betray him. He makes off for his birthplace and on the way is joined by a mestizo (half-caste) who, he suspects, intends to sell him to the police. He escapes and goes to the capital of the state, Las Casas. There he must surreptitiously obtain wine for communion; this is a dry as well as a godless state. A man professing to be the cousin of the governor sells him wine and brandy for his last pesos. He has to offer a drink to the chief of police and his friends in his hotel room where the alcohol has been provided. In a ludicrous and pathetic scene they drink the wine away. Drunk on brandy he is picked up by the Red Shirts (the atheistic vigilantes) and spends a hideous night in prison but is released in the morning, undetected by the lieutenant.

After a dreadful journey he escapes over the mountains into the neighboring state. On the way he finds the dead body of a child who has been shot by an American gangster on the run. With the child's mother he buries the body in an Indian cemetery. Across the border of the state he is nursed and sheltered by the American Lutheran brother and sister, the Lehrs. He is able to celebrate Mass openly and to baptize and hear confessions.

He prepares to leave for Las Casas, but at his departure the mestizo reappears with the story that the gringo, the American gangster, is mortally wounded and, since he is Catholic, the priest must go back across the border to hear his confession. Not deceived by his betrayer but unwilling to neglect the possibility of a duty to the dying man he goes with the mestizo. He reaches the American who dies without confessing and soon afterwards the lieutenant and his men close in and arrest the priest. That night he has a conversation with the lieutenant who feels a grudging respect for him. The priest is executed in the morning, and although in the eyes of the official church he is a sinner, a drunken coward who had been unable to keep the rules of his faith and even had a bastard child from one of his parishioners, the conclusion is that he is a good, and even holy, man. The following night a new priest, also unnamed, arrives in the town to continue the work of the dead whisky priest.

The novel is Greene's first attempt at integrating theology (the priest) and politics (the lieutenant), even though the two are at opposite extremes and mortal enemies. The setting for the conflict is far more appealing than that of "Brighton Rock." An environment or society enduring religious persecution is far more congenial to theological debate than an oceanfront with holidaymakers and racetrack bettors. Also the novel is a journey, always attractive to readers, which is a standard metaphor for spiritual self-discovery.

One of the major theological points that Greene makes in the novel is that in a priest the man is separate from his office, so that despite being corrupt, or even damned, he can still put God into the mouths of men. The priest explains this to the lieutenant and that the same cannot be said for the so-called 'religion' of politics and socialism. The secular ideals of the political party are founded entirely on man's capacity for good, and thus can be irreparably damaged by the weakness or corruption of the individuals. When the priest is arrested and the two of them have a discussion, the priest says: "That's another difference between us. It's no good your working for your end unless you're a good man yourself. And there won't always be good men in your party. Then you'll have all the old starvation, beating, get-rich-anyhow. But it doesn't matter my being a coward—and all the rest. I can put God into a man's mouth just the same—and I can give him God's pardon. It wouldn't make any difference to that if every priest in the Church was like me." (We see here that Greene's whisky priest is no Donatist, a heresy that Augustine had to grapple with during his life as a prelate. See the chapter on Augustine in this volume.)

The novel continues with its ironies and paradoxes. The lieutenant's compassion for the poor is contrasted to the heartless and uncharitable piety of several of the religious characters, including the pious women the priest meets, especially the pious mother of the boy Luis. She reads aloud to Luis the fictional life of the saint, Juan, from a book filled with smug holiness and spiritual self-satisfaction. It only buttresses Luis' hate for the whisky priest, since quite obviously, the two, Juan and the unnamed priest, are being contrasted.

So Greene here is dealing with the complex issue of an antagonist in the plot who has admirable and sometimes enviable qualities. The Lieutenant is committed, he is obedient to his superiors, and there is no reason given in the novel to suspect that he is not sincere about his politics. And his extreme position as a socialist may have come from the fact that the Church in this society never did deal adequately with the problem of the poor and disenfranchised. He more than likely sees himself as representative of a State that will bring a better life situation to the people, indeed compensating for the Church's neglect. We all know that State failed far more miserably than the Church did, but the Lieutenant does not know that at the time.

As a newly ordained priest the protagonist had had an affluent parish and was as comfortable and complacent as any. His spiritual journey from a similarly naive piety towards true unconditional love reaches its climax at the moment of his greatest degradation: the first night he spends in the prison cell, having been arrested for drinking alcohol forbidden under the new prohibition laws. This is the central scene in the book and one of the most effective passages Greene has ever written.

The priest, who is disguised as a peasant, is thrown

into a common cell with criminals and prostitutes, who urinate and fornicate in the darkness around him. It is in this setting that the priest finally loses his pride and learns instead the power of love and humility; it is here that he learns his true identity. It was John of the Cross who taught in his "The Dark Night of the Soul" that one must reach the pits of degradation before the ascent. With this Walpurgist Nacht, the whisky priest realizes what an unbearable priest he must have been as a young man and comparatively innocent. It seemed that venial sins, sins of little consequence, were of equal culpability as the worst sins of all. Ironically, in his innocence, he had felt no love for anyone; now in his corruption he had learned humility and love, those qualities that make saints. Peguy taught that the sinner is at the very heart of Christianity and closest to the sinner is the saint, and indeed here they are one and the same person. Flannery O'Connor was one day to remark that many people detest the Roman Catholic Church because the Church is always on the side of the sinner. In his youth the priest had been without sin, but also without love. Later, when he is full of sin and totally corrupted, his capacity for love is astounding.

When the priest is back in prison awaiting his execution, in a prayerful dialogue he bargains with God, offering his soul for damnation if the soul of his illegitimate daughter, Brigitta, who even as a child is seen to be corrupt and sinful, can be saved. "Damn me, I deserve it, but let her live for ever." The bargain is seen as a measure of the priest's power of love, the same intense love that Christ taught, "greater love hath no man than this that he lay down his soul for his friend."

The role of the boy Luis is important for the novel's final resolution. Luis admires the police lieutenant and hates the pious propaganda stories read to him by his mother. However, after witnessing the martyrdom of the whisky priest, whom his mother despised, Luis changes his allegiance and it is he who at the end of the novel welcomes the new fugitive priest into his house—the priest who will carry on the solitary and illegal ministry. Just before his death, the whisky priest feels the immense disappointment about going to God with nothing to show for it. However, it is Luis' conversion, unknown to him, which suggests that this is not in fact the case, that despite his miserable example of sinfulness as a priest he has touched the hearts of people and brought them to God.

"The Heart of the Matter" (1948) introduces us to Scobie, the Roman Catholic English policeman, who is stationed in a godforsaken backwater of colonial West Africa. The constant allusions to the oppressive heat, the humidity, the mosquitoes, flies, rats, overall filth and odor create the symbolic landscape that accompanies Scobie's descent into total failure. Major Scobie no longer loves his wife Louise who has become neurotic after the death of their child and further irritated at Scobie's being passed over for a promotion. He feels pity for her and must secure money to enable her to go to South Africa where she can be happier. It is wartime and there is a good deal of diamond smuggling from the interior to neutral ships passing through the port. Wilson, a new commercial clerk, is really an undercover intelligence agent sent to investigate the smuggling. He becomes romantically involved with Louise who finds him a comfort from boredom since they can discuss poetry together. Actually it is Scobie that he is investigating. Scobie goes to search a Portuguese ship in the harbor and finds a letter from the captain to his daughter in Germany. The letter's content is innocuous but Scobie destroys it to save the sentimental captain from losing the right of entry to the port if his offence against regulations is discovered. The episode, although unimportant, is the beginning of Scobie's descent into lawlessness for the sake of pity.

Scobie is refused a bank loan for his wife's trip so he turns to the dubiously honest Syrian trader, Yusef, who is suspected of smuggling and who has often offered Scobie favors that he has rejected. He then investigates the suicide of Pemberton, a young District Commissioner, who was in debt to a shopkeeper who was an employee of Yusef. Scobie visits the local Catholic priest with whom he discusses suicide and divine retribution, which of course is the central moral issue of the novel. Scobie feels that God would forgive Pemberton because he was young, unformed, and inexperienced, "Even the Church can't teach me that God doesn't pity the young." Also God would forgive the sentimental captain because he loved his daughter.

The novel is divided into three books. At the end of the first book, Scobie has acquired enough money to send his wife away. At the beginning of the second book Scobie visits the survivors of a torpoedoed boat and meets Helen Roth who has lost her husband in the open boat. He helps her, they become friends and then lovers. Scobie writes a letter expressing his love for her and it is intercepted by Yusef's servant boy. Yusef uses the letter for blackmail. It is at this time that Louise returns.

The third section of the novel has Louise insisting that Scobie go to communion with her. In the confessional, Fr. Rank refuses him absolution since he will not resolve to give up his adultery. In an effort to insure the happiness of both women, and to keep up appearances, he receives communion with the clear knowledge of his damnation. His betrayal of God coincides with his corruption as a policeman: he delivers diamonds to Yusef and in the ensuing transfer, Ali, Scobie's trusted servant, is killed. Scobie, convinced his life is a failure, finds himself in the conscience-striken situation of seeing himself as betraying his servant, betraying the two women to whom he failed to bring happiness, and of betraying God. He plans for his suicide. He takes an overdose of pills, sits at his desk with a crucifix before him, and begins saying "Dear God, I love . . ." and falls to the floor.

To say the least, the novel is problematic, especially the

controversial ending which introduces Greene's customary moral paradox, Scobie's act of atonement is one and the same with the supreme act of despair, suicide. For years after its publication in 1948, the fate of Scobie was discussed by novelists and critics alike. Is he in Heaven or Hell? There is that wonderful story (I wish I could find verification for it.) of Evelyn Waugh being asked in an airport by a reporter where he thought Scobie is now. Waugh shot back, "In hell. Where do you think he is?" It is interesting to note that much the same type query surrounded Pinkie in "Brighton Rock." Was his jump from the cliff a suicide? Maybe not. But if so, did he whisper a final word of repentance? Did he say "Dear God, I love . . ." in his final moments? There is that possibility when we speak in terms of the holy sinner.

If we accept the theory of the holy sinner, then "The Heart of the Matter" belongs with the two previous books. First the depraved criminal in "Brighton Rock" who, despite deterministic social circumstances, at least experiences the passage of holiness; then the ordinary sinner in "The Power and the Glory" whom God and circumstances compel into sainthood; and finally Scobie, in "The Heart of the Matter" a good and honest man who sins to avert pain in others and sins out of pity for the sufferings of others.

Scobie is undoubtedly a good man, an honest man who is corrupted not by money or power but by sentiment and a sense of responsibility for the happiness of others, which leads him to the extreme of wishing to damn himself not so that others will be saved, as was the case with the whisky priest, but so that they will not suffer in this world. He cannot bear the sight of another's pain and what is ironic is that he himself is the instrument that causes pain. He is caught in an emotional dilemma which can only be solved by betraying and therefore hurting either Louise, his wife, or Helen, his lover.

Scobie's strange sense of pity leads him to blasphemy when, in writing a note to Helen sparing her from pain, he assures her that he loves her more than he loves God; and in protecting Louise from the truth he goes to communion with her even though he is in the state of mortal sin. Even God becomes a victim of Scobie's pity, for his final decision to kill himself is as much due to wishing to spare God further suffering as to spare Louise and Helen further unhappiness.

Scobie's sense of pity and responsibility is a form of spiritual egotism which of course is pride. He is not only his brother's keeper but petends to be God's keeper as well. Critics have judged Scobie to be a moral failure, an inferior person, a self-destructive neurotic. Another described him as a lover who loved too well but not wisely. The final pages of the novel are important but seem placed there as an afterthought. Louise, his wife, concerned that Scobie has committed the unpardonable sin of suicide, goes to the priest, Father Rank, who sums up in the manner of the old priest in "Brighton Rock" whom Rose went to in the end. Father Rank says, "The Church knows all the rules. But it doesn't know what goes on in a single human heart." He adds that he thinks Scobie really loved God and when Louise breaks out bitterly, "He certainly loved no one else," he replies that she may after all be right.

Of all Greene's novels, this is the one he disliked the most. His original intention in writing the novel was to show that such intense pity, or even self-pity, was a form of pride that leads to despair. Maybe he felt that he had failed in this narrative undertaking since Scobie had become a much-beloved protagonist to some readers while to others he was a damned fool. Maybe his dislike for the book was due to the fact that his "The Power and the Glory" had just been put on the list of forbidden books by the Vatican; he didn't need any more grief.

"The End of the Affair" (1951) has for its setting London in the war years and immediately afterwards. The peculiar atmosphere, especially of the period of the blitz when ordinary life and personal relations co-existed with sudden death, is brilliantly evoked in Greene's "London Journal" based on his experience as an air raid warden at a post in Bloomsbury. Greene's narrator in the novel is Maurice Bendrix, a novelist who is also an air raid warden in the blitz. He cultivates the friendship of Henry Miles, a civil servant, because he wants to put a civil servant into his next book. He and Henry's wife Sarah become lovers and she visits him in his house opposite theirs on the other side of Clapham Commons. During one of the first flying bomb raids in the summer of 1944 they are together and Bendrix is buried under the front door but only slightly grazed. Sarah makes a vow that if Bendrix lives she will believe in God and she will give up her lover forever. She keeps the vow and avoids him.

Insanely jealous, Bendrix can only think that she has gone with another man. He hires a private detective to watch her, and a fragment of a letter salvaged from her wastepaper basket seems to confirm his suspicions. The message of the letter can easily be interpreted that she is in love with another but that is not the case. She is making weekly visits to a man named Smythe who lives with his sister in a neighboring house and has a hideous birthmark on one side of his face. Bendrix confronts him out of morbid curiosity, going to the house with the private detective Parkis's little boy. Parkis insinuates himself into a party at the Miles's house and manages to purloin Sarah's diary.

The diary is reproduced in full and reveals what really happened. She has kept her promise to God and stays away from Bendrix in unwilling agony. Equally grudgingly she is drawing nearer to God, going into churches and buying a crucifix. Smythe turns out to be a militant atheist of the old school who addresses the crowd on the Common and hands out tracts. Sarah goes to him in the hope of shaking the unwanted faith that is making inroads into her life.

Bendrix is relieved that Sarah has not taken another human lover. He feels competent that he can compete against God in whom he does not believe. He visits her in order to persuade her to go away with him; she escapes from him and enters a church where he follows her. She is tired and already sick from exposure to the cold rain; he agrees to stop badgering her. This is the last time he sees her. A few days later Henry phones him to tell him she has died of pneumonia.

After her death, the two men are drawn closer together (Henry already knows of Sarah's unfaithfulness) and Bendrix goes to live in the Miles house. They learn from a Catholic priest, Father Crompton, that Sarah had been receiving instruction. He had advised her that she must not leave Henry and marry Bendrix, though she desperately wanted to, if she wished to become a Catholic. Bendrix in his bitterness advises Henry against a Christian burial and Sarah's body is cremated. At the cremation Bendrix meets Sarah's mother, Mrs. Bertram, and has dinner with her. He learns from her that she is a lapsed Catholic and had had Sarah baptized, mainly in order to spite her second husband. Now the coincidences that lead to the edge of miracle begin to build up. They involve both the subsidiary persons outside the triangular drama, Smythe and Parkis, the private detective.

Parkis's boy Lance is severely ill with an undefined stomach complaint and running a high temperature. He dreams of Sarah to whom he had become deeply attached and in order to please and calm him Parkis borrows one of her old children's books from Henry. In the morning the fever has gone and the child says that Sarah came and touched him and took the pain away. He also says she had written in the book for him. It remains an open question whether the childish scribble Bendrix reads in the book when it is returned was there before or not.

The other coincidence is much more startling. During Sarah's visits to Smythe he had fallen in love with her. His disgust at his own deformity provides the incentive for his evangelizing rationalism. He confesses this to Sarah and in pity she kisses his deformed cheek. After her death he visits the house and takes away a lock of her hair. Soon afterwards, his face clears up in a single night. At first he is too embarrassed to tell Bendrix when he meets him and pretends that he has had electrical treatments, but later he phones while Bendrix is with Henry entertaining Father Crompton, and tells him the truth.

So the word 'miracle' is never heard though it would have been if Bendrix had continued the phone conversation. But the inference is there and the evidence is greater than that of these two 'cures'. Father Crompton and others speak consistently of Sarah's goodness, and among the others is Parkis who does his job of spying with reluctance, and always contributes the voice of common human decency since Bendrix, the chief witness, is so biased.

Then there is the evidence of Sarah's journal, quite apart from its record of her developing trust in God. Her unselfishness is shown by her staying with Henry when he needs her, against her own happiness and when her suitcase is already packed. She describes her emotion about Smythe as envy, rather than pity, of one who carries the mark of pain around with him reflecting the suffering of Christ. Finally there is something peculiarly selfless and unworldly about Sarah's complete neglect of her own health which brings on her fatal illness. The incidents and her behavior combine to furnish corroborative evidence of supernatural intervention. In the end, Bendrix is still hating but now hating the God he has come to believe in.

The reaction on the part of many Greene fans to this new work was mixed. Many felt that the theological aspects were not subtle or nuanced enough. The novel which begins as a story of a love affair becomes the story of two miracles and sainthood. The curing of the boy's stomach ailment and then the healing of the birthmark, along with a piece of hair as a relic, was pretty heavy-handed for many readers. Yet, the conflict that Sarah experiences is a very credible one. To convince herself that the 'miracle' of Bendrix's survival of the bombing was merely coincidence and the vow was just superstition, she goes to Smythe, the consummate atheist (very much like the baker in "The Hint of an Explanation"), who has an intense intellectual hatred for God and a self-proclaimed mission to convert others to atheism. This flight of Sarah from God is typical of the chase motif and the material in the diary reveals much about her progress in sanctity.

Bendrix, who is the first person narrator of the novel and through whose eyes we sees much of the action, is caught in the end in the web of hating the God he now believes in. He is not too unlike Charles Ryder in the end of Waugh's "Brideshead Revisited," caught up in the working of grace and possible conversion and salvation. In a sense, "The End of the Affair" considered Greene's most Catholic novel, is his most unorthodox. It is the story of sainthood achieved through the sin of adultery.

There are two filmed versions of this book and they make an interesting study in contrasts. The first came out some ten years after World War II and it has a certain immediacy about it, but for the most part it fails because of the weakness of the actors portraying Bendrix and Sarah, Van Johnson and Deborah Kerr. The second version came out in 1999 with Ralph Fiennes and Julianne Moore. It was very well done with fine acting, excellent cinematography, and a credible reconciliation of the problem of faith and miracles with the novel's realism. Jake Heggie's new opera based on the Greene novel, composed in 2003, was commissioned by the Houston Grand Opera Co and has been generating quite a bit of attention since its premier.

"The Quiet American" (1955), Greene's 'Vietnam novel' dramatizes the necessity of disloyalty in the face of a destructive idealism. The novel opens and closes with the political assassination of an idealistic young American official led by Mr. Heng. What comes in between is the reconstruction, in Fowler's mind, of the events leading up to the murder.

Pyle and Fowler represent opposite values between innocence and experience, idealism and realism. Pyle has come to the war in Vietnam full of idealism and zeal about the political situation in that country—in particular, the need for an arbitrator in the struggle. He is, however, extremely naïve and is responsible for more harm than good. With his government's backing he finds, and finances, this arbitrator in an unscrupulous General The, whose first action is to explode a bicycle bomb in a crowded square, killing and wounding a number of innocent people. It is at this point that Fowler, a typical Greene reticent protagonist, and who has been deliberately uninvolved, feels he must act to prevent Pyle from putting any more of his policies into action, and he cooperates with Heng in the planning of the murder of Pyle. To compound the conflict is the fact that Pyle has recently robbed Fowler of his Annamite mistress, Phuong.

The main theme of the novel is commitment. Pyle, through his commitment to rectifying the situation by a form of democratic action, becomes a messianic figure enforcing the responsibilities of the West. Fowler, on the other hand, has washed his hands of politics and has resolved himself to non-involvement. He learns, however, that one cannot absolve himself of personal responsibility when innocent and harmless people are victims of evil.

The central scene of the book is the night Fowler and Pyle pass together in the watertower, hiding from Vietminh snipers, with two frightened Vietnamese peasant soldiers. The suspenseful scene reminds the reader of the remarkable exchange between the whisky priest and the police lieutenant in "The Power and the Glory" as they express their conflicting ideologies. This is interrupted by an attack of the snipers at which time they manage to escape with

Pyle saving Fowler's life. At this point Fowler becomes aware of a wounded soldier crying in the dark and realizes he must assist in alleviating another's pain and suffering. "I made an effort to get over the bank into the road. I wanted to join him. It was the only thing I could do, to share his pain." It is this succession of events that leads Fowler to "hate war" and ultimately to become involved by collaborating in the murder of Pyle.

The novel branded Greene as anti-American, although eventually with the passing of time, he was seen as having foresight. It has all the thriller aspects of his early experiments in intrigue and espionage. The first film made of the book in 1958 was unfaithful to the text with all kinds of changes which made the American look better. The second film, done in 2003, was far more realistic and closer to the author's intent. I recall a stranger leaving the cinema and turning to me and saying, "You know, we are going through the same thing all over again." I suspect he was referring to American involvement in Iraq. If Greene were living today, we can be sure he would produce something about the political situation in the world today. "The Quiet American" is the best of his group of novels dealing with British and American involvement in foreign political affairs. It has one of his favorite themes, the betrayal, indeed the painful betrayal of someone who has saved the betrayer's life. And it gives us the reluctant hero who is compelled to become involved in order to alleviate pain and suffering.

"Our Man in Havana" (1958) is one of Greene's 'entertainments' but with a difference. The thriller aspect is there but it is all very funny. The setting is the corrupt Batista regime with the Castro rebels waiting in the mountains. Wormold, a vacuum salesman in Havana, allows himself to be recruited as a British secret agent in order to provide some extra money for his much loved and extravagant daughter Milly. He sends bogus reports based on a book code taken from Lamb's "Tales from

Shakespeare." After a time his scheme rebounds on him. He has supplied imaginary plans of military installments based on vacuum cleaner designs. An unspecified hostile agency becomes interested in the names of real persons he has given in his reports. His friend, the ex-Prussian officer Dr. Hasselbacher, and others are killed, and he himself is in danger. He enters into the stream of events and revenges Dr. Hasselbacher by killing his assassin. He is not acting for the British Secret Service or for any other organization but to assert his individuality. "If I love or if I hate, let me love or hate as an individual. I will not be 59200/5 in anyone's global war." However, ironically enough, the authorities reward him and he happily marries his secretary.

What is significant in this truly entertaining novel, which has rapid pace and great satirical humor, is the importance of the moment of transition from ordinary life to a world of danger and violence; Greene describes it in terms of crossing a frontier, and of course it echoes the trauma of the green baize door in the 'childhood' fiction. Also, once again the innocent man, reluctant to become involved, demonstrates his power to create havoc, but this time he collects himself to meet the challenge and goes some way to redeem the harm he has caused. As with Fowler, it is an individual commitment, not a service to a particular cause, that Wormold finds he must choose. The novel combines exciting satire on the exploits of the British secret service with wry commentary on Fulgencio Batista's decadent Cuba and its stupid bureaucracy.

The film version of this book with Alec Guinness and Noel Coward was faithful to the novel's satiric humor. It expressed Greene's support of a Castro take-over and looked at the Khruschev-Dulles, Batista-Eisenhower world situation in absurd terms.

In "A Burnt-Out Case" (1961) Querry, who was once part of the Catholic establishment, has lost his faith in God. Because of this emotional and spiritual crisis he goes to a remote African leper colony where he joins a group of missionaries experiencing great difficulties in ministering to the physical and spiritual needs of the lepers. The priests at the colony are assisted by Dr. Colin, an atheist, yet a man of great humanity and compassion. During his stay among the lepers, Querry rediscovers a reason for living by joining the doctor and the fathers in their work. However, near the colony lives Rycker, a frustrated man who once aspired to become a priest and now harbors great bitterness because of his failure. Querry feels sorry for Rycker's lonely, frustrated wife, Marie, and tries to help her tolerate her abusive husband. Rycker, however, although at first impressed by Querry, now suspects him of having had an affair with his wife, and the novel ends with Rycker arriving at the leper colony in a state of fury, armed with a gun. Querry laughs at the absurdity of the misunderstanding, but Rycker, thinking he is laughing at him, shoots and kills him.

In this novel, the setting acts as a metaphor for the protagonist's spiritual and emotional atrophy. Like one of the burnt-out lepers whose stage of the disease is such that mutilation is the only recourse for relief from pain, Querry is spiritually mutilated by his crisis of faith but finds in this environment of misery goodness and charity which help him recover. As his name suggests Querry is a man who asks questions of life concerning its meaning and in the characters of Rycker, Dr. Colin, Father Thomas, and the priests, he finds various states of belief and disbelief. Rycker and Father Thomas are extremist Catholics and Father Thomas inflicts his own psychological problems on Querry who has enough of them already. The other priests in the colony are exemplary and become an inspiration for Querry as he begins to move away from his state of emptiness to one of recovery. But it is Dr. Colin, the atheist, who truly understands Querry's spiritual dilemma better than anyone else at the colony. Despite his atheism, he is religious in his concern for man and in his understanding of man's spiritual state. It is Father Thomas with his text book theology and Rycker, the failed priest, who fabricate the adulterous affair between his wife with Querry. They abrogate Dr. Colin's and the priests' influence on Querry. Rycker, the evil force, interferes in Querry's life and destroys it.

"The Comedians" (1966) opens with a prologue on board the Medea, a ship bringing the four central characters, Mr. and Mrs. Smith, Mr. Brown, and Major Jones, from the United States to Haiti, the poorest country in the Western hemisphere and at the time ruled over by the ruthless dictator 'Papa Doc' Duvalier. Under this regime there are no human rights; constitutional laws have been suspended; and people live in the fear of his secret police, the Tontons Macoute, who with their black sunglasses deal in mindless brutality. (In the 1960s Haiti was one of Greene's political interests; he visited the country several times and witnessed the brutality.) The names Smith, Brown, and Jones are significant. Like the initials in "The Confidential Agent" and the nameless protagonist and antagonist in "The Power and the Glory" the names serve to universalize the situation, showing no particular time or place, but emphasizing the tragic situation.

Mr. and Mrs. Smith are going to Haiti for the first time and have no idea of the horrors that await them. They are innocent Americans and wholly committed to their belief in vegetarianism. They want to open a vegetarian centre since they feel that the main source of the society's woes is eating meat. The Smiths attempt to do so much good, but they are stunned at the corruption of the officials who offer them a grant for the centre which the officials have no intention of honoring honestly. The reader genuinely admires their sincerity as naïve as it is.

Brown, the narrator of the novel, is middle aged and rootless, totally uninvolved and uncommitted, like Fowler in "The Quiet American." He is returning to Haiti to look after the Trianon, a hotel left him by his mother, the Countess, and which she has been trying unsuccessfully to sell in New York. He is also returning to a dying love affair with Martha, the wife of a South American ambassador and daughter of a Nazi war criminal.

Major Jones is an ex-actor who boasts not only a false military record, but a false record of heroism in the war. Actually he was rejected from military service because of flat feet. He is a con man who has come entirely for self-interest, to plan an arms deal with the officials whom he knows are corrupt. The volatile world of Haitian politics is so unstable that his attempt to swindle the government backfires and he is forced to take refuge in the embassy with Martha and her husband. As fraudulent as he is the reader likes him because he is truly funny.

When Brown returns to the hotel he finds the dead body of Dr. Philipot, the ex-Secretary of State for Social Welfare, who has taken his own life because he has fallen out of favor with the existing regime. The suicide in his pool gets him involved in politics, however reluctant he is. He does eventually join a revolutionary group founded by Philipot's son but for personal interests not ideological ones. He suspects that Jones is having an affair with Martha and Brown is determined to expose him for the phony military man that he is.

All the characters are important in this novel, and it is through Brown's eyes that we see all the action. He feels that God is the ultimate joker who has made the world a humorless comedy, or better still a black comedy, with actors and actresses ('comedians') acting out their lives in absurd fashion. Again commitment is the novel's central theme and the 'comedians' are Brown and Jones, who have no true commitment, although they pretend or act as if they do. As a matter of fact, they avoid their true selves. On the other hand, the Smiths, with all their eccentricities about vegetarianism and their comic ridiculousness, are not 'comedians.' The Smiths are comedians only in their bizarre ways, not in anything important like commitment. When Mr. Smith says, "Perhaps we seem rather comic figures to you, Mr. Brown, the answer is not comic . . . heroic." Their dedication to vegetarianism is a laughable substitute for true faith, but at least they are sincere in their belief. At least they have commitment.

Greene was up front about "The Comedians." He asserted that the book is written from a particular partisan viewpoint, "to fight the horror of Papa Doc's dictatorship." It is a scathing commentary on the conditions in Duvalier's Haiti, the poorest country in the Western hemisphere at that time (the 1960s) ruled by the world's most ruthless dictator. Greene had a genuine interest in Haiti and a strong criticism of American foreign policy underlies the story, a criticism aimed mainly at U.S. fear of having a Communist state in its back yard. The State Department saw Papa Doc as a force against communism, and was therefore supportive of him. No one can ignore the scathing irony of the Smiths, representative of America, setting up a vegetarian centre in Haiti because the people, many of whom are starving to death, eat too much meat. It certainly implies that American foreign aid policy is a farce.

The priest who appears at the end of the novel (priests seem to show up at the end of most of Greene's novels) delivers a liberationist sermon to the survivors of Santo Domingo. He is a liberationist, part of the originally South American movement of Liberation theology which links the teachings of the gospels with political involvement, as taught by Gustavo Gutierrez. Christ's message, according to the liberationists, is political and social as well as spiritual, intended to disturb the powerful and give hope to the powerless. This Haitian priest is one of those rare instances in Greene where the priest adequately rises to the occasion.

He preaches on St. Thomas the Apostle's words "Let us

go up to Jerusalem and die with him." by saying, "The Church is in the world, it is part of the suffering in the world, and though Christ condemned the disciple who struck off the ear of the high priest's servant, our hearts go out in sympathy to all who are moved to violence by the suffering of others. The Church condemns violence, but it condemns indifference more harshly. Violence can be the expression of love, indifference never. One is an imperfection of charity, the other the perfection of egoism. In the days of fear, doubt, and confusion, the simplicity and loyalty of one apostle advocated a political solution. He was wrong, but I would rather be wrong with St. Thomas than right with the cold and the craven. Let us go up to Jerusalem and die with him."

This literary denunciation of the Haitian government had a direct political effect. Duvalier brought an action against Greene in the French courts and was awarded one franc damages. He also, in 1967, issued an official pamphlet accusing Greene of all manner of perversities, including drug addiction. The incident is significant because it exhibits a twentieth-century writer making effective protest against tyranny. It proves that the pen can be used as a sword. Greene was a strong believer that good writing, being truth speaking, has a function in the public world.

"Travels with My Aunt" (1969) is a novel in which Greene's wonderful powers of pure comedy is dominant. Henry Pulling, as he begins retirement and old age, is liberated at the eleventh hour from a lifetime of conventionality and boredom by his outrageous, Auntie Mame-like, life-loving septuagenarian aunt. In the rough process of liberation Henry discovers not only that she is his mother, but that her lifestyle, of which he had disapproved, is at leas preferable to the empty bland respectability of his own life as a bank manager. Their adventures together also enable Aunt Augusta to tell Henry her life story, and thus a series of vignettes in the present are interspersed with a series of vignettes from the past giving the book a picaresque flavor.

Henry and Augusta represent two opposing attitudes to life in some of the most hilarious dialogue Greene ever wrote. Augusta's pursuit of love and amusement, and her determined liberation of Henry constitute a celebration of individualism, as opposed to dull conformity. Henry is one of Greene's long list of reluctant heroes who gets dragged into the world not of politics and violence, but of sexuality and law breaking, marijuana and tobacco smuggling. He begins to enjoy the incursion of the world into his own world, and half way through the novel when he leaves Augusta for a life of quiet retirement he realizes the emptiness of his life. He again seizes the bid for freedom. Through his aunt he sees his past life as a prison and he frees himself from it and his negative sense of morality. He is elated at being alive, as was Wormold in "Our Man in Havana." The journey theme, turned upside down, is an adventure in fun and hilarity. The film of the book in 1972 with Maggie Smith, Alex McCowan, and Robert Stephens captured the madcap eccentricities of Augusta and the whirlwind pace of the European travels and despite the miscasting of Alec McCowan, who was too old for Pulling, the film was a popular success.

"The Honorary Consul" (1973) is as so often with Greene about commitment and in it he fuses the various forms of commitment—political, religious, and emotional. Greene's epigraph from Thomas Hardy is, "All things merge into one another—good into evil, generosity into justice, religion into politics."

The novel is set in Corrientes, a small town in northern Argentina, near the border of Paraguay. Again as in "The Comedians" the action revolves around three main characters: Dr. Eduardo Plarr, Father Leon Rivas, and Charley Fortnum, the Honorary British Consul. Plarr, a middle-aged doctor, is indifferent., like Greene's Querry,

Fowler, and Brown. He is incapable of any form of commitment, be it religious, political, or emotional. Typical of a Greene reticent protagonist, he becomes reluctantly involved by helping an amateurish group of Paraguayan Marxist freedom fighters in their attempt to kidnap the American Ambassador to Argentina. Plarr's motives for helping them are mainly personal: the group is led by his old schoolfriend, Leon Rivas, a liberationist priest who has sided with the poor and the oppressed to the extent that he has taken up arms in the struggle for their liberation; also, the freedom of Plarr's English father, a political prisoner in Paraguay, is part of the exchange deal demanded by the kidnappers (though this is a trick on Plarr, for the kidnappers know that his father is in fact dead).

The guerrillas in their ineptitude kidnap and seize by mistake the Honorary Consul, Charles Fortnum. He is a listless character, an alcoholic farmer, who has found new reason for living in his love for Clara, a whore whom he has married and who is, unknown to him, Plarr's pregnant mistress. In the end both Plarr and Fortnum are trapped in a hut with guerrillas who refuse to believe what is in fact the truth, that the British Government will gladly sacrifice Fortnum in order to make a show of firmness in not giving in to the terrorists. The kidnappers announce their intention of killing Fortnum if their demands are not met, but before then the police discover the hideout and arrest Fortnum, killing in the process Plarr, Rivas, Aquino and the other guerrillas—all of whom, and especially Rivas, are good men.

This brief outline of the plot cannot convey the structural richness of this mature and accomplished novel, nor the depth and range of the characters. This, like "The Human Factor," was written in Greene's mature years and he considered it his best work. It contains all the familiar themes that we have come to expect from the novelist. The theme of political commitment and the political duty of a Christian in an unjust society is even more to the fore here than in

"The Comedians." And the liberationist priest here is further developed because he is one of the main characters; his prominence here makes him a very telling subject of dramatic contrast with the whisky priest in "The Power and the Glory." The Church of the 1940s when Greene introduced us to the renegade priest became a far different Church from that of Father Rivas in post-conciliar 1973. And one has to assume that Greene was very satisfied with what had happened. Just as Catholicism underwent great changes and matured under a series of five pontiffs so did Greene in scope, style, and subject matter.

"The Human Factor" (1978) is about espionage and spies, people who happen to be spies and not about spying itself. They are dull commuters, unhappy, aging divorcees, middle-class bureaucrats, or careerists without ideals, The novel is about the human factor in the lives of the people in this line of work. Greene's portrayal of day-to-day espionage in the office scenes, between dull, contented Castle and his restless, bored colleague Davis, is one of unglamorous and tedious routine. One thinks immediately of John Le Carre.

A security leak is discovered in a small sub-section of SIS dealing with African affairs. Of the two suspects, Maurice Castle is ruled out by Dr. Percival, the sinister and ruthless senior officer in charge of the investigation, because although he is an excellent office worker, Castle is too dull to be a double agent, and too close to retirement. Castle's young colleague Davis, on the other hand, seems to be a classic suspect: intelligent, restless, and with a life style seemingly beyond his income. On the basis of little more than a hunch, Percival concludes that Davis is the mole and decides that yet another security scandal would be damaging to the Service and that therefore Davis should be quietly eliminated. Davis, however, is entirely innocent and it is Castle who has been feeding the classified information to the Soviets over a number of years. He has done this not out of any ideological support for the Soviet cause, but because his black South African wife Sarah, and her son Sam, were both aided in their escape from the South African security forces by a Communist friend, and Castle's only means of repaying the debt of gratitude he owed him was by passing information to his Russian master.

After Davis is murdered, and after Castle has fallen into a trap set by Percival, Castle realizes that he has been discovered and escapes to Moscow with the help of the KGB and of Halliday, a Communist bookshop owner who has been Castle's contact in the field. In making his escape Castle is forced to leave behind Sarah and Sam, on the understanding that they will follow on afterwards. But they are refused passports by the vengeful Home Office. In Moscow Castle has learned the same and the book ends with a desperately frustrated telephone conversation between husband and wife in which they exchange unconvincing hopes for reunion in the future until the line goes dead.

It is interesting that "The Human Factor," his last really major work, takes place for the most part in Berkhamsted, where Greene had grown up as a boy, had the experience of the green baize door, became convinced that innocence can become consumed by evil forces, and where he played at spies on the Common. There are noticeably autobiographical elements in the novel and often there are recurrences of situations and events that have occurred in the early works. Some critics have seen the book as self-parody which is a charge I feel simply does not hold up. Greene is using many of his themes, such as treachery and betrayal and certainly the transition from innocence to experience, in such a mature manner, fashioning them into a whole new construct. Just as Father Rivas of the 70s is seen in a whole different light from the whisky priest of the 40s, so too the theme of treachery and betrayal is presented in a much more mature fashion for the audience of the late 70s.

"Dr. Fischer of Geneva or the Bomb Party" (1980) is the longest of Greene's short stories which was published as a volume and requires some consideration here. He called it a 'black entertainment.' It is unlike anything that Greene ever wrote and it makes a reader wonder if Greene had lived longer and continued to write, would this be a new direction in his fiction. There are any number of characters in the story but the protagonist, Dr. Fischer, is a figure of the most chilling cruelty. He has made millions by Dentophil Bouquet, a tooth paste which keeps at bay the infections caused by eating too much Swiss chocolate. His home is in Switzerland and he maintains a certain neutrality towards all human affections. His wife has found affection and a shared love with a clerk called Steiner. Dr. Fischer breaks up the relationship, has Steiner dismissed from his job, and hounds and nags his wife to her death from misery and neglect. He has one daughter who marries a clerk but they live without any support from the father. Dr. Fischer surrounds himself with "toadies" whom he delights in teasing and tormenting at his famous parties while he plays on their greed with luxurious presents and the promise of more to come. These parties are the occasion for every kind of humiliation and insult to the guests, which they accept for sheer greed. Dr. Fischer sees God in his own image as a giver of presents, bribes in between the endless humiliations he inflicts on the human person

There is a last party to which all the toads are invited and at which time Dr. Fischer shows absolutely no emotion whatsoever. It is Christmas and there is snow on the ground and the dinner is held outside by a large fire. There is a Christmas cracker for each guest to be taken from a tub and each cracker but one contains wrapped round its paper motto a cheque on Credit Suisse for two million francs. The remaining cracker, declares Dr. Fischer, contains a lethal device. But Dr. Fischer has the last joke: there are cheques for all, but no bomb. At the end of the party, Steiner who feels so disgusted by all that has happened, feels that he must deliver the final insult to the great insulter, Fischer. "Now, I want to get near enough to him to spit in God Almighty's face." But it is too late. Though there was no bomb there is a shot. A hundred yards away they find the body of Dr. Fischer who has blown his brains out.

"Monsignor Quixote" (1982), an imitation of Cervantes, is a picaresque journey along the Spanish roads bringing into being a loose chain of anecdotes and incidents. For the most part it is a dialogue between two men, a priest and a Communist ex-mayor, representing two points of view, two differing twentieth-century attitudes to the human condition.

Greene's Don is a parish priest of a small village in La Mancha. His friend is the communist mayor who bears the same surname as Sancho Panza. The Don, after assisting an Italian bishop with his car, is made a monsignor. His promotion to Monsignor sets off a whole series of adventures. The Don is able to leave his parish now and go on leave, taking with him his friend who has been defeated in the local elections. He drives a little car named Rocinante, the name of knight's horse in the original source. They go to Madrid, Salamanca, Avila and Valladolid; they see the Valley of the Fallen, the grandiose shrine built by Franco for the dead of the Civil War, and the simple sepulchre of the man of letters Miguel de Unamuno. They stay a night in a brothel. The Don does not know where he is and can only say how quiet and well behaved the servants are. This along with the joke about the bidet in the room bring home the Don's priestly innocence. The Don hides an escaping thief in his car and they find themselves in trouble with the police.

As well as the general pattern of knights errantry and the arguments between idealist and materialist, the original Don Quixote provides sources for particular episodes. And as interesting as these parallels are, the conversation between the Catholic and the Communist is central to the thematic structure. The conversations explore the relationship between religious belief and political commitment, features that have been part of Greene's work from his earliest days. Sancho argues for a political, historical remedy to the problems of human society. He is a rationalist humanist who sees the root cause of the problem in social injustice and the only solution is in the practical application of Marxist theory. Monsignor Quixote, on the other hand, has no confidence in anything but the power of faith and prayer, and in the reward of eternal life beyond this world. But as they travel together and continue to converse, both begin to become insecure in their respective beliefs and their growing doubts serve to bring them closer together. (This is a far gentler relationship than that of the whisky priest and the police lieutenant in "The Power and the Glory.")

As Monsignor approaches death and in his delirium celebrates Mass, he shows that his dream of understanding and reconciling the two faiths has been achieved. He consecrates an imaginary host and presents it to the Communist, whom he addresses as 'comrade,' and Sancho accepts. The mayor's motive for accepting the host from the Monsignor was love for his friend, and through this love he is brought back to God despite himself. It is a beautiful story giving us Greene in one of his gentler moments. A wonderful television adaptation was made of it in 1991 with Alec Guinness, Ian Richardson, and Leo McKern.

Conclusion

Graham Greene has to be one of the great writers of fiction of our times. This study has concentrated primarily on the novels, giving brief consideration to three short stories as being a microcosm of what is happening in his vast output of short fiction.

His plays include "The Living Room" (1953), "The Potting Shed" (1957), and "The Complaisant Lover" (1959), none of them great financial successes but honorable enough to qualify him as a thought-provoking dramatist. His travel books, describing journeys in Liberia ("Journey without Maps," 1936), Mexico ("The Lawless Roads" 1939), and Africa (In Search of a character: two African journals, 1961) have given vivid background material of the many places in the world he has taken his reader.

His work as journalist stands out for embracing left-wing, liberal causes, often getting him into trouble with leaders of countries who took exception to his politics. Greene was of the generation of Burgess, Maclean, and Philby, and himself served in the intelligence services during the war. He was a friend of Philby of whom he had written an account. ('The Spy', Introduction to Kim Philby, 1968.) His wide range as a writer, geographically, is astounding: London, Liberia, Sierra Leone, the Congo, Haiti, Argentina, Cuba, Belgrade and the stops on the Orient Express, all can provide the young reader with a mini-world tour through fiction.

His thematic interests are not only universal but revert back to the beginning of time: the reluctant hero who can change the world or destroy it, the chase, the pursuer and the pursued, the green baize door of innocence and experience, the corruption of the innocent, treachery and betrayal, and commitment. But his preoccupation with moral dilemma, personal, religious and political, his attempts to distinguish 'good-or-evil' from 'right-or-wrong', and his persistent battle with God and with what Augustine called 'primordial evil' give his work a highly distinctive and recognizable quality.

Greene's heroes carry the scar of a primal wound and he has exposed his own in his autobiographical memoir "A Sort of Life" and elsewhere in his fiction. He is particularly attracted to characters who are on the spiritual borderline, on the fringe of society, (he once used the word 'sleazy' and regretted it), and who embody some form of paradox, such as 'holy atheist,' 'Catholic agnostics,' and 'sinful saints.' Such oxymorons are part of the loyalty and betrayal themes so central to Greene's work.

In his essay on Francois Mauriac, Greene said that with the death of Henry James the religious sense was lost to the English novel. This was a 'disaster' for "with the religious sense went the sense of the importance of the human act." Right to the very end, Graham Greene was concerned with the 'human act'; he never lost his religious sense.

Selected Novels of Greene

The Man Within (1929)
Stamboul Train (1932)
It's a Battlefield (1934)
England Made Me (1935)
A Gun for Sale (1936)
Brighton Rock (1938)
The Confidential Agent (1939)
The Power and the Glory (1940)
The Ministry of Fear (1943)
The Heart of the Matter (1948)
The Third Man (1950)
The End of the Affair (1951)
The Quiet American (1955)
Our Man in Havana (1958)
A Burnt-Out Case (1961)
The Comedians (1966)
Travels with My Aunt (1969)
The Honorary Consul (1973)
The Human Factor (1978)
Dr. Fischer of Geneva or the Bomb Party (1980)
Monsignor Quixote (1982)

Selected Plays

The Living Room (1953)
The Potting Shed (1958)
The Complaisant Lover (1959)

A Sort of Life: Autobiography (1971)

NOTE ON SOURCES

Chaucer's "The Canterbury Tales" is best served for the modern reader by Nevill Coghill's lucid translation of the work into Modern English. Professor Coghill, who died in November 1980, will always be best remembered for this translation. It is clear, understandable, and retains all the nuances, both comic and sad, of the original. Most of my observations here about the tales are from graduate classes I had with Dr. Catherine Dunn and Sr. Emmanuel, OSF at The Catholic University of America. I have used the Norton Anthology of English Literature: Major Authors edition, an ever reliable college text, for its introductory notes to the Chaucer section, and "Masterpieces of World Literature," edited by Frank N. Magill (1989) for the observations on Chaucer as character and Chaucer as narrator in the Tales. Richard West's "Chaucer" (Carroll & Graf Publishers, 2000) is good as popular history. Ruth Margaret Ames' "God's Plenty: Chaucer's Christian Humanism" (Loyola University Press, 1984) is exceptional in placing Chaucer in the context of his times.

I have used "The Complete Pelican Shakespeare," (general editors, Stephen Orgel and A. R. Braunmuller, 2002) for all quotations from the plays. The magnificent "The Oxford Companion to Shakespeare" (edited by Michael Dobson and Stanley Wells, 2003), which covers every aspect of Shakespeare imaginable, is a miracle of scholarship. It is a volume that should be owned by anyone interested in Shakespeare. I have relied on it in discussing details of Shakespeare's life and in understanding the Elizabethan theater, its construction, its audiences, its actors. Roland

Mushat Frye's book "Shakespeare and Christian Doctrine" (Princeton, 1963) is still the best of its kind and has been a great help to me; Roy Battenhouse's "Measure for Measure and Christian Doctrine of the Atonement" (*PMLA*, 61, 1946), early as it is, is still the best theological approach to the play. Peter Milward's book "Shakespeare's Religious Background" (Loyola University Press, 1973) is excellent for background on the Bard's religious formation, the Catholic clergy, the English Jesuits, and the Anglican liturgy. The best introduction to Shakespeare for the beginning student is John F. Andrews' "Shakespeare" in the *Dictionary of Literary Biography*, (vol. sixty-two, under "Elizabethan Dramatists," edited by Fredson Bowers.)

The primary source for Augustine's life is his "Confessions," especially the beautiful edition by the Catholic Book Publishing Co., 1997. There are many biographies of Augustine but one cannot do better than to go back to the author's own words. For "De Civitate Dei" ("The City of God") I have used J.-P. Migne, Patrologiae Cursus Completus, series latina (New York: Adler Foreign Books, 1965-71). Quotations of Augustine in English are pretty much my own translation, although I have used "The City of God", edited by R. V. Tasker, translated by John Healey (Everyman's Library Edition) for verification. Garry Wills' "Saint Augustine" (Penguin Lives, 1999) is a must for the contemporary student interested in Augustine. I have also referred often to my own "Milton and Augustine" (Penn State Press, 1982) in discussing Augustine's teachings on the Fall of the Angels, the Incarnation, and the Redemption. With the many years of reading Augustine I have always returned to "Augustine the Theologian" (Herder and Herder, 1970). It is such a thorough study of the Father's theology, an old reliable. The best introduction to Augustine is R. J. Teske's "St. Augustine" in the *New Catholic Encyclopedia*, second edition, (The Catholic University of America). Mary R. Reichardt's chapter on

Augustine in "Exploring Catholic Literature" (Rowman & Littlefield Publishing Group, Inc. 2003) is excellent as are all the other essays in this stunning book which is a fine resource for Catholic Studies Programs, a growing and healthy trend in colleges and universities today.

The best introduction to Newman's life is James Forsythe Hazen's "John Henry Newman" in the *Dictionary of Literary Biography*, (vol. fifty-five, 219-247.) An excellent introduction to his thought is the article in the *Dictionnaire de Theologie Catholique*, 1931, by Joseph Bacchus and Henry Tristram. However my most valuable source for biographical material has been the "Apologia pro Vita Sua"; that and other works quoted here are from "Collected Works." New York, 1890-1927. "John Henry Newman" by Charles Stephen Dessain of the Birmingham Oratory is an excellent study for its brevity yet its thoroughness. (London: Thomas Nelson & Sons, 1966).

The definitive biographical study of Chesterton is Michael Ffinch's "G.K. Chesterton" (London: Weidenfield and Nicolson, 1986). Ffinch has taken every two years of Chesterton's life and has imposed some order on this often disorganized, enormously prolific, and flamboyantly public, giant personality. The material he has unearthed about Gilbert's and Frances' life is very valuable for a true understanding of this remarkable love relationship. Chesterton's own autobiography does not come up to it. Maisie Ward's book "Return to Chesterton" (New York: Sheed and Ward, 1952) brings a certain intimacy to her study since she was such a close friend of the family. This is a follow-up volume to her "Gilbert Keith Chesterton" and is chiefly made up of unpublished letters, verses, and memories of many who knew him.

A fine introduction to Graham Greene is Richard Hauer Costa's essay in *Dictionary of Literary Biography* (vol. 15, edited by Bernard Oldsey). Greene's autobiography "A Sort of Life" (New York: Simon and Schuster, 1976) is invaluable for the personal reflections. Paul O'Prey's book "A Reader's Guide to Graham Greene" is exactly that, a 'guide' and an exceptional one at that. His tracing the 'green baize door' in Greene's fiction is fascinating. Roger Sharrock's "Saints, Sinners and Comedians" (Kent: Burns & Oates, 1984) is a must. A professor of mine, Sharrock investigates thoroughly all the novels, chronologically, and highlights Greene's religious imagination and the Christian tradition.

Over the years of teaching these authors I have used innumerable books and articles, far too many to mention here, that have in one way or another indirectly shaped and influenced my thoughts and judgments of the writers. The above are the immediate sources I have consulted.

BVG